MEN AT PEACE

Dick Brian Klaver

THOMAS NELSON PUBLISHERS
Nashville

Published in Nashville, Tennessee, by Thomas Nelson, Inc., and distributed in Canada by Lawson Falle, Ltd., Cambridge, Ontario.

All scripture quotations are from THE NEW KING JAMES VERSION. Copyright © 1979, 1980, 1982, Thomas Nelson, Inc., Publishers.

Library of Congress Cataloging-in-Publication Data

Klaver, Dick Brian.
   Men at peace / Dick Brian Klaver.
     p. cm.
   Includes bibliographical references.
   ISBN 0-8407-7795-7 (hard)
     1. Men—United States—Psychology.   I. Title.
HQ1090.3.K59   1993
155.3'32—dc20   93-19451
                                              CIP

Printed in the United States of America

1 2 3 4 5 6 7 - 98 97 96 95 94 93

To Kriste,

My greatest love and friend.
I brought Tupperware to this marriage,
you brought Life.
"She sows the seeds of kingdom dreams,
and plants them in my heart."

Contents

Introduction

1. You Can Be Right or You Can Have Peace 1
2. Power and Passion: Cravings that Clash 18
3. Walking Toward the Pain 31
4. Steps to a Lifestyle of Peace 45
5. Step 1: I Am Responsible for My Behavior 59
6. Step 2: I Am Responsible for My Anger 79
7. Step 3: I Am Responsible for My Anguish 99
8. The Origins of Our Fears and Hurts 118
9. Step 4: I Am Responsible for My Fear 124
10. Step 5: I Am Responsible for My Hurt 147
11. The Antidote to Fear and Hurt: Forgiving
    Yourself; Reconciling with Others 167
12. Step 6: I Am Responsible for My Grief and
    Gratitude 176
13. Step 7: I Am Responsible for My Passions:
    Our Passions for Women 196
14. Step 7: I Am Responsible for My Passions:
    Our Passions for Work 214
15. Step 8: I Am Responsible for My Feelings
    and Thoughts 226
16. Step 9: I Am a Peacemaker 243
17. Men at Peace Groups 249
    — Men at Peace Group Rules 269
    — Men at Peace Registration 271
    Endnotes 273

Acknowledgments

My heartfelt gratitude to:

Those who have taught me to seek the Truth which sets us free.

Men at Peace: Bob, Jack, Dennis, Steve, Ernie, Richard, Dave, Lee, Dick, Jim and all the brothers who teach me peace. They have courageously lived this material.

Lew Smedes, who dared me to be free.

Thom Fiet, true friend, great mind and player.

Sheila Coleman, encourager and wise editor.

Elsa and Rob Deyell, Cindy and Allen Tapang, who endure my wild stories, and who pulled off our men's conference.

Henk DeYoung, who instilled me with joy and passion.

Family Life Ministry, pastors and friends at the Crystal Cathedral who laugh and cry in community for Christ.

Friends in Loveland, Colorado and Chino, California, who conceived ministries of peace and let me administer them.

Jane Jones, Karen Linamen, Ron Haynes and others at Thomas Nelson, who breathed life into this project.

Brad Francisco and Jim Whiting, who taught me about men.

The First Reformed Church of Glenville, New York, with whom I now share a great adventure in the life of peace.

Dad, Mom, Linda, Valerie, my first family. I love you.

Kriste, Matthew and Micah, who love me each day, and who reveal the person I truly am. The book is done! Let's get pizza!

Ken Medema and Beverly VanderMolen of BrierPatch Music.

Peacemakers for the Prince. Wait . . . I hear something! The One who whispers through the ages . . . do you hear something?

Introduction

I work with men troubled by anger/rage or depression in weekly groups called Men at Peace. I began men's groups with a partner, James Whiting, in Loveland, Colorado, in 1984. When, in 1987, I was called to be Family Pastor at the Crystal Cathedral in Garden Grove, California, I began Men at Peace groups. I love being with Men at Peace brothers for two hours each week.

You might picture groups of men as raucous, loud, cursing, abusive, and crude. But just the opposite is true for Men at Peace. In fact I prefer these times to some church leaders' meetings, because they are often more consciously and purposefully peaceful and dignified. Further, we don't allow alcohol or drug abuse; we confront our addictions. We don't allow abusive language. We don't talk about women or anyone but ourselves, except as we discuss the dynamics of a member's "problem." We don't just talk about peace; we practice peace.

Through sensitive stories, tenacious personal growth, and profound love and care, hundreds of men have changed their lives in incredible ways. Men at Peace is a powerful personal change agent.

At last Tuesday night's group, for example, one brother described how he put away his guns rather than use them after he lost custody of his son. Another held his head up high after admitting he was molested as a child. A younger man, who had experienced two failed marriages, decided to remain single and learn to channel his passions into music and faith in God. Another found the support he needed to love his continually depressed wife. A middle-aged man learned to forgive the driver of the car who permanently disabled his son.

Another admitted his problem with rage and began to learn alternatives to battering his wife. Another decided to begin looking for a vocation which is less competitive and more joyful than his present job. There were other stories shared and discussed that same night.

Most men cannot admit they have trouble with anger/rage or depression. Some say, "Sometimes I get a little angry," or "Sometimes I feel a little down." Most think they are fine, but quickly add, "I know someone else who needs help." Unfortunately, we see others' issues more clearly than our own. It is just as Thoreau said: "The mass of men lead lives of quiet desperation."

The same pioneerish, individualistic, competitive spirit that drives American men to success, can also quietly devour joy, peace, and love. Faustian bargains are made imperceptibly. Of course, few *consciously* choose to give up true joy and peace for quick, shallow "happiness." The problem is that hypermaterialism has our society by the throat and is choking out transcendent values.

The good news is that change is happening! American men are asking new questions and seeking new answers. They are awakening to significant values and character traits that go beyond success, such as love, joy, peace, patience, kindness, goodness, faithfulness, gentleness, and self-control.

This book proposes one path for acquiring these values and traits: learning to live at peace with God, one's self, and others. While learning, we will delve into the common sources of male anger/rage and depression, and we will renew ourselves with the healing art of peace-living.

Women tend to have a firmer grasp of relational and transcendent values. They seem to more readily learn to express a wholesome variety of emotions. Still a number of women have told me they find themselves in this book. Others say this book was useful in understanding their partners in particular or men in general. I am grateful. Male and female socialization are interrelated; yet intentionally, I speak first to men and acknowledge male socialization nuances. Men need to converse more self-consciously with men to help each other.

This book teaches a process. It does not provide simple answers. It advocates social change, and it is a resource to facilitate personal healing and recovery in the ways of peace. Two hurtful consequences of our male dilemma are that we launch into abstract thinking because we have not learned "emotional thinking," and that we want to "fix" human problems. But relationships rarely thrive on, or repair with, rational thinking alone, and they do not "fix." Relationships always involve ambiguity and process.

Women have been telling us this for years. Now we just might be beginning to understand.

A final note: The need to reveal the dark side of human nature objectively has been necessarily tempered by the demands of propriety in this book. The danger of cleaning up language and sanitizing stories is that the offenses are made palatable. The harm seems excusable; the evil is winked at; the horror is dulled.

May God keep us from aiding and abetting denial. I am speaking of our collective denial. I have worked with aesthetic felons and prominent Christian men. Both proclaim, "I am not one of those violent men." Violence takes many forms and some of these forms we have gotten used to. God's standards have not changed; we have. May God help us to see the blinding logs in our own eyes. Thereby we can experience the profound joy of our own healing by the God of mercy and grace. We all have this dark side. We need freedom from its shackles. Peace begins at home.

The stories in this book are parts of true stories, woven together. Through them you will meet my Men at Peace brothers. Let them teach you the ways of peace.

May God be with you.

You Can Be Right or You Can Have Peace

Al was "right" for thirty years.

When he met Marie, she was bright-eyed and attentive, attractive and vivacious. Her warm smile made him melt. Her beauty made him feel like a king. Her rapt interest in all he said and did persuaded him that she was the woman of his dreams.

Al worked at capturing Marie's heart by showering her with gifts and being very good to her. Marie felt cared for, and thought of Al as a very special man. She said he was not like all the others.

Then they married.

According to Al, shortly after their June wedding he "woke up" to some of Marie's "foolishness." He told his buddies that it was nothing big, just that Marie had some dumb ideas. For one thing, she liked him to call her sometimes while he was at work. When he scoffed, "I don't have time for that!" his buddies laughed and told stories about their wives. Al was not worried. He would educate Marie.

Three months into their marriage, Marie told Al she wanted to visit her parents, who lived two hundred miles away, for her father's birthday. She was also very excited about telling her folks that she was pregnant. Al took a look at their budget and decided that—technically—they could afford the trip, but that it would require some trade-offs he did not want to make. He thought they needed to save "every penny" to buy a house. Except for a few beers now and then (after all, a man deserves some breaks, Al reasoned), and some tools he needed, he figured they should forego all else until they had a house. "The tools are totally necessary," he explained. "How am I supposed to fix things without tools?" He wouldn't admit that he was buying more than basic tools. Some of the tools were toys. But in the end, he told Marie, "It's a nice idea to visit your folks, but it makes no sense to take the trip right now. It's not that I don't want you to—it's just that we can't afford it."

Marie thought Al had their lives a bit too well-planned. She felt tied down by their tight-fisted drive to buy a house. "Let's slow down the house plans," she said. "This trip is more important to me."

Al felt Marie was challenging him and that she didn't appreciate his efforts. After all, he was sacrificing to get the house for *her*! He was irritated by her attitude.

He told his best friend, "Marie just doesn't know what it takes to accomplish big things. She doesn't appreciate what I'm doing for us. If I left it up to her, we'd never get a house." What Al didn't admit was that he felt threatened by Marie's closeness to her parents. He was especially convinced she was too close to her mother. In his mind, the trip was more of "that problem." But instead of telling Marie what really bothered him, he kept arguing their lack of money.

The argument heated until their words sizzled and stung. Eventually Marie gave up her plans to visit her parents, but Al didn't feel satisfied. He felt only resentment and frustration.

The argument established a pattern in Al and Marie's relationship. Not, of course, that the pattern was entirely new to them: they had learned it from their parents. Both sets of parents had demonstrated that each partner must compete with the other and fight to win an argument by being right. The one who is right then has "the right" to pummel the other with demeaning words disguised as logic, honesty, or common sense which "anyone can see."

This pattern favors the most verbally persistent and stubborn partner. It short-circuits the healthy interchange of subjective emotions and objective negotiation which are essential to sustaining commitment. This pattern unravels the supporting strands of relationships.

Al was the more stubborn partner, although not by much. Through the years he won most of his arguments with Marie. And through the years Al and Marie grew increasingly bitter toward each other.

Having disagreements which occasionally turn into stubborn fights because "I am right" is one thing. These differences usually can be forgiven. Developing obsessive patterns of fighting to win because "*I am right!*" is something else. This obsession eats away at trust. Neither partner knows whether or not the other primarily wills the good of the relationship and is working to that end. The uncertainty and continual confrontations burn away energy and the hope of forgiveness.

True to his obsessions, Al did not see his habit for thirty years. He was too busy being right. He was right with his kids, who felt distant from him. He was almost always right with Marie, who gave up all hope for closeness with him. He was right with his few remaining friends, who kept a cautious distance.

One day, however, all was not right. Al was about fifty-two when, without warning, he had a sharp pain in his chest while at work. With the pain digging in his chest, he tried taking more antacid, but the pain got worse. Then he decided that the best medicine was to ignore the pain. That worked until Al fell on the floor, gasping for breath, and his coworkers called an ambulance.

Al's heart had carried too great a load for far too long, and he had suffered a mild heart attack. Loneliness, bitterness, and general depression had overtaxed Al's heart. Most of all, it was exhausted with the I-must-be-right disease.

Marie and the children spent the evening with Al in the cardiac care unit. They were worried and scared, even though the doctor assured them Al would recover. Eventually, convinced that Al would be all right, they left.

Once he was alone, Al began to cry. Tears were new to him, for he had never allowed himself to cry or even to acknowledge that he wanted to. He felt relieved and then refreshed by his tears, but he also felt some fear and confusion. He began to wonder:

- How could this happen to me? This only happens to other men.
- Is there anything I could have done to avoid this? Is there something wrong with my life?
- I don't want to die. What can I do to live?

These honest thoughts and questions were the beginning of Al's new life. Because all new beginnings are awkward, they require perseverance, and Al's stubborn persistence became a great strength in his healing process.

Al's cardiologist was wise. He referred Al and Marie to a marriage and family therapist who recognized right away that Al was fighting people everywhere in his crusade to be "right." She saw that Al's self-esteem was weak, and that instinctively, whenever he was challenged, he fought to win to preserve his fragile feelings of self-worth.

For the first few sessions, the therapist helped Al and Marie learn to grieve the years they had lost to bickering. They cried many hours over the hurts and pains they had inflicted on each other. This was an important step for both of them, for grief had to precede or be concurrent with learning new ways to befriend each other. The grief would continue as Al and Marie awakened to the damage they had done: yet as they learned to grieve together, the grief no longer threatened their relationship.

The therapist was grateful Al and Marie had the resilience to do this together. With many couples, one or both partners give up when the healing process hurts, thinking wrongly that pain, which does not feel good, means the relationship is not good.

Then Al experienced a watershed awakening. Marie told him she was going away for the weekend to visit her mother

(her father had died previously). Angry adrenaline shot through Al's body. For fifteen minutes he shouted heatedly that he had counted on Marie being home that weekend. He even upped the stakes by claiming he had planned to take her out for dinner on Saturday night. Showing her newfound relational skills, Marie calmly insisted she needed to go. She suggested that Al visit their grown children and grandchildren for the weekend, and she began to pack.

Fuming and remembering the therapist's prescription to "take time-outs when you feel angry," Al went for a walk. After twenty minutes, he turned a corner and walked into a new housing development. Suddenly Al felt great sadness. He remembered the tension he and Marie had felt as they saved for their first home. He felt tears running down his cheeks. And he knew he had been wrong—almost dead wrong.

Al raced home to tell Marie he was sorry. He gave her a kiss and wished her well as she left for the weekend. Marie felt grateful for Al and his encouragement. Al felt a new freedom. He was free *not to be right*.

THE IMPACT OF OUR CONTROLLING STYLES

The constant need to compete and control produces two emotional cycles—rage and depression. Although men are scorned for behaviors and attitudes that arise from being full of rage or depressed, American society continues to socialize boys toward these emotional patterns. Parenting styles also tend to train young males in these ways, and American business and consumerism promote them as a lifestyle.

Rage

Perhaps you struggle with anger. Most anger that leads to conflicts with others, however, is actually rage. The distinction is important. Anger can be felt and spoken of calmly; rage occurs when anger inflames our bodies. When *experiencing rage*, we react with aggression—verbally and sometimes physically.

How can you know if rage is a problem for you? Some men just know it. They know they are "ticked off" much of the time, often for little things. A great testing ground for rage is the highway. Think about these questions and be honest with yourself while you are responding:

- *How do you respond to a slow driver?* Do you scream at the driver? Do you wave or gesture madly? Do you tailgate and then ramrod around the driver at the first opportunity? Or can you relax and slow down?
- *When a driver cuts you off on the road (this happens to all of us!), how do you respond?* Do you scream at him, but soon thank God you are alive? Or do you scream profanely, then race to catch him—nearly killing yourself and others in the process—so you can show him what you think of him? Do you give him a piece of your mind? Are you dominated by his action? Ironically, all of this only proves to the other rotten driver that you are emotionally reactive. Think of it. By your reaction, he "wins." He couldn't care less what you think. But in the heat of the moment you have spent immense amounts of emotional energy "to get him back." Yes, he might be an insensitive fool, but are you behaving foolishly too?
- *You arrive home from work and walk through the door emotionally spent. Your wife (or child) says "the wrong thing." How do you respond?* Do you blow up and ventilate verbally? You might excuse yourself by saying, "She sure knows how to press my buttons," but that excuse ignores the fact that you chose rage as a response. The behaviors of rage are always your choice. No one forces you to act that way.

Some men get violent. Touching or threatening another person with harm is violence. It is an attempt to control people (whom we treat as objects) by force and to make them be or do what we want. Controlling others with violence or the threat of violence might work for awhile. But you also create bitterness, hostility, lack of trust, deceit, and a host of other negatives. Controlling people does not work in the long run.

After episodes of rage or violence, usually the raging person cools down and quickly begins feeling guilty or ashamed. He wants to "make up." Sometimes he makes rash promises, such as "I will never do it again—I promise!" But it is a promise he usually cannot keep. The "problem" arises from old unresolved wounds, and a quick promise isn't powerful enough to heal them. Promising not to do it again is like putting a Band-Aid on a cut and then declaring the cut is healed. He is anxious to get over the embarrassment and wants the incident forgotten.

Mere words, however, are not enough; we must suffer the pain of patiently practicing our promises. Only then will they be validated. There is no way but this heroic way!

Sometimes we try to buy love by buying something for the one we harmed, such as appliances, jewelry, or flowers for the wife, or toys or clothes for the kids. We might not see the motive as trying to buy love, but it is. This might work in the short run, but in the long run, buying stuff wears on human dignity—ours and theirs. Oddly, buying things eventually feels cheap as the thrill of the new toy wears off. Until the real issues are sorted out, understood, and discussed calmly, we cannot reach lasting, peaceful solutions.

Some men demean themselves as a ploy to make up, saying, "I don't know what's wrong with me. I am such a fool. I always mess up. But I don't mean it. It just happens." By this tactic, you put yourself down as you prove how rotten you are. Self-proclaimed rottenness, however, is highly selfish and manipulative. You are not selfless, but actually thinking a great deal about ourselves as you beg sympathy or mercy. This, too, might work, for a few hours, maybe even for days, if you are skilled at it. But rottenness won't kindle passion or build trust. It won't build your self-esteem or hers, and it won't build your relationship.

Do you think she wants to be married to humiliated "junk" for the long haul? Your wife (girlfriend/boss/child/friend) is going to wake up to this gimmick.

Depression

Some men are deeply steeped in feeling rotten, to the extent that they believe the lie. They truly believe they are worthless!

They have stuffed so many emotions deep inside—saying to themselves, "I'm no good," "I don't care," "Nothing bothers me," or even "I'm not angry!"—that their hearts disconnect from their bodies. Disconnection leads to depression. Their bodies generate the chemistry of depression, their minds become dull, and their hearts become numb. They find no joy, no hope, and sometimes little or absolutely no reason to live. Life becomes a chore.

When we are depressed everything we do can be a burden. We have little energy or reason to get up in the morning. What we do gives no satisfaction. That in itself breeds depression, and we become depressed about our depression. The web entangles us ever deeper and surviving becomes a major chore.

True depression is different from pseudo-depression. Some men pretend they are depressed, which is depressing in itself! They do it with mournful eyes, talking endlessly about the latest sad story of their woeful lives and eliciting whatever sympathy they can from their wives or others. People with addictions tend to use this ploy. It is more subtle than simply demeaning themselves with raw humiliation because a man does this with a conniving twinkle in his mind's eye. He carefully and willfully contrives his stories to get what he wants. Often he plays this out with a woman, while remaining highly functional at work. At home he becomes a helpless little boy, incapable of self-care so that his wife is set up to be his mother. If she responds the right way, he reaps comfort such as food, rest, sex, drugs or alcohol, or new toys. If she responds the wrong way, he becomes resentful: "How dare she not comfort me!" he rages.

I am not saying that all depressed people are wholly responsible for their depression. Body chemistry, which is sometimes out of our control, plays a part. Experts have differing theories about the causes of depression. The primary debate is between those who stress psycho-social causes and those who stress physiological causes. Arguing exclusive forms of treatment, however, such as *only* psychotherapy or *only* drugs, is not helpful; although, I am concerned with Americans' tendency to over-medicate depression.

In this book I am using the word *depression* with a less clinical definition than the psychiatric community prefers. I am more concerned with personal and social healing than clinical diagnosis. If you feel depressed, a doctor can help to evaluate your needs.

Rage and depression are the two primary emotional responses to the unresolved wounds of our hearts. These are the two emotional lifestyles men are socialized to use as ways to escape dealing with vulnerable emotions. Often functioning quite well in many areas of their lives, some men choose cycles of rage. Others choose depression cycles. Many choose mixtures of both.

There are two styles of "being right," or controlling communication. The first is the *correcting style*, which is aggressive, perhaps even raging. The second style is *silence*. It is passive and rooted in depression. In this scene between Dotty and Joe, Joe is using the correcting style to control Dotty.

> *Dotty:* "We need to be at the Smith's at five."
> *Joe:* "Five-fifteen is good enough. The Smith's are always late."
> *Dotty:* "I'm going to wear my red sweater."
> *Joe:* "That sweater is too light."
> *Dotty:* "But I like red with this dress."
> *Joe:* "That's not a true red. It has orange it in."

The second style of controlling communication is *silence*. Silence wields a lot of power because when you choose not to participate others are uncertain about you. This style of controlling also is an attempt to protect yourself from hurt. In the same scene Joe is now using this depressive style.

> *Dotty:* "We need to be at the Smith's at five."
> *Joe:* (no response while reading the paper.)
> *Dotty:* "Joe, did you hear me?"
> *Joe:* "What?"
> *Dotty:* "We need to be at the Smith's at five."
> *Joe:* "Yeah."
> *Dotty:* "I'm going to wear my red sweater."
> *Joe:* (mumbling) "Fine."

It may seem peculiar to think of rage, and even more of depression, as a choice or an escape. Yet both derive from the same root: wounds of the heart. Rage is an aggressive, external reaction; depression is a passive, internal reaction. The two go very much together, and often one feeds off the other. Remember, having a feeling is different from acting on the feeling. Behaviors are choices; feelings are less controllable.

Contrary to myth, men who have episodes of rage much of the time are passive and depressed, not aggressive. They have short outbursts of aggressive rage, but most of the time they do not know how to take care of themselves. Most American men suffer bouts of depression in varying degrees, but we describe it in generous ways: "Things are just going bad"; "I'm having a mid-life crisis"; "The kids are giving us trouble."

Others patterns or cycles result from a constantly competitive and controlling style of life, such as broken relationships and loneliness.

INNER WOUNDS FUELING RAGE AND DEPRESSION

Broken Relationships

An in-depth analysis of what causes divorce is not within the scope of this book. However, we can simply state that, since about 50 percent of all American marriages end in divorce (approximately 1.2 million a year), men (and women) are not doing well at keeping commitments in marriage.

Perhaps we are the victims of our parents' divorces or their deadly marriages. We suffered wounds. Perhaps we did not learn well how to communicate, affirm ourselves or others, resolve conflicts, express affection and vulnerability, or forgive—all skills that make a marriage work. Fundamentally we never learned intimacy. We learned to be protective, defensive, or perhaps, superficial. We learned that relationships are tenuous commitments based on our feelings of satisfaction. Divorce has become a social malaise, but that is not our fault. Still *we are responsible for our present choices.*

The results of our choices may be that our marriages have ended in divorce or we are suffering in our current relationships. We can feel lonely, scared, or bitter, and we do not know what to do about it. Some of us control our partners with blame by lashing out at their imperfections. Some men become infuriated when their wives gain enough emotional strength to leave them. I always say to a man whose wife has left: "That she left you may not be fair or morally right, but it is reality. She has made that choice. You cannot make her stay with you. And you have no right to threaten or manipulate her or the children. Your pain gives you no right to force her to do anything. What you can do is grieve, learning through this pain about yourself." These words are profoundly difficult for a man dependent on his "woman" to accept, particularly if he feels enraged or depressed.

Other men hate all conflict. They walk on eggshells in relationships, trying not to inflame anyone. Conflict can hurt terribly so these men live with constant internal tension, trying to avoid it with the people around them. Caring deeply about what others think and feel, they try to make everyone happy. Unfortunately, we are poor judges of others' thoughts and feelings. We exaggerate and fantasize and obsess about what others think or feel. If they are not happy, we take the blame (or blame them). At some point, we might reject the pain by rejecting the person, even if he or she is someone we love.

We just don't know how to make relationships work. We have a problem. We long for someone to care for us passionately; at the same time, we are terrified of someone who knows us too well. We're in a catch-22. We are lonely and stuck, and there seems no better way.

Loneliness

Loneliness is an ache that will not go away. It is a void or empty place we cannot fill. We hurt too much to deal with its sources. We feel loneliness as boredom, meaninglessness, insecurity, the need for a woman or sex. We try to dull it with chemicals or experiences—anything that will take the edge off the pain or cover it up for awhile.

Some men try to deal with their loneliness by using drugs. Some use women. Some become obsessed with business deals or corporate ladder climbing. These behaviors all begin with emptiness and become behaviors that are driven, obsessive, addictive, or abusive. We allow anything that gives us "a high" and temporarily fills the void to control us. Sometimes the energy we use to fill emptiness makes us incredibly successful in the business world, and the admiration others have for our workaholism and accumulation persuades us we are okay. Society rewards us, so we convince ourselves we are doing things right. We ignore the fact that our personal lives are a mess.

Our Need to Control

Men learn to handle inner feelings and wounds through control. Primarily we control our emotions. Most American men have learned to control two sorts of emotions: those that cause us to feel vulnerable, that is, hurt and fear; and those that cause us to feel childlike, such as playfulness and joy.

Still we are capable, at least theoretically, of feeling a whole range of emotions. Men have just as much emotional capacity as women. The issue, then, is not ability but control. We have learned to rationalize or think our emotions. We talk about how we feel and filter emotions through our brains. Rarely do we allow ourselves to feel what we feel with spontaneity.

Think about these examples of men having trouble feeling their feelings.

"Tom, do you love me?"
Tom: "Of course I do! You know that I do. Why do you even ask?" (But Tom rarely says, "I love you.")

"Jim, how did you feel when Wendy said, 'Leave me alone—I don't want to talk to you'?"
Jim: "I felt like I wanted to grab her."
"Well, that is what you thought you wanted to do. What did you feel?"
Jim: "I'm not sure what you mean. I felt that she turned her back on me!"
"And how did that make you feel?"
Jim: "That ticked me off."
"Aha! So you felt 'ticked off.'"
Jim: "Of course. Anybody would feel that way."
"So what did you feel under your anger?"
Jim: "Nothing. I just felt ticked off."

"Did you feel frustrated, irritated or hurt?"
Jim: "No, just ticked off." (Jim is unaware of his deeper feelings. He is disconnected. He can feel and talk about his anger/rage, but feelings of vulnerability lie beneath his anger. They always do.)

"Bob, are you depressed?"
Bob: "No, I just don't know what to do."
"What is it you think you must do?"
Bob: "Well, maybe if I just think positively, my problems will go away. Or maybe it's just my body. If a doctor could just prescribe something, I'd be okay. Maybe I just need a few more business deals, a little more money . . ."

CAN I CHANGE?

We have just taken a look into some of the wounds of men. But our larger purpose is reconstruction. American men are under reconstruction. Many have been rebuilding for months or years. As you read the wonderful, painful, through-it-all hopeful stories in the pages of this book, you will find a creative plan for your personal reconstruction.

Still, very few people are motivated to change by truth or insight alone. Most people hit rock bottom before they are willing. Only then does the pain of changing become less than the pain of staying the same. Arrest and jail time, job loss, bankruptcy, illness, marital separation are rock-bottom motivators. Unfortunately, people often avoid change until it is too late.

Many men see themselves as doing quite well. Surely most men's lives are peaceful and significant in many ways. Genuine strength of character and emotional expressiveness deserve affirmation. Many marriages are quite strong, loving, and resilient. Nevertheless, are there areas of your life in need of growth and development, not only for your own benefit, but also for others?

Men tend not to see their weaknesses clearly. Part of the American male style is avoiding or denying weakness. Many wives have told me how they endure their "wonderful husbands'"' glaring weaknesses. Wives often give up and accept our relationship inabilities.

The truth is that we don't have to grow. But it surely would be a courageous step for us and a gift for others! And the personal rewards are great as we get lives with more depth and color.

Occasionally personal growth involves therapy and/or medicine, but often it doesn't. In Men at Peace groups we teach what you can do to heal yourself by following a personal path of healing, particularly in cooperation with other men.

You may still be resistant, thinking I must be talking to "those men" who have real problems—those who drink too much, or work too much, or hit their wives. You might be thinking, "That is not me."

If that is your thought, maybe you are right. Maybe you are an exceedingly peace-living person. Maybe I, and many other men, have something to learn from you. If so, I challenge you to get involved with other men who are reconstructing their lives simply because they are your brothers. We need each other, and you will benefit, too.

But if you are not peace-living, let your brothers help you rebuild your life.

RECONSTRUCTION

To rebuild we must first understand what needs to be done and know the plan. If you were hired to do a remodeling job, first you would listen carefully to your customer describe what is wanted. Sometimes customers know specifics; sometimes they have only general ideas. Then you would translate the customer's ideas and assess what specifically needs to be done with walls and objects removed or added. Next you would draw up a good set of plans and evaluate the costs. (In this reconstruction you need no permits—you give yourself permission!) You would sign a contract satisfactory to all, and finally you would do the job—taking out the old, adding the new, and finishing the project.

Rebuilding your life to become a peace-living person follows the same general steps of assessing, planning, and doing, only you are both contractor and customer. This book is your builder's guide. In the beginning chapters, the issues and the scope of the reconstruction are broadly outlined. As we look into male socialization, listen well to understand what you can change to build a more sane and enjoyable personal and relational life. This will require removing some old things, putting in some new things, and sometimes adding whole new areas.

Be patient and disciplined. You will discover that your discoveries and processes—the changes you will make—are more than this book can define. This book teaches processes, but you provide the personal materials. This book gives general plans (with options!) to frame the project. You provide the significant, specific materials. With hope, discipline, and support, you can and will build peace.

Some men have had a kind of conversion or awakening experience in the course of their reconstruction. You could too. You might begin to see your reconstruction as a work of art, and then discover *you* are the work of art! You'll learn that your process, the story of your reconstruction and personal growth, is more important than the end product when it comes to human relationships. Jesus of Nazareth taught us this. We are still learning.

You'll probably find that this book is worth reading through once. Then perhaps you'll come back to it from time to time as you work through the stages of your reconstruction.

What are we working toward? What does this book teach?

First, *you will learn awareness.* You will learn more about who you are. You will hear how common American male socialization patterns (that is, how we were raised) have hurt us, pushing us into cycles of rage and/or depression. As you gain awareness you will begin to grieve. You will know you are experiencing grief. Grief will not hurt you (it has been hiding in you all along), but you might need a friend or two to travel with you.

Second, *you will learn to stop controlling what cannot be controlled.* We can learn to stop rigidly controlling our emotions, minds, bodies, and souls and to stop trying to control other people. Most of all, control devastates our relationships with the people we love—our wives, children, families, and friends. When we try to control all aspects of our lives, we isolate ourselves. We might "function" all right in isolation in some areas of life, but not in relationships.

Trying to control too much leads us to be obsessive about our work, because that is usually the place we try to build our ego kingdoms. When work is going well, we feel in control and good. But that lasts only as long as work goes well.

Control is not all bad. Self-control is a particularly necessary tool of discipline, and discipline is part of growth. But control for the sake of control has no heart, no soul, no hope, no character, no significant purpose. Just as laws only work if citizens accept the spirit and intent of the government, control needs heart, soul, and vision.

Third, *you will explore your emotional life*. How have you shut down your emotions? What can you do about that? How have you disconnected from your body? Have you lost touch with your soul? Touching our hurts and fears unlocks our need to control and opens new doors to joy and peace. We can find new purposes for our roles and commitments. We will discover significant new choices.

Fourth, *you will reconstruct your relational life*. We will explore personal and spiritual renewal, love for God, trust and care for a community of men, love for our wives, families, and friends.

Finally, we can dedicate ourselves to be peacemakers.

WHAT CHANGE WILL THIS REQUIRE?

A ten-year-old boy went to the theater one Saturday afternoon to watch a movie about space aliens. The aliens were slaughtered by earthlings, and this upset the boy terribly. He decided to see the movie again the same day. In fact, he returned ten more times during the following week. Eventually the ticket-taker stopped the boy and said, "Son, I've seen you at this movie about ten times. Don't you think that's enough?"

The young fellow replied sincerely, "Sir, every time I see this movie the aliens are slaughtered at the end and I don't like it. I figure that if I just keep coming, one of these times the ending will be different. That will make me happy!"

I have heard many men say, "I have tried it all. Nothing will change!" Yet when I hear their stories, I discover they keep trying to change others (and a little of themselves) using the same old dysfunctional styles and systems.

The first step toward change that works is to admit *this movie will not change, but I can change.* Then get serious, saying, "Whatever is wrong with me is not her fault, the kids' fault, or the boss's fault. Sure, they have problems too, but I cannot control them or fix them."

The next step toward change is to go to a different movie. You can try a whole new way. So, once you have set your resolve and formulated your plan, do it! Don't expect magic; expect change. Change takes time and needs to be rooted. Yet every bit of change is significant. These two steps can provide significant change.

Some men reach a third level of change. This occurs when a man says, "I can actually write the script and direct the movie! That is, I can create a healthier life for myself which will impact others for good too!" Then, control, in the service of commitment, becomes a healthy tool for good. We experience true self-control in the service of God and others.

I pray for all men seeking personal peace, including you.

Power and Passion: Cravings that Clash

Men desire power and long for passion. These needs are natural and legitimate. We need power to accomplish deeds and to have a sense a purpose and pride in ourselves. We need passion to experience warmth in a cold world and to feel secure and loved. Having our needs for power and passion satisfied is the basis of our sense of dignity, contentment, and personal significance. It is basic to our humanity and feelings of self-worth. How we satisfy these needs, however, is a problem.

Men learn to fight for fulfillment. Most of us try to satisfy our desire for power by competing with other men for money, material accumulations, and position. We say we're not comparing ourselves to other men or competing with them, but we are. Usually we compare ourselves to others subconsciously and, when we feel we don't stack up well, try to step up the competition by increasing our drive to succeed.

When we want passion, we tend to try using the same methods to get it. Instead of looking for affection and intimacy, we demand physical and/or emotional care from someone—usually a woman. Instead of offering and finding warmth, we make conquests. We don't mean to, but we do.

The fight to satisfy our needs for power and passion becomes an internal battle as these needs compete for fulfillment and contradictions form in our souls. Meanwhile the needs are unfulfilled. We tend to blame others for this, and unable to quench the smoldering fires within us, we feel guilty and vulnerable. These drives seem so natural that we have difficulty understanding how we missed our cues. We sense we are acting in the wrong show or drinking water that looks good and smells sweet, but is laced with poison.

In these days when men are being unfairly maligned for seeking power and passion, it is fair to say that we need to learn alternatives to fighting and forcing to satisfy our needs. We need to learn greater civility and peace.

THE TENDER KING

"What can we do?" cried the commoners of the kingdom of Chimeras. Gathered late one night by a flickering fire, they discussed their serious predicament.

"Our leaders have gone mad!" one said. "There is no one to trust! No one! They demand our money to subsidize their pointless plans. They send our boys to war for hollow victories against paper enemies. They battle, bicker, and blame, while the spirit of our people collapses. Our neighbors are getting meaner and nastier. We barely trust each other. We are fast losing hope!"

"All my neighbors are infected by this Delusion of Powerful Appearances," mourned another. "They steam and rage about who is greatest or, depressed and full of dark-eyed confusion, they wallow in failure."

Then a quiet commoner spoke up. "What about the Book?" he asked.

"What book?" the others demanded, mumbling and grumbling among themselves.

"The Book of our Fathers. It says, 'One day, when things look the worst, a Tender King will arise from among the commoners. This King will lead us but not as we might expect.

Regarding appearance, he will have no outstanding traits or handsomeness. Regarding our security and desires, he will not always give us what we want. His power will be in tenderness and peace.'"

"What kind of king is that?" the group bellowed. "We need a king with power. Our neighbors and leaders would crush him!"

"There is more," the quiet one replied. "He will salve our inner wounds and share our sorrows. He will suffer tortures for us, both physical and spiritual, before the authorities. He will give vision to our powerless souls, proclaim our worthiness before the leaders, and fill us with joy. By his presence we will be able to carry on with dignity. He will quench the deepest longings of our souls with the waters of truth which will satisfy us eternally."

"We want a king who looks like a king, sounds like a king, and acts like a king!" The mass of commoners cried and charged away, bitterly mocking the quiet one's tale.

But a few men remained and began to weep. Something long forgotten had been awakened within them. It may have been the memory of the Tender King stories they were told as boys by their faithful fathers. Or maybe they had grown tired of the endless battle. Whatever the reason, deep within themselves they each knew they longed for the Tender King.

All men long for the Tender King. We admire the power and authority earned by truth. Yet truth requires submission, and we fear giving up the fictions and myths of our lives. We long to follow and serve significant purposes and eternal principles. At the same time, we also starve for caresses and warmth, affirmation and acceptance, kindness and gentleness, respect and dignity. Beneath our cool exteriors we long for God and to have God's ways revealed to us.

Today American men are under reconstruction. Across the country men are rebuilding their masculine identities with new ideas and experiences. Knowing that true intimacy empowers us, we desire the passion and validity of love. The Tin Man has found a heart.

What are men discovering that is significant? We've discovered we can admit to other men that we are lonely, hurt, and insecure. We've discovered we can listen to each other's stories about failure and fear, care for one another, hold one another, and feel supported and encouraged. We are giving up cut-throat competition, material accruing, and physical games as the primary measures of masculinity. Men are making commitments to God and their wives, families, friends, and communities.

THE KINGDOM OF TYRANNICAL APPEARANCES

Finding our hearts and minds does not come easily. We have been trained to control, deny, or squelch most of our inner longings. Consequently we build pride in being logical or rational, calling that *The Male Way*. We fantasize about being powerful and coldly decisive, seeing ourselves making brilliant decisions in the heat of business without flinching. We long for applause.

Still the longings for inner peace keep tugging at us, until the moment arrives when we decide to uncover pulsations of inner joy, or we dare to admit we are lonely.

Then, just when we are about to express our joy or emptiness, *The Male Way* kicks in and our defenses against primary inner feelings take control. Anxiety or awkwardness or embarrassment overwhelm us. Joy is overpowered by the fear of being seen as emotional. The embarrassment of being seen as weak causes us to ignore our loneliness. Re-exerting control, we go back into hiding. After all, why be vulnerable? Why reveal anything about ourselves?

Certain occasions seem to validate our fear of revealing our inner feelings. For example, your wife says, "You never show your feelings. You are just heartless and cold!" Or one day you risk telling her about your feelings and blurt, "I am not happy with my job anymore. I feel trapped." But she doesn't listen or try to understand. Instead she says, "Quit your belly-aching. At least you *have* a job." Or perhaps one night spontaneously you say, "How about a hug?" but she says, "Get away from me! All you want is sex!" You feel stupid, and you re-learn to keep quiet and stuff your feelings into the slowly boiling kettle in your gut. Thoroughly pummeled, you go back into hiding.

Some of us are just plain exhausted. We have been performing roles and tasks without personal reward for so long, we don't know who we are. We feel empty, spent. The pump cannot pull out any more water.

You are a father. You are a husband. You are a truck driver, or a doctor, or a minister, or a carpenter. These are things we do. They help form our identities. Some days these roles give us purpose and reward. Other days we secretly assess how we could disappear to a faraway tropical island.

We ask, "Shouldn't I be happy? I have so much." Yet there are days when we wake up and know we are not happy. We are stressed, acting out our roles without heart or desire. We are trapped by others' expectations and their needs. We don't have time to know what we think or feel. Maybe we keep busy because we are afraid of finding out how hollow and empty we really are. We know that bright, youthful dreams fade into hopeless nights.

Too many of us also have deep, dark secrets. The little boy in us was deeply wounded, yet we are afraid to tell. When we were young and the secret was happening, we couldn't tell, because no one would believe us. We were very ashamed, and some of us still feel the shame. These are the ones who were molested, by their fathers, other family members, friends, or strangers.

Current estimates are that one of seven American men was forced into sexual encounters as a boy. For some it was a one time experience; for others it was or is an unending nightmare. Some brothers have been suffering quietly ever since.

Others, like Louis, were physically beaten. I met Louis in a Men at Peace group. He had been arrested for hitting his wife and charged with third-degree assault. The group asked Louis about his childhood. We said, "As a boy, when you did something wrong, how did your parents respond?"

"Oh, I got punished," he said.

"What do you remember about your punishments?"

"Well, my dad whipped me a few times, but that was just normal. I deserved it!"

Louis did not understand that violence begets violence. Lou's father beat him because he "deserved" it. Now Louis beats his wife.

Other men were forced to do evil, scary things—maybe even by Dad, or Mom, or an uncle, or a person they trusted, or a friend, or a stranger. They have carried this secret alone for many years, and it still haunts them. If this describes you, you are not alone.

Perhaps as a young child you were verbally berated and constantly criticized. Your self-esteem was shot through and through, until now it is full of holes and gaps. The result is a porous confidence and a fragile sense of self. That makes the cover up—the facade you present to the world—all the more exhausting to maintain.

Maybe you were neglected. You had to create an identity. Unfortunately, hiding behind a mask of confidence does not give anyone genuine confidence.

Our secrets affect our personalities, our relationships, our bodies, our minds and hearts—our entire lives. Secrets wear on us. Hiding or denying them takes a great deal of energy. But the tragedy of secrets is that those who have them often are the last to see the profound effects they have on our personalities and our social styles. We think the past was past, but others know we have wounds. The words "I am just fine" sound a hollow echo in the huge cavern of truth.

MALE BASHING

"I am sick and tired of male bashing!" That is what an acquaintance said to me recently, and I feel that way too. Men are victims also. But we are resilient. We are capable of taking responsibility for ourselves. We can define and admit what is not okay with *The Male Way*. In the 1990s we are discovering that what used to work no longer does.

One man said, "If discovering and expanding our feelings requires opening up to pain, why do it? Pain is pain. I don't want it." But we must discover our feelings, because fearing and avoiding emotional pain will control us and narrow our choices in life. We must walk toward our pain and face it. When we don't, we are emotionally handicapped. When we do, we can venture into a world of wonderful emotions. We can generate new ways of seeing life and making creative choices. If we don't fear the pain, we might even feel love.

Ernie, a friend of mine, tells the story of a man whose little boy was bitten by a poisonous snake. The stunned father knew that to save his son's life, he had to lance the bite with a knife and suck out the poison. But the father could not cause his son pain—it would hurt the father too much! Horrified, the father put the boy in his truck, raced to the hospital, and arrived just in time . . . to carry the limp body of his dead son into the emergency room.

Like this man, we avoid dealing with the pain we know about because the unknown pain of the cure scares us. Meanwhile, we die a little inside.

THE MEN'S MOVEMENT

There is hope! The movement of the '60s and '70s, focusing on human potential, introduced American men to the experience of sharing their feelings. Not many men dared try this "touchy-feely" experiential stuff. But in the late 1970s a small number of men's groups began through agencies devoted to helping battered women.

Seeing violent men charge from one relationship to the next, leaving a trail of wounded women and children, a few people understood the need to help victims of violence by treating the perpetrators. They said, "If someone were pushing people over a cliff, first we'd treat the injured. Then common sense dictates that somebody ought to stop the person pushing people over the cliff!"

Still, not many men voluntarily admitted they needed help. They reasoned to themselves that only men who were violent needed help, "and I'm not one of *them*." Therefore, most of the participants in early men's self-help groups were ordered by the courts to attend as a diversion from trial and sentencing. Still, the threads of a men's movement formed, as treatment professionals and recovering men began networking.

In the late '80s the movement expanded its themes. Robert Bly, described as a "mythopoet," and others began to teach men to get in touch with their "inner warriors." Using mythology, poetry, singing, rhythm, drumming, strumming, and movement, men began to understand that their inner warriors were not macho and violent. As men tried to touch their emotions and souls, they began trying to live to the rhythm of nature, to grieve the loss of their fathers, and to seek to rewrite their stories with a new sense of their primitive masculinity and brotherhood.

Since most movements "jump start" with romantic ideals that shock a dulled society into realizing the extent of the dilemma, some of the inner-warrior ideals and behaviors seem rather eccentric. They pulsate off "mountain-high" experiences. A friend of mine, after seeing a "20/20" television segment on Wild Men weekends, commented, "That's downright weird, but it shows how wounded we men really are." Now, having changed the mainstream, the movements are beginning to merge into the mainstream.

Introspection helps some men begin the process of grieving the past, releasing their emotions, and clarifying issues. Yet the "find-your-inner-self" approach, by itself, is not enough. Mountain-high revelations don't last long down in the valleys of life.

So what works in the valley?

Commitment.

Men need not just to find themselves, but to *commit themselves. The most significant questions each man must answer are: To whom have you committed your love, faith and hope?* and *To what have you dedicated your abilities and time?* In the valley we find ourselves through commitment more than through isolated, idealized selves.

What unifies the men's movement is that men are asking new, fundamental questions about the dark side of basic American male values. The questions deal with neurotic competition, mad drives for "success," obsessive greed, deification of the self, quick-fix solutions to problems of the soul.

WE MARRY WORK AND USE WOMEN

When we disconnect from the lives we were meant to live, we ache and become angry. We feel restless, anxious, short-tempered, and depressed. We become anxious, role-performing adults, disconnected from our bodies and souls. We trade the hope of love and the creativity of heartfelt work for immediate, short-lived rewards and pleasures.

Men learn to try to fill their emptiness with work and women. In fact, a man's "success" with work and women tends to become the measure of his worth. This fallacy forms the fabric of a shallow identify.

Work

What we do to make money or to earn power and prestige is what we call "work." Many people work their jobs detached from the joy of living, simply having a job that pays the bills. I don't mean to discount the importance of paying the bills. It is, after all, a necessary thing to do. After graduating from college, I spent months anxiously unemployed and unsure what I wanted to do. Since then I have grabbed jobs from time to time simply to have money to pay bills. Yet if we never escape the urgent trap of just paying bills (and bills multiply in proportion to the comforts we require), we miss the joy of living blissfully according to our gifts.

Some of us are controlled by our careers. Consequently we've made careers of feeling anxious. We thought we were preparing to become doctors, carpenters, pastors, or painters. But actually we became puppets playing roles. Our careers are a constant throb of anxiety played out in the theater of our jobs. We perform in order to measure ourselves by what we accomplish. But each accomplishment only feeds the need to do more. Our egos become addicted and the applause we receive is never enough.

Genesis, the first book of the Bible, reveals that God intended work to be an expression of creativity carried out in fulfilling behaviors. He meant us to use our potentials, gifts, abilities, and desires creatively in the betterment of other people and the earth. But after greed took hold of humankind, work became *toil*.

We can recapture the fulfillment God meant us to receive by doing our work to create rather than working our jobs only to make money. For example, a carpenter *creates* and earns legitimate power by building a structure he is proud to put his name on and happy to watch his customers enjoy. Or, a carpenter *works a job* by finishing a task in a hurry to make the greatest profit. A surgeon *creates* and earns power by investing himself in the wellness of people through continual learning, keeping up with research and new techniques, and taking an interest in his patients. Or, a surgeon *works a job* by performing as many surgeries as possible to make more money or to impress his colleagues with his performance.

We men need to get our work in perspective.

Women

Some men try to fill their need for passion with a woman. We hope a woman will give us two magical things: security and ecstasy.

We want to be mothered. We want someone to take care of us, to fix our meals, clean up our messes, raise our children, and comfort us when the cruel world wounds us. We think that some woman out there, the magical woman, should fill the void we have. These magical women will hold us and understand us. Hopefully, they will love us even better than our mothers did!

To be perfect they must also be sex goddesses. If they don't give us great sex then they won't be fulfilling their "womanly obligations." We somehow believe that good sex happens when a woman is willing to be invaded as our impulses drive us. We say we can't help it—we cannot control our urges.

Not only do we expect women to play these absurd and incredibly incongruous roles, but we believe they had better figure out *when* to play *which*. If they get it wrong, we might discover ourselves in bed being passionate with Mom! Or we might feel disgusted if, while playing Aphrodite, they fail to adequately clean up the messes in our castles. These expectations are inhumane. How crazy can we get!

Enduring love involves two people sharing deep commitment. The commitment includes sharing mutual passion and affection and sharing many other emotions and ideas, tasks, and common experiences, such as accomplishing mutual goals and rearing children. United efforts toward these commitments build greater and deeper love. But lack of effort, particularly as we use a woman to fill our individual needs, creates distrust and separation. Lasting passion builds on mutual commitment, emotion, dreams, and goals. Ironically the terrifying choice we make to sacrifice *I* for *we* liberates *I* to live and feel a more significant life—the life we long for.

WHAT DO MEN TRULY LONG FOR?

Like all people, we men seek meaning in the ordinary moments and purpose in our actions. We want our lives to count. We want to impact our communities for good. We long for genuine love and friendship with women and men. Many men are choosing more than financial success to feed their egos. We are ready for a change. We are ready to find significant purposes for our lives! We might fear the commitment and responsibility that comes with love and friendship, but we will keep trying! We fear losing the fragile selves we have carved out of our psychic stuff, but we will risk it.

Today men are asking better questions:

- Which of my dreams are possible and which are delusions?
- Since I cannot have everything, what can I practically attain in my life?
- What am I willing to give up to simplify my life?
- What are the fears and hurts that provoke my rages and depressions?
- What makes me afraid of commitments?
- What am I willing to do to be committed?
- What will be the cost, both personal and financial?
- What are the foundational principles on which I base my decisions?
- Is a personal God alive and active in our world, or not?
- If I am not God, what is my place in this world?
- If God is active, then how am I to respond?

We need to develop new social beliefs and behaviors which are consistent with our created purposes and potentials. We must stop stabbing our own hearts with delusions of ultimate control and power.

Of five hundred American men surveyed, over half said they would cut their salaries up to twenty-five percent if they could have more time alone or with their families. Forty-five percent said they probably would turn down a promotion if it meant spending less time with their families. [1]

Most men will be forced to find new sources of dignity and esteem outside their jobs. For example, few baby boomers or busters, despite their degrees and expectations, will make it to the top of any corporate ladder. In her article entitled "The Dead-End Kids," Karen Tumulty cites this prediction by Barry D. Leskin of the USC School of Business: "While there were about ten potential candidates for every middle management opening in 1975, the number will rise to thirty in 1995 and fifty by the year 2000."[2] Work "success," at least that defined by climbing the corporate ladder, will be less available to most of us.

Put simply, our access to wealth and prestige will decrease in the 1990s and beyond. Studies show the relative economic standard of living in the United States is decreasing for the first time in history. We must find new measures of personal significance and satisfaction.

Even for the few who climb high on the ladder of success, there are costs. "I think half the successful work force is depressed," claims Douglas LaBier, a Washington, D.C., psychoanalyst who treats stressed executives. Men succeed by overachieving. They drive themselves to achieve to please or impress others (often parents or peers). Having reached a level of success, they must work even harder, "fearing their inadequacy will be found out," says Gerald Kraines, a psychiatrist who treats CEOs.[3]

Many of us work at everything we do. We even "work" at playing. Play means working out at a health club. If we play a sport, we compete to win, and if we lose, we feel badly. Even with our relationships, we work at them but rarely play. True play, on the other hand, has no goals. Play is what you do just for the pleasure of it. We must learn again how to play, perhaps from our children before they are taught not to.

This book is for men who dare to ask new questions. It is for men who dare to walk the higher path—the path toward their pain.

Walking Toward the Pain

In September 1983 I was just beginning my internship as a marriage and family therapist. I was filled with anticipation, and I had a bag full of skills and techniques to rely on. Most of all, I had a great desire to help people. I was terrified but ready. I soon learned there was much to learn, particularly about the depth of men's wounds.

Eddie, escorting his vivacious wife, Sarah, came into my bright therapy room. He was twenty-four years old, a little under six feet tall, muscular, and blonde with piercing brown eyes. He had a steady job as an auto mechanic. He looked like the all-American male. Sarah was twenty-one and full of life. She had short brown hair, big brown eyes, and she energized the room. They were the parents of a sweet new baby girl, Rachel, and they attended church regularly. Seemingly full of potential, I thought they were a beautiful family.

After a bit of small talk, I asked what had brought them to therapy.

"He didn't want to come with me to see you," Sarah said tersely, nodding toward Eddie. "And he warned me not to come either. I told him you wanted to see us together, but if he wouldn't come, I was coming anyway. At the last minute he came. And he's been cussing me out every step of the way."

Eddie's face flushed crimson. "I said I didn't think we needed this," he retorted to his wife. "Just get off my case!" Then Eddie shot his eyes at me and said with precision, "I don't like being told what to do."

Eddie felt caged and under attack. He was setting ground rules for Sarah and me. And that made me feel even more nervous. I had just heard about a therapist being shot by a client, and I glanced at Eddie's pockets looking for weapon-shaped bulges. A knot was growing rapidly in the pit of my stomach. We were not getting off to a good start.

"Eddie is dead!" Sarah said coolly. "He doesn't seem capable of feelings. He doesn't love me. He can be sweet to Rachel, our baby, but sometimes I get scared at how mad he gets when she cries. Mostly, though, he just sits around at home being depressed."

Uh-oh, I thought. *She's a grumpy, nagging wife. Well, at least we have something to explore.*

"How do you know that?" I challenged Sarah, hoping to gain Eddie's favor and slow her assaults. "How do you know exactly what Eddie feels?"

Although I was a novice, I had already observed this scenario many times—emotionally absent husband married to lonely wife—they were Mr. Distant and Mrs. Smother. Still, my intuition told me that Sarah loved Eddie and would work at therapy, so I listened to her.

"His home life consists of watching sports on TV, tinkering in the garage, or mowing the grass. Outside the house, when he's at work, for instance, he puts on his happy face. Everyone says, 'What a great guy Eddie is. You must really be thrilled to be married to him!' I just laugh. I'm hardly thrilled."

Eddie's face got a little redder. "What do you know?" he growled. "You're too busy nagging me to know anything. I get along fine with most everybody. *You* are my problem!"

Sarah shrugged. "Rather than get help, Eddie tells me it's all my fault. He says I'm a nag and that I gripe too much. He says he was just fine before he met me. The truth is, he's married to his work and works like a dog, or maybe like a robot. At work he's great. He's great with his friends. But at home he wants his sexual needs met and that's about it. He doesn't get it, though. I can't just turn on, you know. He's just like his dad. And, I'm sorry to say, he's just like my dad too.

"Right now I like Eddie best when he's working," she snapped. "I mean that I like him best when he's not around me. And someday I hope to have a life after he's dead. Working and being dead, that's what he does best. I think it's the way all men are."

That did it. So much for compassion, empathy, skill, and technique. I was ticked off. Her shots at the brotherhood of men tore through me and apparently they got to Eddie too. He looked ready to explode. Quickly I tried to light a backfire.

"Do you say this stuff to Eddie a lot?" I asked.

"Yes, sometimes. Why?" She answered me calmly.

"Well, it would bother me if I were Eddie. I like your energy, but your verbal shots are awfully sharp. I'm not sure I would feel real safe being close to you!"

My backfire didn't diminish Eddie's rage. He jumped in and launched a verbal torrent at Sarah that included expletives and name calling. That made me feel sympathy for Sarah and a desire to challenge Eddie.

I had lost control. A bit unsure of my role in this triad, my bag of skills suddenly seemed empty.

That session began weeks of therapy. I felt like I was working with a bucking stallion and a wild mare. Sarah had her quirks, of course—she could stab with words as well as Eddie could—but mostly she tried to be positive and work a plan. She had the personal self-esteem and emotional resources to try again and again with Eddie. Sarah could be nasty, but she was committed to her marriage. At least Mrs. Smother had a heart. But not Eddie. If their problems were as simple as being Mr. Distant and Mrs. Smother, there would be hope so long as each of them had an emotional pulse.

For weeks, though, I couldn't find Eddie's emotional pulse. He was not only distant, but relationally he was defensive. Eddie simply wasn't there. He wouldn't reveal or commit himself. He was hard, but very fragile. He couldn't bounce back; he had no resilience, and he couldn't forgive. He held on tightly to his depression and rage. Sarah was hurt but flexible; Eddie was rigid.

I will never forget the day Sarah came in looking haggard. Her words were uncensored and hopeless. She looked Eddie straight in the eyes and said, "Eddie, I realized something this week. I am not your wife. I am just your mistress. I am waking up to the fact that you will probably work yourself to death—just like your dad and just like my dad. I'm afraid our marriage is going nowhere."

For ten sessions we had tried marriage therapy. We had experienced moments that seemed to indicate we were making progress. We'd had some deep dark moments too, but Sarah's words articulated a profound truth. Eddie was *stuck*.

As time passed and I saw more couples, again and again I encountered something I had felt in myself and in men in general. We (and some women too) can be downright emotionally deprived except in ways of rage and/or depression. This social malaise inhibits our ability to commit to relationships. It is an illness that has passed from one generation to the next, until our generation is struggling with knowing our most basic intentions—that is, who God meant us to be.

A little more honesty flowed in the following sessions. It became clearer that Eddie had "a little trouble" with his temper. He was, of course, not like those violent men. "My father taught me never to hit a woman," he explained. Somehow in Eddie's mind verbal assaults, controlling behaviors, and in general neglecting his wife technically weren't "violence." In fact, Eddie denied all of these behaviors. He said, "Sarah exaggerates all the time," which was the greatest exaggeration of all!

Eddie would not give his heart to anyone, not even himself. And he couldn't keep a commitment to himself, much less to his marriage. He had "tried a little cocaine," and he drank "a little once in a while, nothing serious."

Underneath Eddie's solid male exterior, he was in great pain. Like many men, he had trouble with addictive behaviors, which almost always are used to divert the hurt. He had chosen to anesthetize his pain.

Sarah's sizzling tears flowed. "I really wanted you, Eddie, but things are so bad between us, I like it better when you are gone. At least then Rachel and I have some peace." Sarah was bitter. Only her moral commitment and her wedding vows kept her with Eddie.

Eddie's parents were mentioned often. They had powerful influence over Eddie, although Eddie denied this even while speaking of them frequently. I asked Eddie and Sarah to invite his parents to meet with me. Immediately Eddie was aghast at the idea, and I challenged him about his fear of it. He decided to meet my challenge and ask his parents to meet with me before our next session. I was already slightly acquainted with them since they were greeters at the church I attended. They always smiled and greeted me kindly at the church door, but the real people were anything but smiling and kindly. They were Mr. and Mrs. Aloof.

Eddie's father turned out to be a Milquetoast workaholic, but at least he shook my hand. Eddie's mother glared at me with icy eyes. She had come with an agenda—she planned to set me straight. How dare I pick on her son and, furthermore, she didn't think much of counseling or "people who counsel." She wanted me to know that Eddie was reared in "a fine Christian home, and he never gave us real trouble." I wondered how she defined the word *real*.

Trying to let Mrs. Aloof's verbal shots fly by, I asked Mr. Aloof what he saw in his son's and daughter-in-law's marriage. He said he thought they could make it, although he knew they had problems "like most young couples."

Then Mrs. Aloof dropped a bomb. "We were not real happy when Eddie and Sarah got serious," she said, "but we tried not to interfere. We told Eddie what we thought—they had just too many differences. She comes from a little different background. But when they married, we accepted her."

I detected not-so-subtle maternal prejudice against Sarah. It meant, "Sarah is not like us."

"Mrs. (Aloof)," I said, "the way I see it, Eddie and Sarah are similar in maturity, but Eddie has a real problem with commitment and expressing love. I wonder if you see that."

The question aroused Mr. Aloof. He felt I had challenged his wife, and he told me they were not there to be challenged. From their perspective, he said, Eddie was just fine, but Sarah was immature and demanding. They wished Eddie had not married Sarah, but since he had, they "would accept it, especially for the grandchild." Then without further comment, Mr. and Mrs. Aloof stood and left in a cold silence.

I sat silently for about ten minutes, partly marveling at the way they had left the room. It was as if they'd had a secret code to signal each other when to leave. They had stood in synchronized fashion and marched in formation to the door. It was a remarkable performance.

Mostly, however, I was shaken by the depth of illness I had just observed. This kind of relational illness, prejudice, and judgment without understanding, wisdom, or compassion runs rampant in our society known for its freedom and peace. I understood far better the source of Eddie's illness. He was both an innocent victim and responsible perpetrator.

Speculating about the entrenched nature of generational illness of emotions and relationships is painful. Is there any hope?

THE MALE MALAISE

There is much to say about what is right with American men. Through the years, we have helped to create the most technologically advanced and economically comfortable society in the history of mankind. We have contributed toward creating government and corporate structures second to none. These achievements have been earned with blood, sweat, tears, and outright brilliance.

Lee Atwater is a good example. He ran President Bush's presidential campaign in 1988 at the tender age of thirty-seven. Later President Bush tapped Lee to be chairman of the Republican National Committee. Lee was on top of the world.

Then on March 5, 1990, Lee was at a breakfast fund-raiser for Texas Senator Phil Gramm. As he cracked jokes about Michael Dukakis (Bush's opponent in the 1988 election), Lee's left leg began to shake. Within seconds, he fell to the floor. In minutes he was on a stretcher in an ambulance, being raced to a hospital. The doctors soon discovered that Lee Atwater had an inoperable brain tumor.

What did this young man, in the prime of life, learn as he faced death head-on? He said, "My illness helped me to see that what was missing in society is what was missing in me: a little heart, a lot of brotherhood. The '80s were about acquiring—acquiring wealth, power, prestige. . . . But you can acquire all you want and still feel empty. What power wouldn't I trade for a little more time with my family? What price wouldn't I pay for an evening with friends?" Lee warned us to watch our own "tumor[s] of the soul." He warned that these tumors grow in the "spiritual vacuum at the heart of American society."[1]

Was Lee right? We Americans pride ourselves on being a civilized, peaceful nation. Then why does the United States rank eleventh among all nations in crime and murder rates? Our country ranks fourth in drug-related offenses (buying, selling, and using) and juvenile crime.[2]

The murder rate among young American males is twenty times higher than that of Western Europe. The death rate for young men in Harlem is greater than in Bangladesh.

A Senate Judiciary Committee report on 1990 crime data concluded that the United States is "the most violent and self-destructive nation on earth."[3]

Who makes the United States violent? Consider these statistics?

- Approximately ninety percent of all "serious" or "violent" crimes, such as homicide, rape, robbery, assault, are committed in the United States by men.
- About eighty-three percent of all "nonviolent" crimes, such as drug abuse, driving while intoxicated, carrying weapons, disturbing the peace, offenses against the family, and vandalism, are committed in the United States by men.[4]
- Three to four million American women are beaten by men every year.[5] ("Beaten" means being assaulted severely enough to require police or medical attention.)
- The F.B.I. estimates that only one in ten incidences of domestic violence is reported to police.
- Data shows that twenty-five percent of all wives will be beaten severely at least once during their marriages.

- Twenty percent of all visits by women to hospital emergency rooms are the result of male battering.
- Forty percent of all female homicide victims are killed by a husband, boyfriend, or other male family member.
- Fifty-five percent of all suicides attempted by women relate to incidences of being controlled or battered in the home.
- Ninety-five percent of all assaults on spouses are committed by men.
- At least one-third of the domestic murders committed by females relate to violent men.
- Over fifty percent of homeless women are fleeing a violent man.
- At least thirty-three percent of all men who hit their wives also hit their children.
- The U.S. Surgeon General has proclaimed domestic violence the number one health problem in the United States.
- One in four females under the age of eighteen is sexually abused by a male.
- One in ten males under the age of eighteen is sexually abused. (Usually the perpetrator is a male family member or friend.)

Violence crosses boundaries of age, race, income, and religion. It is particularly prevalent during crises or changes in the family, such as pregnancy, separation, or divorce. Daniel G. Saunders has observed that "if men who batter have a common trait, it is probably low self-esteem. The jealousy, depression, and sensitivity to criticism often noted in these men seem to stem from low self-esteem. . . . In such men, hurt and fear are quickly converted to anger and aggression."[6]

Are violent men wholly unlike all other men? Is there just a small group of bad apples, or is this a male malaise? Saunders says that men who batter "can be viewed as being on one end of a continuum of male socialization. To paraphrase one expert in the field, *men who batter are like all other men, only more so.*"[7]

The point is not that all American men practice violence. No one of sound mind endorses random violence, such as gang violence, murder, or rape. The real point is that American male socialization patterns violate natural emotional development which, in turn, violates male emotional and rational choices. So, while few of us get violent in the criminal sense, most of us bear the wounds and damaged choices of being violated. In turn, too often—even unintentionally—we violate others. In other words, *most of us are messed up.*

HOW FEAR AND HURT CONVERT TO RAGE OR DEPRESSION

Men avoid feeling fear and hurt. We run from these emotions, dodge them, and fight them. These are antimale emotions, or so we think. The truth is that fear and hurt are intrinsic human emotions. We are all born with fear and hurt, and we feel these emotions every day because life is not always fair or kind. These feelings are as natural to us as breathing. Just as inhaling and exhaling air is crucial for physical health, inhaling and exhaling vulnerable emotions is crucial to mental health. Holding emotions in is like holding your breath. You can do it for awhile, but not forever. At some point the emotions either explode or leak out in odd ways and places.

Roger claimed he wasn't bothered by losing his job. Yet he began fighting with his wife and children. He was in conflict with his friends, hollering at store clerks, and drinking a few extra beers alone. Three months later, he was having mysterious dizzy spells.

Unfortunately, our society teaches young boys to hold their emotional breaths by denying and rejecting vulnerable feelings. We teach young boys to pretend they don't have emotional pain.

Our rejection of vulnerable emotions seems to have some basis of logic. Who wants to feel the pain of fear and hurt? And even if we feel it, what are we to do with it? Thus men make Faustian bargains. By rejecting these emotions, we also learn to reject a whole range of powerful, passionate emotions, such as profound joy, soothing peace, wondrous awe. We learn to reject our own hearts! Oh, we might be aware of these emotions because we see others having them, but we don't feel and express them ourselves. The unused "muscles" of these emotions atrophy.

Many escape acknowledging fear and hurt by having fits of rage or bouts of depression. Some have both. By raging we externalize our pain; with depression, we internalize it. We choose the tortures of avoidance and denial rather than deal with our wounds. Consequently many of us live a black-and-white photograph life in a color-movie world. By missing the splendor of life and aging too quickly, many of us starve the person we were meant to be until emotionally we are dead.

The good news is that we can recover. We can connect again with our hearts—the source of our emotions, whether painful or joyful. Learning to feel and articulate a range of emotions might not be easy; difficult changes may be required. But you must be courageous. You can do it, for there is a reward.

You get a whole life. You hear the rhythm of your emotional breathing. You feel the beat of your emotional heart. Your life takes on bright colors, refreshing sensations, and renewed energy. People respond to you more openly. You feel alive!

Healing begins by facing your fears and hurts, and healing begins today. The past is not your master. It has no choke hold on your present. You are free to choose a new future. Living on the path of personal peace transcends self-power, prestige, or aggrandizement. We do this by taking one step at a time.

Each step makes a difference.

THE IMPACT

American men tend toward patterns of socialization that judge "manliness" on the basis of control, performance, and competition. We find ego gratification based on values which force many, if not a majority, to sell their souls in order to be "successful" men. Because many fail to reach a satisfying level of success, it's time for us to calculate the costs of success to our sanity and the sanity of others. Do we use success at work and/or control of women and children as techniques to avoid facing personal responsibility for our unhappiness? Are our obsessions with toys, sports, sex, and chemicals—both alcohol and drugs—simply means to dull our emotional inabilities, insecurities, and pain?

Why do men in the United States live about seven years less than women? According to Dr. Redford B. Williams of Duke University Medical Center, "Angry, cynical people are five times as likely to die before age fifty as people who are calm and trusting. People who are hostile are more likely to suffer premature death from all causes."[8]

From ages twenty-five to sixty-four, men are twice as likely to die as women are. Men die of heart disease, clogged arteries, strokes, cirrhosis of the liver, cancer, and accidents. Men die four times more often from suicide and two-and-a-half times more often from homicide than women do. Could these incidences be linked to repressed emotions and obsessive drives? We know the immune system can handle only so much stress and physical/psychological dissonance before it weakens.

In the brilliant movie *Dad* the father lived a "normal life." He stayed married to the same woman for his whole life and reared a daughter and a son who both became successful adults. But Dad wasn't happy all those years. To survive, he became a "successful schizophrenic." In his fantasies he lived with his wife and four children on a beautiful, tranquil farm in New Jersey. The dream was vividly real in his mind and emotions. It was his escape. Dad felt blocked in real life, so he found joy and contentment in his fantasy.

His only adult son was highly successful in the financial world. The cost he paid for success was a divorce and a distant relationship with his only son. The movie portrays these three men struggling to overcome their relational barriers as Dad is dying of cancer. Their potentials were violated by learned fears and awkwardness. They struggle to learn to freely and honestly love each other and other family members. Often only death or the prospect of death will soften our rock-hard barriers.

Aliens to Ourselves

Robert Bly says that men suffer profound emotional wounds.[9] Unable to express our deepest longings and feelings, we live alone with the people we love. Perhaps this begins with massive emotional walls being built between fathers and sons. Conversations with Dad that ought to be meaningful, instead are superficial and scripted. Sad, we are stuck and alone with our pain.

In a PBS broadcast interview with journalist Bill Moyers, Bly claimed that we are a nation that has lost the ability to grieve. We experience emotional pain, but to survive, we deny our wounds. We think that if we deny pain, then maybe it doesn't exist. Too afraid to feel, we get busy.

Bly wondered if Abraham Lincoln were alive after the Vietnam War what he would have done to help this country grieve. "He would have said, 'We've killed so many people, and these veterans are here, we have destroyed them.'" Then Bly burst into a gut-wrenching, anxious howl. "Aah! Let's all weep. Aah! Aah! Aah!"[10]

At first I thought Bly was nuts. He howled like a wounded coyote. But those crazy, haunting, mournful wails echoed powerfully. They reverberated in my emotional caverns. Long forgotten chords resonated tunes deep within me—first softly, then with increasing volume. I did not know what I was feeling until I recognized the tunes. Then I found myself crying.

My mind and emotions drifted to parched memories, and I felt tremendous sadness. I ached at the unfairness of life. Good people suffer. Cruel people succeed. I know so many wounded souls. I wept for myself and others—those who are driven, self-centered, greedy, isolated, lonely, afraid.

I remembered seeing Glenn, my twelve-year-old neighbor, lying dead in a casket. I was nine or ten then. We had folded and stacked Glenn's *Orange County Registers* in neat rows in his newspaper bags just minutes before a speeding car clobbered him. The impact with the pavement smashed his brain. As I looked at him lying there, white and stone cold, I hated his lifelessness. I hadn't seen a dead body before. Death belted me in the stomach, taking my breath away. I gasped for air and nearly passed out.

I remembered my mom's face, flushed with disappointment, moments after I ripped up my first grade papers before she could see them. I was mad at her. I don't remember why, now, but I remember standing in the kitchen and sobbing because I had robbed my mother of the chance to see what I had done.

Even patching the papers together didn't make it all right. I loved to see her look proud. I had robbed both of us, mother and son, of that moment of pride and joy.

I remembered disappointing my dad by not being as good a ball player as I wanted to be for him. My coordination and confidence just couldn't do it. I was a junior in high school and I was pitching in my first baseball game ever. (I had been too afraid to try as a freshman and sophomore.) People's stares bore into my psyche as my mind scrambled to relay to my body the memory of how to pitch. I stood alone on the mound, shaking like a leaf, while the coach screamed at me, "Get outs!" Each pitch was an immense undertaking. Oddly my mind chose that moment to think, "This must be what people with cerebral palsy feel." While I tried to read the catcher's signal, the kid I had just walked stole second. After a few walks and hits, mercifully the coach sent me to left field. I'd never played there either, so I prayed for hits to right field. Perhaps the most significant part of this memory is that I disappointed myself by quitting the team the very next day. My low level of confidence did not match my dreams of baseball heroics.

Through Robert Bly's mournful wailing, something deep and vulnerable inside me was called out. Through my soft weeping, I felt release. The aching sighs brought relief, and I breathed deeply. After a few moments, I felt awkward about what had happened, and my typical male defenses kicked in, saying, "Pretend this never happened! You should never be so vulnerable! Are you crazy?" But it was too late. My defenses had been washed clean with tears. I would not go back into hiding.

Unplugged Emotions

Having our emotional wires unplugged has long been the standard for American males. We are a nation of pioneers and immigrants. We are "tough." Our mythologies immortalize the rugged, passionless, individualist pioneer. The cowboy loved his horse and cared for "the little woman." Ian Fleming's fictional character James Bond calculated the enemy's demise and used women for pleasure. Even modern American athletes alternately kiss and throw right crosses.

Glamorizing emotionally detached heroes cannot mask our collective and personal wounds. Perhaps the emotionally distant male was necessary in an agrarian, survival society. But times have changed. Our relational society demands emotion. Even our greatest external successes can toll the deaths of our souls, for all the wealth, power, and prestige we can hoard will buy only transitory gratification.

That is not what God meant us to be.

Remember that we learn best in dialogue. So find a committed partner to work with you or start a group for mutual support. That's risky? Or different? Perhaps, yet risk and trying something different are parts of the healing process. And you will be amazed. The reward is within your reach. When you try, you will only gain. There is no failure in the process. *You can become the person you long to be!*

Zusya, a famous Jewish rabbi, wished he were someone other than who he was. He moaned, "Why could I not have been Moses?" Then he realized that in the life to come, "They will not ask me, 'Why weren't you Moses?' They will ask, 'Why weren't you Zusya?'"

Who are *you* meant to be?

Steps to a Lifestyle of Peace

"It takes a very long time to grow young."
—Pablo Picasso

As you venture into the chapters ahead, you are about to embark on a life-changing journey. Others before you have blazed this path in their lives, and now it is your turn. No one can take this journey for you. But this can be the beginning of *your* path to personal peace.

The *Men at Peace* steps are like a map. These steps will guide you into unexplored places in your life, particularly in the realm of emotions. The journey can be exhilarating. But we need to be honest: taking these steps will be hard work and sometimes they will be painful. To make the journey, you must become a pioneer, and take on the spirit of one who is willing to explore the untouched wilderness in your heart, mind, and spirit. This is not a journey everyone dares to make, but with courage you'll complete it and be glad you did.

These are the steps of the journey:

Step 1: I am responsible for my behavior.
Step 2: I am responsible for my anger.
Step 3: I am responsible for my anguish.
Step 4: I am responsible for my fear.
Step 5: I am responsible for my hurt.
Step 6: I am responsible for my grief and gratitude.
Step 7: I am responsible for my passions.
Step 8: I am responsible for my feelings and thoughts.
Step 9: I am a peacemaker.

Each step is discussed in a chapter that gives insights into how males are socialized, how this socialization impacts men on a day-to-day basis, and how we can change. Each Step also recounts stories of men who are pursuing peace.

These Steps are the building blocks of peace for life. Each builds on the previous, so that you take this journey one step at a time.

The title of each Step serves as a daily reminder of your stage of peace-work. A few times each day, speak aloud (or in your mind) the Step you are working on. Simply say, "I am responsible for my behavior," or "I am responsible for my anger."

The *Men at Peace* Steps are more than chapters to read and get through. Too many self-help books pretend that simply by reading the book, you will change. Significant healing does not come from reading, but from reflection and working on behavioral and attitudinal changes. Significant healing comes from conscious, intentional effort to change. By *conscious*, we mean that you purposefully give your best effort. *Intentional* means that you are willfully making changes in your behaviors, feelings, or attitudes.

Did you notice that each Step mentions that you have some responsibility for doing what you do? Many people confuse responsibility with guilt, but they are *not* the same thing. The great lie of guilt is: "I am incapable of goodness in feeling or behaving." Guilt likes black-and-white judgments. Guilt can paralyze us from taking action. Guilt is the enemy of responsibly getting well.

Responsibility, on the other hand, means we do today what we can to get well. We need to understand personal responsibility since for most of us the word "responsibility" has negative connotations, particularly if it is personal.

Perhaps that perception began years ago when large persons of great authority said to you in crisp voices, "*Who* is *responsible* for this mess/disaster/hole in the carpet/broken window?" Less often did the large person of authority ask in a voice that was soft and filled with pride, "Who is responsible for this clean room/wonderful report card/perfectly cut yard?"

We began to get the idea that under no circumstances should we ever admit to having done anything important enough to be criticized later. It was the way the large person said "*Who* is responsible" that made us want to avoid being responsible and to find someone else to blame it on.

Saying that Jerry broke your Tonka truck, or Susan said bad words to you, and therefore you had to hit him or her is not acceptable here, even though it may have worked when you were six.

It's time to grow up. Positive changes *can* happen in your behaviors, feelings, and attitudes—as long as you are willing to take responsibility and make these changes a priority in your life. Best yet, these changes will not detract from your freedom or power. On the contrary, learning to take responsibility for your attitudes, emotions, and behavior can make your life freer and more powerful. The genuine changes you make will feel profoundly rewarding. Furthermore, you will gain a sense of pride, contentment, and peace.

Dealing straight with your wounds will also positively impact others, and they will begin to notice the change in you. When someone compliments you for your new self, remember to say thank you!

Sometimes your progress will be dramatic and quick; other times you may work on a Step for a long time without sensing much progress. Yet patiently persevere! Fast growth is encouraging but barriers cannot be gone around—they must be gone *through*. Actually, barriers are opportunities. They help you to build greater strength and skill.

If you become discouraged with your progress in a given Step, move ahead. Sometimes breakthroughs happen later, and may allow us to return to an unfinished step with greater understanding of its implications and requirements.

Remember that old patterns can be hard to break. Change, even good change, can cause anxiety. You may find yourself saying, "Is this really me? When will I fail? Maybe I should fail now and get it over with. I am more comfortable with my craziness!" Don't be surprised if feelings like these creep up on you while you change and grow.

Progress requires process, and process takes time. You are making progress when you see yourself going in the right direction. But making progress doesn't mean you are done. We are never done! Remember that progress does not mean just answering the questions. Progress is reflecting on the questions and gaining insight into your life. This, and only this, is what makes a difference. As Walker Percy said, "Some people get all A's and flunk life!" You see, answering the questions "correctly" is not as important as what you decide to do with your answers.

Your progress in each Step will continue even as you progress through other Steps. Sometimes you will seem to be losing ground, and this will feel discouraging. It will seem like you are taking two steps forward, one step back. Just keep facing the right direction and keep moving forward as best you can.

Picture yourself building a pyramid of progress. You start at the bottom by building a solid foundation. Solid foundations take time to build. As you build each level, the previous levels expand in depth, and you continue to mature previous levels without conscious awareness. Be encouraged!

Some try to do each Step perfectly. Others rush and do not dig deeply enough. Just be honest—neither too harsh nor too hasty. Don't judge yourself too exactly. Be gracious. Tough, yet tender. Don't excuse your faults. Don't bail yourself out with reasons for your mistakes. Face slip-ups truthfully. Then be forgiving.

Let a trusted, objective friend or the members of a men's group help you evaluate your progress. Men's groups work particularly well as confidential objective friends.

An "objective friend" is someone who tells the truth, as he sees it, without needing something in return. Objective friends tend to be good listeners. Often they only help us with personal growth: we don't play golf with them, or work business deals together. Objective friends are usually people with wisdom or skill in personal growth. Therapists, ministers, rabbis, or people who have worked through some of their own life issues can make good objective friends.

If an objective friend is to be truly helpful, you must tell him the truth—the good and the bad. If you present this friend with an image—a facade of yourself—then your progress will crumble. You will dig a deeper hole of self-deception. Facades are part of what we are trying to get rid of.

Mark Twain once said, "I always tell the truth so I never have to remember anything." He meant that when you tell the truth, you no longer have to remember what image you were trying to put on—what lies you were weaving—at a particular time or in a certain set of circumstances. Usually the only ones fooled by our facades are ourselves. Others smile sadly, quietly recognizing our fakery and foolishness. Lying does not work in virtually any area of our lives—it particularly does not work in the realms of mental and relational health.

At the same time, honesty requires emphasizing the good as well as the bad. Be affirmed. An objective friend knows to affirm you! Choose trusted friends who will do just that.

Some men want to conquer each Step. This impulse is particularly true for men who work in sales. They "manage" or "sell" themselves on their progress, thinking that if they control this well enough and persuade themselves of great progress, then they will have accomplished something grand. The thought is, *If I conquer, I win and I succeed!*

Wrong. This is not the way this works. This is not a business venture. You are not out to win a prize for selling something. You need to dig deeply and discover your soul. Period. Wrestle with yourself. Don't try to fix, acquire or win. Don't try to become a veteran without doing a few real inner battles.

A few men have come to our group saying, "I am here because I want to help other guys." After a week or two, these brothers become great salesmen for the group, saying, "I just want to tell you new guys how great this group will be for you. It will change your life just as it did mine." After a few weeks or months, with little of their selves exposed, such brothers often leave, their personal wounds still running deep. Being scared is okay. Being upbeat is even okay. But you must dig deeply into your own soul.

Our goal is not to conquer the Steps. Our goal is to grow at peace-living. These Steps are only tools. The process is only as good as your will to dig deeply.

Objective friends can help you because they see what you do not see. They can help you see your barriers and blind spots. An objective friend balances your extreme positives or negatives. An objective friend will understand and may have a similar experience to share. An objective friend will say something you had not considered. Or, he can put into words something you have been unable to say.

Many men come to group, saying, "I am not into groups." We simply say, "Welcome! We are a group for men who are not into groups!"

Others say, "I am not into talking about myself." We say, "Good. We talk about not wanting to talk about ourselves."

For many, allowing someone to help is a dramatic step. Many are not used to trusting. These men can begin by talking about their fear of trusting. Trust requires vulnerability and risk and it takes time to develop. The power of a Men at Peace group is that we are all equal in need but each person can contribute in special ways. We act as mutual supporters of one another. The power of community is great.

We are all afraid to be vulnerable. My secret fears, hurts, or problems are the worst—or so we imagine. Then we hear others' stories. Their problems may seem much worse, or their stories are like ours. Either way, we find comfort.

Your spouse or partner may be your best friend. That is terrific! Yet that also makes her your poorest objective support. Since your relationship is deep, that person can be "too close" to help you in some ways. She might not perceive your progress or weaknesses clearly.

It is okay to ask your partner for a sense of your progress. But watch the intensity of your reaction to her comments. You might soar too high with her affirmation; you might sink too deeply into despair or resentment with criticisms. *Your partner has her own agenda tied into your progress, and therefore your partner cannot be your best guide or most objective friend.*

You also deserve warning that occasionally a partner might try to unwittingly sabotage your progress because your progress will expose her weaknesses. Your partner is used to you as you are, and your change can be scary. Sometimes she might even test your growth, asking, "Is this for real? How long will it last? When will you go back to your old ways?"

Be patient with your partner. She may have tolerated your quirks for a long time. Remember, you cannot fix your partner. The painful truth is that you can only change yourself! Your change is enough to handle. Over time, your partner will have room to change herself if she so chooses.

So respect your partner's valid concerns and modestly enjoy her affirmations. Bear her criticisms gently. Most of all, keep responsibility within yourself.

As you begin to experience the benefits of change, you might find yourself tempted to try to change others. But be careful—never tell an acquaintance how to live his or her life. Do not give advice unless it is clearly asked for, and even then be very careful! Never copy these pages and tell someone to do this or that. You might help a brother "fix" or cover up his problem, thereby preventing him from true personal and relational growth. Some men are not ready for change. This might sound tough, but some people need to suffer more pain before they are ready to change. Pain is a great motivator.

You can help friends who are not in your group, as well as those who are, primarily by doing one thing: *Listen!* Listen well! Hear what they say, then tell them what you heard. You can ask questions if you do not understand. You can ask them what they are feeling. You can ask what they plan to do about their situation. You can tell them that you care.

Perhaps you can give a friend a simple suggestion. For example, you might say, "It seems to me you could . . ."

Or "What I hear you saying is . . . "

Or "Do you think you might . . ."

These suggestions are cautious and subtle. Because men are prone to give "fix-it advice," it might feel good to you to give advice—especially if your advice is accepted! But too much hard advice can diminish the respect your friend feels from you.

Perhaps the best thing you can do for another person is to tell him that you are working on personal growth. Invite him to join your group. Or begin a group with him! (Later we will tell you how.)

As you work through these Steps, be sure to affirm and validate yourself. Do this by allowing yourself to feel pride about your progress. Walk with your head up. Give yourself a day of constant verbal strokes ("I am a good person!" "Thank you God for giving me such a wonderful day." "I did it!") A sign of pride with humility is that you can share your pride with a friend without embellishment or embarrassment. He or she need not be impressed. You just need and want to share something you are proud of!

This entire program assumes that a key to our growing in peace includes building self-esteem. Dignity helps us feel better about ourselves and gives us the security and energy to change! We don't have a step on self-esteem because the entire program builds self-esteem. The skills of esteeming yourself are built-in without buzz words.

Thank God and congratulate yourself for your commitment and progress. Each step you take, each task you venture through, adds another blessing to your life, your family, your friends, your neighborhood, your country, and even the world. On these seemingly "small" steps, God builds the Kingdom of Peace.

Am I fantasizing? I don't think so. Your children will be blessed, and their blessings will pass to their children. The greatest gift you can give your children is a life at peace. The greatest part of this gift is to help them know the great Peacemaker.

Wouldn't it be wonderful if someday your grandchildren call you blessed? "My Grandpa practiced peace. . . . He began this way of life for us!"

Bless you, friend, on your journey as you venture into peace!

TIME-OUT!

Time-Out is a technique that interrupts the stress and tension that tend to build in the early stages of conflict, enabling the people involved to stop the momentum before rage or depression sets in. Time-Out provides guidelines to help you structure your behavior and release tension. It also provides an alternative way of responding, rather than simply reacting. The goal is to decrease friction in yourself and toward others, thereby enabling you to make better choices.

It is important that you follow Time-Out procedures carefully. Many think they have used this technique before, yet often their actual motive and use of the Time-Out was to escape, manipulate, or get revenge. Time-Outs, used appropriately, are for *you*: they are never to be used as a tool against anyone else.

Time-Out is not used to avoid difficult issues, or to escape conflict. Partners agree to come back after the time spent away, check in with each other, and attempt to settle the disagreement if possible. To settle a disagreement means you can agree, compromise, disagree, or agree to disagree— peacefully.

You may need to adjust the Time-Out procedure to fit your circumstances and schedule, but stick close to the purpose of the Time-Out.

Time-Out Steps

1. *Be aware of body tension.* Your body tells you what you feel. In the midst of a disagreement or confrontation, do you have shaky, sweaty palms? Tight muscles around your forehead, jaws, neck, or shoulders? Tense stomach? Do you feel numb? Hot? Cold? If your body is sending you signals, this tells you that rage (or depression) is not far away. You need to take a Time Out.

2. *Choose a Time-Out Indicator.* Prearrange, with your partner, a simple statement to be spoken aloud: "I am feeling angry/tense/overwhelmed. I need a Time-Out for myself." Then take a Time-Out immediately! Some men are helped by visualizing a Stop sign to help them stop themselves, to interrupt their process, or to prompt them to say the Time-Out indicator.

3. *Leave the room immediately.* It's important to leave the presence of the other person in order to practice the Time-Out.

Don't escalate the situation by slamming the door, getting in the last word, punching the wall or giving nasty glances! Remember, a Time-Out is for *you*. No excuses! Leave the premises complete and *stay apart for a least half an hour*, if at all possible.

4. *Allow your body to expend some energy.* Do the following during the Time-Out: walk briskly, run, ride a bike, lift weights, or other physical activity. Do not drive a vehicle, visit a person of the opposite sex, or use alcohol or drugs. In addition to physical exercise, you may want to try to release the energy in your body through relaxation techniques.

5. *Assess the following:*

- "What am I feeling?" (What are the feelings beneath your anger? Fear? Hurt? What form of fear or hurt? What is your body telling you? Make a mental note of the signals.)
- "What do I truly need?" (Do you need respect? Do you need not to be yelled at? Do you need more time to yourself? Articulating your needs to yourself during Time-Out will help you articulate them to your partner when you resume your discussion.)
- "What am I willing to do to get what I need?" (This usually requires a compromise. Think about what you can give up, how you can compromise, or how you can help your partner better consider your need.)

6. *Be aware of your self-talk.* Negative self-talk escalates tension. Listen closely to the "quiet" negative background messages in your head. Do you hear any of the following? *I hate her. If she says one more thing, I'll explode. I'm stupid. I always screw-up. I'm bad. I'm wrong. I'll never get it right. Nobody cares. I can't stand this anymore.*

Some of these negative messages are so deeply engrained—often from childhood—that we may not even hear them! They are like tape-recorded messages in our minds, running on fast forward, making squiggly sounds. But the messages are there. Stop and listen to your mind.

Replace negative messages with positive messages: *I am okay. I have choices. I can stay calm. I will be peaceful. I am a good person.* Saying these new messages aloud helps to "tape over" the old messages. I know one man who practiced one positive self-statement at every red light.

7. *Decide what the issue or issues are and think of positive solutions before you return.* Discuss these solutions with your partner when you are ready. If tempers flare, take another Time-Out. If you think this sounds foolish, remember that rage or depression is far more foolish! One man had to take four consecutive Time-Outs. Then he and his wife made a major breakthrough. They realized how silly they felt and they admitted that their arguments were, in fact, usually about silly things. As a result, they simply quit arguing about most things. They felt wonderful!

8. *Identify the fear and/or hurt which led to your anger and/or anguish.* You'll be learning more about this in the following chapters.

9. *Practice Time-Outs* for ten minutes at least twice each week until they become an instinct. If you do not practice Time Outs in calmer times, they are difficult to use when tension rises.

How to Make Time-Outs Fail!

If you *don't* want your Time-Outs to benefit you or your partner, do one or both of the following:

1. *Don't make a conscious effort to practice Time-Outs* during some of your less intense arguments.

2. *Say, "She won't let me do a Time-Out!"* Usually this means you haven't honestly helped her understand the purpose of the Time-Out. It betrays your lack of commitment. Did you let her know she can take a Time-Out too?

Even if our partners don't like Time-Outs (some of our members have heard the phrase, "Stay and work this out like a man!") we do them anyway. Remember, a Time-Out is for you.

One fellow I know insisted that he could not get away. His wife blocked the back door.

"You could have run out the front door," we advised.

"I did, but she stood behind my truck so I couldn't get away."

Remembering guideline number four—get some exercise and don't drive—we asked, "What were you doing in your truck!"

"Well, if I walked, she would have followed me."

"Then run!"

"What!" he said aghast, "I'd look crazy!"

Time-Outs can change your life. But you have to be willing to use them!

JOURNALING

Time-Outs are necessary tools. A journal is another important tool. As you begin this journey, consider writing down your thoughts and feelings along the way. A self-record will help you track your progress in the days ahead. As you look back and remember, be grateful for your growth and progress.

Journals are friends. Each day spend time with your private book to say what is really on your mind and heart. Give yourself a chance to vent a little or to express what you wished you had done or said earlier in the day. Affirm yourself for a good day. Say a prayer. Make a plan for tomorrow. Take notice of one small, new step.

Because journals are best kept private, don't write what you hope others will read. A journal is not a place to perform. There is no need to impress yourself or others with your writings.

Journals make great "feelings diaries" as you sit quietly alone and explore feelings you didn't have time to recognize or explore during a busy day. Exploring and articulating feelings are critical skills in personal and relational growth.

Best yet, journaling is relatively simple:

- *Just find a time.* Some people like to journal in the morning; some evening; some lunch time and others during a break at the office. Consistency is more important than when.
- *Then find a place.* Staying in the same place can be helpful. But more important is having a quiet place without interruptions.

- *Buy a book.* I like the ninety-nine cent stenographer notebooks or small loose-leaf binders with pages I can remove. Sometimes I splurge and buy a brand new ninety-nine cent pen, but that is strictly optional. Occasionally I write on napkins. These tend to get stuffed into my pockets. Sometimes the napkins end up in the wash, where they break down into hundreds of little white pieces that cling all over neatly washed laundry. My wife . . . Well, stay away from napkins.
- *Sit down.* Take a deep breath; inhale through your nose and exhale through your mouth. Write the date. Then begin writing what comes to you easily at first. What thoughts occurred to you today? Where does that take you? What else happened to you today? What angry or anguished feelings did you have? How did you handle these? What were your fears or hurts?

If you prefer, you can try making a journal using audio cassettes with a tape recorder.

Don't spend long hours at this. Fifteen to thirty minutes should be adequate. Some people write too much and then burn out. So pace yourself, focus, and let journaling be a valuable, satisfying tool.

ALCOHOL OR DRUG USE

Abuse of, or addiction to, alcohol or drugs lessens the value of attempting this program. A person must face his chemical problem before other significant recovery can occur.

There is no other way.

Signs of trouble include the following. Do you . . .

- Often drink to avoid problems?
- Ever drink alone?
- Want a drink the next morning?
- Ever lose time from work because of drinking?
- Ever promise not to drink, then end up having a drink anyway?

- Ever feel remorse after drinking?
- Find that others notice your personality changes after you begin drinking?
- Ever have complete loss of memory after drinking?
- Neglect your family because of drinking?
- Resent others who advise you to stop drinking?

A "yes" to any of these questions, according to the National Council on Alcoholism, may mean you have an alcohol problem—or that one is swiftly on its way. If this is a possibility in your life, see an alcohol or drug counselor immediately. Or, call a Twelve Step program (Alcoholics Anonymous, Narcotics Anonymous, or others). Let someone evaluate your use of chemicals. Follow a recovery plan.

Once you establish yourself in such a program, you may enter the Men at Peace program concurrently. Be sure you face your chemical problem honestly and boldly, and admit that you are in recovery.

CHRONIC VIOLENCE OR PROFOUND DESPAIR

If violent behavior is common in your life, or if you are loaded with tension and live on the verge of explosion, you should seek the help of a trained domestic violence counselor immediately. He or she might recommend additional help as you begin the Men at Peace Steps.

If you feel despairing, if suicidal thoughts plague your mind, or if you wonder if you are experiencing depression, you would be wise to see a professional therapist or doctor for evaluation. Once you have a sense of your situation, the Men at Peace Steps will be of greater value to you.

Step 1: I Am Responsible for My Behavior

Responsibility is not a popular topic. After all, America is a nation rooted politically in a "Bill of Rights." We are highly individualistic in thought and life-style. We have a right to demand our rights, right?

I fear that we have missed the point. Have we forgotten that our nation was founded on the fundamental principles of equality, justice and the common good? The "Bill of Rights" is a document clarifying a few specific exceptional rights—it was not meant to outline a predominant philosophy of society.

Perhaps the time has come to write a "Bill of Responsibilities." Let us start with ourselves.

Learning to be responsible is the foundation of the entire Men at Peace life-style. We are responsible to make wise and peace-living choices in a morally teasing and conflict-oriented world. Unfortunately, apart from other "responsible" people, we might not receive applause for making responsible choices. Many cynical people applaud using others for short-term gain.

Yet responsible people make the best employees and marriage partners over time.

"I am responsible!" is simple to say and difficult to master. Every Step depends on your taking responsibility. Persevere and be proud of your progress.

TAKING RESPONSIBILITY IS A POSITIVE STEP

Admitting responsibility does not mean you are a bad person. To the contrary, knowing your intrinsic self-worth is a significant aspect of learning to be responsible! A healthy self-esteem gives you the power to make healthy, responsible choices! Remember, you are a creation of God, made in the image of God. (See Psalm 139 for more light on this subject.)

Being responsible does not mean you do everything wrong. Unfortunately, many men associate the word "responsible" with having done something wrong or bad. Maybe as a child, you heard the phrase, "You are responsible," only when you were being told you were at fault. Being responsible also means admitting you do many things well! What do you do well? Remember—doing something well does not mean doing it perfectly. I don't believe that anyone can perform many tasks with perfection; but there are any number of things that we do well. Take responsibility for these things. In fact, this would be a good topic to spend a day writing in your journal.

Taking responsibility does not mean that other people are okay, but you are somehow not okay. Others have problems too. They might be far less responsible than you, but that is their issue, not yours. Sure, their craziness may affect you, but you can only take responsibility for your response to their problems—you cannot fix them. This is a powerful lesson to master.

Some men come to Men at Peace saying, "I am not responsible!" They might add, "I will not take responsibility for what Dad/Mom/my wife did to me!" If someone hurt you, it is true that you are not at fault. You are not responsible for being abused or mistreated. You are not guilty. There are many things in life—emotional wounds included—over which we have little control. Yet this is precisely why it is critical that we take responsibility for the things over which we *do* have some control.

Taking responsibility is the first step to stopping our victimization from past or present wounds. Taking responsibility is the only way to begin to build peace today and in the future. Today we say "No!" to the power of victimization. As one brother said, "Today I choose a life in which no one has the right to hurt me or abuse me."

Responsibility empowers us to build the life we choose. We will, with support, choose to get well. This is true for a victim, or an abuser. Responsibility empowers us to choose peace.

CHOOSING RESPONSIBLE BEHAVIORS

Our first Step is: "I am responsible for my behavior."

We use the word "behavior" broadly. First of all, we mean we are accountable for our actions. We will learn not to react destructively to situations which bother us. Instead we will learn to slow down, sort out our feelings, and to consider our choices. This is power.

Our behavior also includes what we think, the attitudes we choose, our responses to the behaviors of others, and our responses to our own emotions. Of course, you are free to feel what you feel without judgment, but you must take responsibility for the choices you make in response to your feelings.

For many of us, the first step in taking responsibility boils down to the following realization: "I have a problem." Perhaps you are coming to this conclusion because conflicts are making your life unmanageable—not completely unmanageable, but significantly so. Perhaps you are willing to accept this realization because an important person in your life is telling you that this is true. You might not completely understand the specific complaint someone has about you, but you understand enough to admit, "I have a problem."

This is your first Step to peace.

Responsibility means facing your obsessions and your controlling behaviors, even if "other men are that way."

Responsibility means learning to have a peaceful inner life.

Responsibility means daring to feel your feelings.

Responsibility means caring enough to listen to others—without allowing yourself to be used or hurt by others.

Responsibility means giving time and discipline to working the Men at Peace Steps to Peace.

Responsibility means saying "No!" to some urgent good choices and saying "Yes!" to significant, lasting choices.

RESPONSIBILITY MEANS MORE THAN CONTROL

In Chapter One we learned the limitations and harm of control. Control works in the short run but hurts us spiritually over time.

One man came to Men at Peace verbally berating his wife. "I am sick of her," he griped. "She needs to show me some love. I tell her I love her, so she'd better give me some love. I told her what I feel, but she still treats me cold. She'd better start responding!"

The brothers in group let him go on for just a bit, then pointed out to him that he sounded angry, if not raging. Further, they suggested that his demands to his wife, though seemingly fair, were spoken in demanding and manipulative tones and words.

"I am not angry!" he fired back angrily. "So you guys think she can do whatever she wants? Easy for you to say. If you were in my shoes, you'd think differently. I'm not putting up with it!"

In a crudely righteous sense, he is correct. He is in a tough spot. His wife might not be fair. She might even be manipulating him. He is hurting terribly and has a point—no one else is in his shoes. No one knows completely the pain that he is feeling. Yet no man can force his wife's love, even if his love for her is genuine and gracious. For this brother, becoming responsible means facing his pain: his frustration, hurt, rejection, anger at the unfairness of life, his desire to force love, his loneliness and emptiness. Becoming responsible also means finding and accepting support from others. It might also mean making some tough decisions.

After all, there is no way he can make his wife become what he needs. He cannot control her. Ironically, most wives respond lovingly as they feel their husband's respect and self-control. Time and experience with a respectful and self-controlled husband allows her to feel safe and enables her to express emotional vulnerability. And, of course, the same holds true for us! When our wives help create this kind of environment for us, we may feel increasingly secure and find it easier to take the necessary risks for personal growth.

Unfortunately, some situations are a far cry from the esteem-building scenario I have just created. Terry, for example, came to group with this story: "I can't believe it. My wife is ice cold to me. She's suddenly acting weird. I asked her if she's having an affair but she denies it. But when I try to talk to her about it she won't look me in the eyes. She's acting so strange—I don't trust having sex with her anymore."

Sadly, Terry's instincts were right. Within two weeks, Terry found out his wife had been having an affair for several months. Terry was enraged over the fact that she had been deceiving him. He said, "I should have trailed her every move. I should kill that guy. I hate being made a fool!" Yet, with the help of the group, Terry chose not to seek revenge. He kept working at maintaining his peace through difficult days. Often he was on the verge of violence toward his wife but, instead, he had the courage to bring these feelings to our men's group. Terry learned to use the group and his friends as outlets for his pain, hurt and anger.

Many men would say, "I would get revenge. No man deserves what Terry experienced." Yet, in all honesty, what would revenge accomplish? Release of anger? Time in jail? Revenge gives vent to our immediate rage but also keeps us locked in a never-ending cycle of bitterness. Bitterness stunts our emotional growth—which is tragic since emotional growth happens to be the only pathway beyond the pain.

Terry had the right to vent bitterness, pain, hurt, and anger with people who cared about him. And as he did, Terry slowly began to see how he had not been sensitive to his wife's needs. His irresponsibility had helped create the right environment for his marriage to fail.

Eight months later, shortly after their divorce, Terry's former wife left the "other man" and wanted to come back to Terry. At first Terry was thrilled. Then he began to consider what needed to happen before he could try again. He wanted them to start marriage therapy. When his ex-wife would not agree, Terry saw that she had not grown as a person in the past months and she expressed little regret about her affair. She was looking for a quick fix to her loneliness.

Terry chose not to return to his former wife. His painful progress over eight months had given him dignity, purpose, and self-respect. If he had unleashed his rages, he could have spent years in a jail cell for a moment of revenge. If he had followed his emotional impulses, he would have returned to his ex-wife with no new skills or purpose for their relationship.

A few months later, Terry's former wife saw the wisdom of Terry's request for therapy. Today, their relationship is being rebuilt slowly, and although they have yet to choose to remarry, they are learning a great deal about peace and commitment.

Another man came to the Men at Peace group for a few weeks, then announced: "I think I am done with this program. I have not been angry for a few weeks. When I feel angry now, I have it all under control."

What toxic words! As we have learned, men love to control things. Many men approach Men at Peace thinking we are an "anger control" or "depression control" support group. These men tell themselves, "I know I should control myself better. I just need to control my anger," or "I shouldn't be depressed. I should just pump myself up with positive ideas."

Perhaps. Perhaps control is better than being out of control. Yet manhandling our drives by wielding an even tighter grasp of our emotional reins is expedient at best. Responsibility, on the other hand, couples self-control with "decontrol" as we actually learn to unleash our deeper, vulnerable feelings.

Unfortunately, men overcontrol their emotions, including anger, which leads to more explosive, raging behaviors. Control is a shaky start, at best, and it does not ensure rooted change in the long run. Control stops personal growth.

This is because control means we manipulate something; we manipulate our feelings. Responsibility, on the other hand, means we face and feel what is happening so that we can make peaceful and committed choices. Control tends to be a reaction of force; responsibility tends to be a purposeful, chosen response.

Most men are deeply rooted in controlling. This comes out in our penchant for "fixing," advising, doing the "right" thing, and using cause-and-effect thinking such as "If only I do this, then that should happen." Often in group we allow a man to continue in this mode as part of his first step. Over time he learns that "man-handling" his rage or depression does not work. We control too much!

More than control, we ask you to begin facing the truth about yourself: You are a good person who needs a changed life. Admitting your strengths and your defects, honestly, will help you grow and expand your emotions and your choices.

COMMON WAYS MEN AVOID RESPONSIBILITY

Life is filled with experiences and circumstances that demand for us to take responsibility and respond with healthy choices. Some of these events include:

- Conflicts with your wife or child(ren)
- Conflicts with a person or persons at work
- Conflicts with brothers, sisters, parents, relatives
- Blow-ups with customers, bosses, coworkers, strangers, disrespectful kids, crazy car drivers, etc.
- Feelings that you are a victim: "Life is giving me a bad rap," "Somebody is after me," "The government is ripping me off," etc.
- Unemployment or underemployment
- General hostility
- Feeling defeated or depressed
- Aggressive or passive behaviors
- Low self-esteem
- Hating yourself
- Perfectionism
- Self-punishment
- Treating your partner disrespectfully

Truthfully, these examples represent the tip of the iceberg. When it comes to conflict that demands a responsible response, the possibilities are endless. And yet despite the overwhelming need, we often continue to avoid taking responsibility. I believe there are three methods by which we manage to avoid becoming responsible:

1. Denial or Repression

George came to group saying, "I don't have a problem. It's just that . . ." He went on to describe a life filled with turmoil, including significant conflicts with his wife.

Denial.

George also described a turbulent relationship with his father: "He used to give us pretty good lickin's," George admitted. "But I deserved it. I messed up a lot."

Repression.

George loves his father, yet his father overreacted and over-punished George when he was a boy. George may subconsciously believe that if he admits his father's violence, then his father is a bad person who must be rejected. This is not, of course, true. George must learn to separate his love and his hurt, accepting the fact that both emotions can indeed exist toward the same person at the same time.

2. Blaming

Another method by which we avoid responsibility is simply to point our finger, insisting: "I wouldn't have any problems . . .

". . . if she would just quit nagging me."

". . . if my boss would get off my case."

". . . if only that jerk hadn't cut me off."

We have an answer for every conflict. If we believe our delusions, none of our problems have anything to do with the crazy persons we have become. Our rage or depression must have a reason. Men love to find "reasons."

Our biggest mistake is assuming that the reason is out there, outside of ourselves, when all the while it lies within.

Tom, for example, likes to tell friends, "My wife makes me angry." In reality, his wife may do things that Tom does not like; but Tom is responsible for how he responds. His wife does not have the power to "make" Tom angry or otherwise. The choice belongs to Tom. And Tom's choice, so far, has been to become enraged. Tom's wife may have problems . . . but she is not the cause of Tom's problems. Tom's problem is within himself.

Your problems are within you too.

You might be tempted to respond, "But you don't understand! She—"

Stop right there! She is responsible for her actions . . . but *you* are responsible for your reactions.

You cannot control your surroundings. You cannot control all the events of your life. You cannot control people in your life; they have moods and problems of their own. You cannot control your children (you can love, guide and discipline them, but not control)—or friends, neighbors or coworkers. You cannot even control your spouse. Your spouse, for example, does not *owe* you kindness. You might deserve kindness, but you cannot demand that it be given you. Your spouse has the right to choose behaviors and attitudes and feelings freely.

You cannot control the choices of another person. You can, however, control your response. You can choose. Is your response a reaction based on hurt or fear? Or is your response a choice based on respect for others—even when their choices hurt you—respect for yourself and a commitment to peace? If someone is choosing to hurt you, you cannot change that person. But you do not need to choose to remain in the abuse. You have the right to leave an abusive situation. You do not, however, have the right to blame the situation—even an abusive one—for your problems. Blaming is not taking responsibility.

This can be painful news. You may disagree with it. You may need to struggle with this idea for awhile. We control—or try to control—because we do not want more pain. This is understandable—pain hurts! We wish others would fit into our ideas of the right or the good. Unfortunately, we can't *make* them want the same things we do.

Love, after all, permits space. Love allows freedom. Love is not possessive. It does not force. To paraphrase Paul in the New Testament, "Love does not seek its own way" (I Cor. 13:5).

You may wish for her love. You may tell yourself that you love her. You may ask if she will share her feelings with you. But you cannot force her to love you. Of course, the positive side to all this is that if she chooses to love you, it is love freely given. You can rest assured in her choice. You are loved!

The concept that we cannot blame our problems on anyone else—that we are responsible for our reactions and that we have the right to choose—is not an easy one to master.

I once heard a man unwind a dramatic story about his wicked and manipulative wife. It made for an impressive tale of evil and woe. "She does this . . ." he lamented, "and she does that. . . . You've never met a woman like my wife. . . ." This man did not want our help. He wanted our pity.

Finally, exhausted with this fellow's tale, I said, "Friend, if this woman is so bad, then you must really be sick because *you chose her!* That is your real problem. When you are ready to face up to that, come back to group."

You have felt powerless. Today you can regain power. Not power over someone but power over yourself. Not power to control, but power to be responsible with your behavior and feelings. Not power to manipulate, but power to make healthy choices for your life.

It's time to stop blaming.

3. Crazy Talk

Crazy talk is the most subtle and devious form of avoiding responsibility. It is a blend of the worst of denial/repression and blaming. Everyone talks crazy to some extent. The danger comes when a person makes a habit of crazy talk and begins to believe the lies they are telling themselves. Otherwise normal, healthy, prominent, seemingly sound-minded people can be found manipulating themselves and others with the most disturbing forms of crazy talk.

What is crazy talk?

Terrence, a sixtyish, slightly balding but fit corporate president, was known for his adventurous corporate decisions.

He frequently hit the nail on the head with his bold business sense. His company's profits doubled during his six-year presidency. Younger executives revered him. Whatever he touched seemed to turn into gold. Yet it was his kindly face and kindlier demeanor that won the hearts and loyalty of his employees. He was the toast of any company party.

But not at home.

His wife, Bea, was a petite, pretty lady, always immaculately dressed. She did whatever Terrence wished. She admired him greatly. She watched his kindness to people everywhere.

Except at home.

His son, Lawrence, single and a picture of his father thirty years ago, honored his dad. He modeled his life after Dad. He revered Dad. Every part of Dad's life he admired.

Except for what he saw at home.

Cara, the gorgeous blonde daughter, a senior in high school who was sought after by all the boys at school, charmed the socks off the corporate execs. She was the sweetheart and co-host, with Mom, of their lush parties. She had great memories of her dad.

Everywhere but at home.

At home, Terrence turns off the charm. His soul grows dark. He spits demands and inane thoughts at will.

When Lawrence took a different job in a distant state, Terrence became distressed—but he would not admit his feelings. Instead, he plunged deep into a kind of communication that relied not only on denial and blaming, but also on projection, verbal smoke screens, and defensiveness. This style of communication is enough to drive anyone crazy—those who use it, and the loved ones they use it on.

Late one night, for example, Terrence entered the family room and sat on the couch across from Cara.

Terrence: "Have you heard from your brother?"

Cara: "No, Dad. He's only been gone a few days."

Terrence: "You know your mother is terribly worried about him."

Translation: I love Lawrence and miss him already. Terrence, who rarely expresses honest and direct feelings, misses his son. He worries for his safety. Yet because the family is so rigid in their closeness—Terrence rarely uses the word love—he is projecting his anxious feelings, like a movie projector, onto his wife. In truth, Terrence—not his wife—is terribly worried about Lawrence. Bea, in contrast, seems to be handling Lawrence's move better than Terrence. In fact, earlier that evening Terrence went so far as to accuse Bea of "not caring for Lawrence." He ragged on her until she left to spend the evening alone in their bedroom.

Cara: "That's funny. Mom told me she trusts Lawrence to take care of himself. What do you mean, 'worried,' Dad?"

Terrence: "Oh, you know your mother. She hides her feelings. Your brother might be in danger!"

Translation: I feel fear for Lawrence's safety. I hope Lawrence has a safe trip. I don't want him to get hurt, but I'm unable to admit any of this. Terrence imagines the worst—he visualizes a drunk driver swerving head-on toward Lawrence's car . . . a burglar breaking into the new apartment in which Lawrence will be living alone . . . Lawrence, lonely and perhaps even victimized in a new city, far from home . . .

Cara: "In danger of what?"

Terrence: (frowning) "What? He's traveling across country!"

Cara: "Yeah. And?"

Terrence: "It's crazy out there! Don't you care? Cara, you only think of yourself."

Translation: I am worried; I am upset. I want encouragement because I am afraid—even though, should you try to encourage me, I wouldn't accept it. I miss my son and will continue to miss him. But I am afraid even to admit this! How am I going to handle this feeling of loss? I feel deathly afraid.

Cara now feels confused, frustrated and even a little guilty. But she is smart enough to ask, "Dad, are you okay?"

Terrence: "Of course I'm okay. It's your mother who's not handling this well."

Cara: "Mom? Where is she? I'll talk with her."

Terrence: "No! She went to bed with a headache. Let her sleep."

Translation: I need to use your mother as the scapegoat. If you spoke with her, she might tell you that I ranted and raved at her all evening. That's how she got her headache.

Cara left the room feeling helpless and worried. And sad. She wondered if *she* was the crazy one. She missed Lawrence too. She would like to have had her feelings heard. She wished she could have hugged her father, and gotten a hug from him in return—but he was too cold.

Talking with Terrence makes each family member feel crazy. In fact, Terrence has the ability to drive *himself* to distraction as well! His talk is dishonest, indirect, blaming, demeaning, and emotionally repressive. He assaults genuine, caring communication. At these moments, he acts and talks like a schizoid and paranoid person.

Confronting Denial/Repression, Blaming and Crazy Talk

Avoidance styles require careful confrontation. The naive innocence of avoidance belies the mad, snarling dog trying desperately to protect his territory.

When a man comes to our group using one of these avoidance styles, I see if a direct approach will help him recognize his own vulnerability lurking beneath the avoidance tactics. The first thing I say to him is: "Is it possible that it is *you* who feels hurt/afraid/lonely/angry?"

If he denies that these are his feelings, I ask repeatedly questions such as: "Then what do you feel?" or "What are your feelings about that?" or "How does that make you feel?"

Our new friend might resist admitting feelings at first. After all, this is new territory! He might say something like, "No, it doesn't bother me," or "Nah, I'm just ticked." Yet in due time, the group—wise to these ploys—can often push him to admit, even if primitively, some vulnerable feelings.

If this doesn't work, a second technique is to use paradox. To a brother I might say, "You know, listening to you makes *me* feel a little crazy!" Then I might explain what crazy feels like to me: "My head is spinning, my stomach feels clenched. I want to holler or scream or run away." Sometimes my friend can identify—"Funny you should say that. That's just how I feel sometimes!"—and we will have created an inroad.

Or I might use direct paradox: "Wow! What power! Teach me how to do that. I want to mess with people's minds like that. That's a great trick—to avoid being loved or cared for, and not to even let it bother you! How do you do that? Teach me!" Sometimes craziness deserves craziness. You have to speak the language!

Breaking through the craziness and learning to be responsible can be hard work. But this is where it all starts. Telling the truth. Owning our feelings.

WHY WORK AT RESPONSIBILITY?

Every man who walks into our Tuesday group, or tells me his story in private, has my utmost respect. It takes courage to open up. It takes courage to admit our rage and/or depression. Admitting this to ourselves, aloud, is our first major hurdle. Many of us have controlled our feelings most of our lives. For some, opening up is scary new territory. Our emotional defenses can resist madly. One man articulated this well: "If I open up, I'm afraid a dam of emotions will burst. It may never stop!"

It takes courage to be willing to uncover the fears and hurts which lie beneath our rage or depression. Some of our wounds are deeply buried. We have built emotional walls to protect these wounds from being seen or touched. Revealed wounds are considered a weakness by too many men. Besides, it's hard to trust anyone with this kind of thing. This includes those we love the most. We fear rejection.

So why try? Why open up at all? Why admit these feelings— especially to another person? Why change what has "worked" for years? Why reveal what we have worked so very hard to hide? Why try when every bone in your body and all of your heart and mind seem to be shouting: "Leave me alone!"

We try because, for some of us, the old emotional system is no longer working. The lucky ones among us simply feel modestly angry or depressed. Others have experienced more severe depression or have even lost their jobs. Still others are unhappy in their marriages or have experienced a painful divorce.

Then there are those brothers among us who are "emotionally paralyzed," suffering profound ache, emptiness or anxiety. Their self-esteem is shaky at best, and performing at work or relating to a woman seems virtually impossible. A few brothers have committed crimes of rage or passion, impulsively, at home or work, and are now serving sentences. Not all had a criminal record before committing a spontaneous crime. One man, for example, told me: "All I did was push her a little. She accidently tripped and cracked her head." Some men are as shocked as you or I would be to find themselves suddenly "doing time."

Then there are brothers whose bodies have suffered a great price from years of emotional repression or stress. The price can be disease, illness, surgeries, medications, and physical limitations. Repression of our vulnerable emotions always exacts a price.

The good news is that *there is hope!* We can begin, whatever our present condition, to better our lives. We can find relief from our ache, substance for our emptiness, rest for our souls. We can live healthier physical and emotional lives. We can live peacefully.

To begin to live responsibly, we must develop a new perspective, a new vision, a new understanding of *what it means to be a man.* As I get to know a brother, I often think to myself, "Who was he meant to be?"

Who are *you* meant to be?

Begin by asking yourself these questions:

- If I were all that I could be, what would I be like?
- What would I look like? Would I smile more? Would my body be stronger and healthier? Would I be more energetic? More calm or relaxed?
- What would my vocation be?
- What would be the strengths of my character?
- What about my attitudes? Would I be critical or encouraging?
- Could I love freely?
- Would I be joyful, peaceful, patient, kind, basically good, faithful, gentle and self-controlled?
- Would I know how to play and enjoy life?
- If I began now to strengthen these traits, what would my life be like?

Then consider:

- What keeps me from being the person I want to be?
- What are my barriers?
- What "rewards" or "benefits" do I get for avoiding responsibility in these areas of my life?
- What are the costs of putting off becoming the kind of man I was meant to be?

As you begin to think about your barriers, what immediate, simple and direct changes can you make? Sometimes we lack clear insight into our bad habits or negative attitudes, losing sight of how these can hurt us and those around us. After all, it is a rare individual who can see his own faults clearly. Perhaps you can begin by confessing your frustration or pain to a confidant. Then you might find the emotional space to try again. Sometimes we need encouragement to try new behaviors or attitudes.

For some men, some things can be changed quickly. If a man is fortunate, he will have a second chance with his wife and/or family. Perhaps modest change will add peace to his life and allow others to live at peace with him.

For many, however, there comes a time when a man must confront significant character defects in order to become responsible. These defects are evident in the ache lying in the pit of his soul, in the rapid-fire tensions in his marriage, or in conflicts with his family or friends. Still, some men continue to dig deep trenches to protect their craziness. They refuse to change. They prefer the familiarity of insanity to inner peace and relational reconciliation. Change is scary.

Significant change in character traits happens through courageous work. Digging out old traits and rooting new ones takes time. Don't become impatient with your progress. Be encouraged. It you want it badly enough, it will happen.

PRACTICING RESPONSIBILITY

Most men begin the program feeling helpless or powerless or just plain "angry."

The first step in Alcoholics Anonymous reads: "We admitted we were powerless over alcohol, that our lives had become unmanageable." (A.A. World Services, Inc.) That is a critical first step in any self-help program.

Men tend to cope with, or control, conflict until their lives become intolerably chaotic or painful. Admitting powerlessness can produce conflicting feelings. For example, when finally admitting powerlessness, it is possible to feel vulnerable *and* relieved.

Vulnerable means we might feel one or more of the following: weak, sad, uncertain, at risk, down, fearful, hurt, rejected, scared, lonely, helpless, guilty, ashamed or disappointed.

Relieved means we might feel one or more of the following: restful, relaxed, hopeful, a load off our minds or hearts, unburdened, peaceful, happy, honest, truthful, satisfied, confident, clearheaded or loved.

There is a paradox: There is power in powerlessness!

When I admit my powerlessness, I am freed from lying to myself and others. No more denial! No more battling. The craziness has been admitted. I give up my anxious way of fixing or controlling or fighting other people. I have hit bottom . . . and I am still alive. I begin to believe: something good *can* come from this.

WHAT DOES RESPONSIBILITY REQUIRE OF ME?

Go ahead. Look it up in the dictionary. R-E-S-P-O-N-S-I-B-I-L-I-T-Y. One definition is that responsibility means to be accountable with patience and perseverance.

Our first Step to greater health begins by saying aloud: "I am responsible for my behavior." What does this mean? What inner tools and resources will be necessary as you begin this life-changing journey? You will need:

1. *Courage.* This is basic to self-acceptance and self-change. For example, will you have the courage to accept yourself, failures and all, as you relearn how to live? Will you stop trying to earn acceptance by pleasing others or performing

to earn self-worth? Will you have the courage to admit your obsessions, compulsions, or any drives that are out of control?

Of course, there will be times you will feel anything but courageous. There will be times you will feel weak or vulnerable. When these moments come, ask for help or support from a confidant. Face your facades. Choose the power of being honest. There is nothing "weak" about asking for help. It takes courage; it shows wisdom.

2. *Truthfulness.* The path of denial/repression, blame, or crazy talk is forever closed. No more lying to others; no more lying to yourself. No more hiding hurts and fears. No more irresponsibility. No more hiding behind blame: "If only she (or he) . . ." Or "I can't help it." Face the behaviors and attitudes behind which you hide.

3. *Grace.* Grace means "gift." We must give ourselves the gift of imperfection. We are not perfect; we are human. The greater your courage and honesty, the more you will need grace. Can you begin to forgive yourself?

Taking one step at a time requires balancing the grace of courage and the grace of raw truthfulness. Be patient. God wipes the slate clean when you come before Him with a humble and honest heart. Can you accept God's grace? Dare you? Many choose to punish themselves with the arrogance of false humility! Do you think God would spend His time to "get you?" Would God spend His time punishing you? Give yourself the gift of grace. God does.

4. *Standards and Disciplines.* Being responsible means we set standards to live by. To fulfill these standards—such as the standard of being a peaceful person—we practice disciplines. A discipline is a consistently practiced behavior and/or attitude. This requires planning, execution and follow-through.

A brother in group recently said, "Discipline is what kicks in when the mood to try fails us."

"I am responsible for my behavior" means I am working at my standard. We practice the skills we are learning in this program. We let others help us grow. We are accountable to others.

Standards and disciplines are not laws to haunt us with failure and guilt—they are opportunities to practice. Visualize yourself living up to higher standards:

- What are these standards?
- What disciplines will build these standards?
- What will you do differently from what you do now?
- What one "different" thing can you do today? This very hour?
- What does this feel like?

5. *Understanding limits.* Freedom comes with natural limits. Goldfish thrive in bowls of water but die when they choose to explore the living room. God gives us limits: limits with money, sex, power. . . . Recognize your limits.

- What are your limits? What are your danger areas?
- What are the consequences when you cross them?
- What are the benefits of staying within your limits?
- How does staying within limits maximize your freedom?

Remember, there is no such thing as complete and absolute freedom. We cannot have it all. All good choices eliminate other good choices. Part of learning to be responsible is accepting the fact that we cannot have it all—especially not all at the same time. As we work our way towards health and wholeness, we learn better how to appreciate what we have and to accept what we don't have. We can always change our choices, as long as we keep in mind that each choice comes with its own costs and sacrifices. These are principles that apply to every area of our lives. By not recognizing these truths, we don't escape their validity—we only make life harder on ourselves. But by understanding—and working with—limits in our lives, we can experience greater freedom to truly enjoy life and many of the great gifts that it has to offer!

Practicing courage. Committing to truthfulness. Accepting grace. Embracing standards and disciplines. Understanding our limits. These are the keys to becoming responsible for our behavior. And with them, it is within our grasp to begin to unlock peace, healing and wholeness in our souls and in our lives.

6

Step 2: I Am Responsible for My Anger

Anger

"C'mon Jan, it's time to go!" Tim shouted. Tim and Jan, an energetic couple in their late thirties, were going to dinner with Tim's boss. Tim was a rising star in his company; everybody liked Tim.

On this day, Tim was anxious about being on time since he was competing for a regional sales management position. He knew his boss liked punctuality. And Tim was feeling the need to make a good impression. He was also feeling the effects of a particularly stressful week. Sales were down. The competition had never been stiffer. Tim felt on edge. Patience had never been one of his virtues—and this evening, with all he was feeling, he was less patient than usual.

"Let's *go*, Jan!" he yelled again.

"Just a minute!" she hollered back.

Tim's emotional "switch" flipped to "mad." His emotional engine starting revving—the "engine" of his adrenal gland began to get hot, ready to pump adrenaline throughout his body.

In addition, Tim's mental "switch" flipped to its "obsessive thinking" mode and Tim began a mental monologue of negative self-talk. He growled in his head: *If she says "just a minute" one more time, that's it! I've had it. I never get any respect. She doesn't give a rip about me! She's always late. I've had it!*

"Goodbye, Jan! I'm leaving!" he belted out as he headed toward the door.

"I'm here," she huffed, running down the hall, still buttoning her blouse.

A few moments later, as he slammed the car door shut behind him, Tim was steaming. "You do this every time. We are *always* late! Will you ever be ready on time? You *know* how much this means to me—to us!"

As Tim ripped through traffic, a heavy silence hung in the air. Jan was seething.

She had gotten the boys ready to stay overnight at her mother's only after they had screamed at her, "I don't want those pajamas!" "This hot dog is burnt!" "He got more soda than I did!" "Why can't I bring my toys!" "He hit me!" "He hit me *first!*"

Driving the boys to their grandma's, Jan had thought to herself: *This is insane. By the time I get home, Tim will be there and uptight; I still have to get ready; I'm exhausted; I don't have anything to wear; and I detest these business dinners anyway! Grrrrr . . .*

Then, five minutes after walking in the front door, as she was racing to get ready on time, she heard Tim holler: "Goodbye, Jan! I'm leaving!"

Most couples face moments of conflict similar to this. We are tired. We feel vulnerable. We are at different places. We have different needs. We have different agendas. We feel hurt and angry. We have no time to talk and understand each other.

Some couples have the ability to understand each other. They have managed to develop the communication skills, empathy, and patience to resolve conflicts. Usually, even under pressure, they can put potentially destructive anger on hold until they have the chance to come back and resolve the issues constructively later.

Other couples, however, do not have the ability to understand each other. They have few communication skills, little empathy and patience. They tend to blame their partners for "what is wrong." During their lives, their self-esteem has taken a beating, so they have little emotional strength to be patient and understanding.

What happened following Tim and Jan's dinner party went far beyond their usual conflicts. In fact, what happened shocked them both. Their relationship would suffer deeply from the incident. Yet it was bound to happen because Tim had childhood wounds which were percolating and which he could no longer repress as he began to experience the stresses of marriage, fatherhood, and a fast-paced career.

Rage

Tim and Jan pulled themselves together for the dinner. They looked a bit tense to their dinner partners—Tim's boss and his wife—but light dinner talk conveniently hid true feelings. After all, Tim's boss and his wife were not particularly happy in their marriage either, and dinner babble was a great way to deny the distress betrayed in their demeanor as well.

Getting into their car to head home, the air between Tim and Jan thickened again. The facades faded. Tim would not look at Jan, but he visualized her face in his mind and thought, *How dare she sit there silent. She oughta be sorry. She ticks me off. Boy oh boy, does she tick me off. . . .*

As the speedometer began to rise dangerously, Jan's anxiety climbed with it. Finally, in fear, she blurted, "Tim, you're driving too fast!"

In a split second, Tim jerked the car to the curb and slammed on the brakes. He turned to his wife, spitting venomous words. His language was demeaning. Cruel. He tore into Jan with tirades on every irksome behavior on his latest grudge list. "You . . . you . . . you . . ." is all Jan heard.

Violence

Jan sat deathly still, unsure of what Tim would do next. She flinched each time his muscular arms thrashed about near her face. He had thrown things in the past, but he had never hit her. Would he hit her now? She was terrified. She managed to blurt, "Yes . . . yes . . . I'm sorry," but the words didn't make a dent in Tim's rage.

Jan felt her soul open the car door and walk into the dark, perhaps never to return again. Her body stayed in the car. Shocked and terrified, Jan tried to concentrate on just surviving the moment.

Tim's tirade continued. What seemed like hours had only been occurring for two or three minutes. Even in the dark, Jan saw the fury in Tim's eyes. Petrified, she could not grasp all of Tim's words but she sensed the volume and rage was still climbing. When would it end?

Suddenly Tim clenched Jan's left arm and slammed her against the passenger door. Jan screamed in panic. Tim stopped. Silence. They sat stunned. They'd had a few venomous verbal fights before—but they had never ended like *this*. The unthinkable had happened. Violence. They drove home in silence, deeply disturbed, confused, isolated in their very separate pain, alone.

Depression

The next morning, Tim awoke with an aching heart, ashamed and remorseful. Jan awoke hollow and numb. Neither spoke. Neither got out of bed. They could hear the boys fighting and squabbling on the couch in the den as they watched Saturday morning cartoons.

Finally Tim whispered, "I'm sorry." Jan burst into tears and hurried from the bed. Neither spoke to the other for the rest of the day.

Tim thought a lot as he did yard work. Even though he had apologized, part of him still felt angry. He thought, *Why does she do that to me? Why can't she act right? It's like she taunts me—she knows how to push my buttons. She doesn't care much about me . . . yet she's a good wife and mother. She does a lot. Works part-time and still keeps up the house, takes care of the boys . . . I just don't get it.*

Without knowing why, Tim suddenly thought of his parents. His past had come to mind a lot lately. He remembered some arguing and tensions between his parents. Mostly they just didn't talk. Dad and Tim weren't close, either, though they liked sports. Their relationship consisted of playing golf and talking football.

I don't know, Tim thought quickly. *We had a good upbringing. Mom and Dad are still married. They gave us a good home. The past is past, anyway. But what is bothering me?*

Later that night, after the boys went to bed, Tim had something important to say to Jan. "I am going to get some help," he announced.

"What does that mean?" she asked.

"I'm going to talk to a counselor."

Jan was skeptical. She had been hurt too deeply. She was nowhere near trying to patch things up. She would wait and see.

But Tim was true to his word. He made an appointment to see the psychiatrist available through their medical insurance. Tim's heart pounded as he walked into the psychiatrist's office. *I'm not crazy,* he thought. *Why am I doing this? Why isn't Jan the one getting help? What if somebody sees me going in here?*

The psychiatrist asked Tim questions about his present life and his childhood. The following picture began to emerge:

Tim was a decent, loving person, husband, and father. He was hard-working and successful in his career. He also suffered with gnawing anxiety and self-doubt.

Mild-mannered in nature, he had occasional bursts of rage. "I just get a little angry," Tim admitted. "I just need to control myself." He had never hurt anyone before this incident with Jan, and he felt embarrassed as he told the doctor about it. He confessed that the whole thing made him feel "confused."

After seeing the psychiatrist three times, Tim quit. He liked talking about himself, but it also made him feel weak and vulnerable. Talking about his feelings was new for Tim, and he decided that it wasn't a helpful exercise.

Still, Tim began to think more and more about his father. On the one hand, Tim had good memories. Dad had taught him a lot of important things about being a man. On the other hand . . . well, Dad seemed so distant.

THE HURTING CHILD IN TIM

One Saturday, while sitting at home thinking about these things, Tim's boys began to bug him: "C'mon, Dad, let's play catch."

"Not now, I'm busy."

"Dad, c'mon! Let's play catch!"

"Yeah, Daddy! Let's play! Get up!"

"Daddy!" "Daddy!" "Daddy!"

Suddenly Tim snapped. "Shut up! Get outta here!" he barked. The boys fled, afraid. Tim collapsed in sadness. He thought to himself, *I have so little patience for my boys, and yet I love them so much. I am just like my Dad! What's wrong with me?*

One day Tim's parents called. They called about once a month; the talk was superficial: How are you? How are the kids? Your sister and her family are fine. Had a great golf game!

This time, though, Tim wanted to talk about something different, something he had just remembered. It happened when he was about ten.

He recalled his father standing by the garage, surveying the lawn Tim had just neatly mowed and edged. Tim had spent several hours trying to make the yard look like a magazine-cover, picture-perfect yard, meticulously mowing in ordered rows. As Tim had surveyed his accomplishment, he'd felt pride. But he wanted something more. He longed to hear Dad's admiration and praise.

Then came Dad's simple, memorable words: "Not bad, but next time cut the grass a little lower, will ya?" Then Dad walked away. Tim held in his tears until his father was out of sight, then ran behind the house and sobbed.

Sitting at the kitchen table, his parents on the other end of the line, Tim took a deep breath and said, "Dad, do you remember that day back at the Rockport house when I showed you how neatly I'd cut the grass in rows, and you said, 'Cut the grass lower next time'?"

Tim's dad grunted, "What are you talking about, Tim? By the way, you see the Bears play last Sunday? What about that third quarter, huh?"

"Dad, don't you remember? Do you remember what I'm talking about?"

"Tim, what is this?" Tim's father sounded irritated. "Ellen, finish this conversation with your son, will you? Goodbye, Tim."

Tim finished visiting with his mother, then hung up the phone and sobbed. Now Tim knew. His father didn't even know him; they were strangers. Jan found Tim at the kitchen table with his head buried in his hands.

Shortly thereafter Tim began our men's group. And this is what he learned:

FACING OUR FEARS AND HURTS

All men feel fear and hurt. As we noted in Chapter Three, these are intrinsic human emotions. Because we have been socialized to deny and avoid these emotions, we must learn to feel again. We begin by searching for our deeper feelings, asking as we go, "Beneath my anger, what is my fear or hurt?"

Sometimes our fear or hurt is immediate and rather uncomplicated:

Fear: "One of my biggest customers is considering leaving us for another company. I'm afraid we might lose them."
Hurt: "It hurts to lose a customer, after I've worked so hard to try to serve them well."

At other times, our fear or hurt runs much deeper:

Fear: "I am not sure I will be a good father."
Hurt: "My father often belittled me. Now I feel ashamed and lack confidence in myself."

HOW FEAR AND HURT BECOME ANGER, RAGE AND VIOLENCE

The word anger derives from the Old English root word *ange*. *Ange* means "to narrow or to tighten." If a man felt *ange*, he felt distress. He felt the tightening of his heart—a pain in his soul.

Every human being "bears the *ange*" at times. *Ange* is our fear or hurt.

Anger is the intensification and externalization of *ange*. Thus, anger can be called a "secondary" emotion because it arises from our fear or hurt. Responding to our *ange*—our pain—we become inflamed. Moving from pain to flame can happen in a millisecond or it might take months. Often it happens in a heartbeat.

Since anger masks our more vulnerable, primary emotions of fear or hurt, to become responsible for our anger we must learn to discover the *ange* that triggered it. Whenever we begin to feel angry, we must be willing to ask ourselves the very hard question, "What am I feeling beneath my anger?"

Many men will insist, "I don't feel hurt or fear, I just get mad! I can't control it! There's no time lapse between what ticks me off, and my anger. I just explode!" If this describes you, then you are masking deep wounds. Your rage may well reflect the degree of abuse or neglect that occurred during your childhood.

Often the man who lives with extreme anger:

- has suffered a great deal of hurt and fear in life, particularly in childhood;
- has disconnected himself from his vulnerable emotions;
- carries a great deal of submerged rage, depression or both, and
- has rather rigid sex-role stereotypes; for example, he may believe that men should not express any vulnerable or soft feelings because these are "feminine."

Perhaps he has been so deeply wounded that he has lost the ability to express vulnerable emotions. He "feels" vulnerable deep within but he has disconnected from these feelings. His capacity for other feelings—including love, joy, and tenderness—has also been compromised. Other than expressing anger, or feeling sexually aroused, he may be living a rather passionless life.

It may also be true that this brother lives in a constant state of anger. Think of it this way. Imagine an "anger meter" on which zero equals "no anger," five crosses the line into rage, and ten and above represents violence. If a "normal" person can drop to zero, there are some men who live perpetually at four or five. In other words, they are "warm" most of the time, and only a little added anger can enrage them.

Anger can function almost like a drug: It can relieve pain—temporarily—and bring momentary control, or at least the feeling of control, to a situation. In fact, American men tend to be socialized to vent pain through rage. We learned from our father and others that we ought not feel emotional pain. Physical pain, yes! Toughing out physical pain is seen as a measure of manliness. We injure our bodies but keep playing the game. In fact, when we get angry about the pain, we can be motivated to play even harder. Anger gives us a rush of pride, invincibility, even godlikeness. American heros are often angry—and they use their anger to get back, get even, or get ahead!

Anger is part of our heritage as American males. And yet, too often, the "way of anger" is the path we follow into rage or violence.

AGGRESSION: HOW ANGER BECOMES RAGE OR VIOLENCE

Anger is a legitimate and useful emotion. Anger can occur when we feel something is not right. It is legitimate to respond to unfair or abusive situations with anger. It is legitimate to draw from our anger the energy to protect ourselves or to motivate us to make things right through nonviolent means. Anger helps us to act and not to be passive victims. Anger helps us to define ourselves and to clarify what we believe in. Anger helps us to take a stand against injustices.

There is a difference between anger and rage.

While it is possible for anger to be a helpful emotion, in the service of aggression, it is easy to slide into rage. While we are venting our pain through anger, it is possible to fall into the attitude or practice of forcibly controlling or offending others. This is aggression. Once we reach this point, the emotions of aggression and rage can begin to control us. In aggression and rage, our bodies become soaked in adrenaline. In rage, adrenaline pushes us into a fighting mode, while the brain becomes sluggish and less rational. We become victimizers.

Thus, anger/aggression/rage violates. It violates others, often those we care most about. It also violates our personal peace and sanity.

It is critical to understand that most of us have learned our aggressive behaviors—we were not born with them. This means that we can unlearn these behaviors. We learn aggression as a defense and a protection for our own pain or fear. And while every man has the potential for aggression, some deeply wounded souls practice aggression as a life-style. Every man's trigger for aggression is different.

Aggression encourages us to reduce people to objects or stereotypes. It's harder, after all, to express our rage at someone we view as a unique individual, with their own personal set of strengths and faults. But when our aggression and rage enable us to depersonalize someone to the level of a "label," it's much easier to act on our angry impulses. For example, for years it was okay to hate and kill a "communist," while no one would think of attacking a sweet, loving grandmother who happens to live in Russia. We can attack a _____—insert any dehumanizing label that comes to mind—yet we wouldn't think of hurting our wives or partners.

It's also easier to blame a "label" or stereotype for all our problems. When we are in the grasp of aggression and rage, it's easy to point fingers at "the establishment," "those foreigners," or "women." But the truth is that the real "cause" is our inability to deal with our childhood victimization. We are wounded boys in adult bodies. For the man who is caught up in rage, someone somehow, at some point in his life, harmed his heart and battered his soul.

OUR SOCIALIZATION INTO AGGRESSION AND VIOLENCE

Television and the Development of Aggression

The National Coalition on TV Violence in Champaign, Illinois, has stated that 70 percent of the most popular children's toys are war toys. Children who play with war toys show an increase in angry behaviors and loss of temper control.

Numerous studies show "that children who watch television violence are more prone to use physical aggression than those who don't."[1]

Yet eighty-five percent of new cartoons in 1987 were violence-based. The average U.S. child sees 250 war cartoons and 800 war toy advertisements on television each year. This is equivalent to twenty-two days of pro-violence classroom instruction annually.

In addition, a University of Pennsylvania study has revealed that by the time the average child graduates from high school, he or she will have watched 18,000 simulated murders on television.[2]

Parents and Aggression

Simple to say, complex to deal with, most men learned aggression from their parents. Many of us, for example, were "punished" in aggressive ways. Aggressive punishment means our parents tended to discipline us when they were angry or full of rage (as opposed to calm and instructive). It can also be applied to parents who used excessive physical punishment such as the hand, a belt or a switch applied capriciously or in rage.

What did you learn in your childhood home about anger, rage, violence? What did you learn about aggression?

MEN AND EMOTIONS: HOW WE LEARNED TO BE "MEN"

For men, sex roles consist of what we learned to think, feel, be or do as boys. For women, sex roles are defined by what they learned as girls.

Traditionally, who has the most influence in the developing identity of a young boy? Most research points to the following:

- Between the ages 0 to 3-5:   Mother
- Ages 3-5 and beyond: Father

Mothering

What did you learn from your mother about being male?

Most babies form their earliest, deepest attachments to mother. Mother provides comfort—milk by breast or bottle, clean diapers, touch, warmth. Mothers and babies seem to have built-in reflexes that respond to one another. They have a kind of shared intuition, perhaps begun in the womb.

During the first months, a child "bonds" to comfort. Later, he will begin to recognize persons—their eyes and faces and eventually the fact that they are separate beings from himself—but in the beginning, he bonds to those who bring him comfort. He coos, cries and finds response in these beings.

In the early years, moms tend to spend more time than dads with their babies. Moms provide the primary nurturing bond. The direct impact is that our first intimate bonds are with Mom.

The hope has been that "modern" fathers are spending more time with their babies. Yet research shows that men still do only "a little more than twenty percent of the total child care tasks by themselves while mothers [do] a little less than eighty percent." Furthermore, these results remain the same whether Mom works outside the home or not.[3]

Mothers also tend to be more emotionally expressive than fathers. Men are object- and function-oriented. Fathers tend to *do things with babies (which we call play)*. And while this is valuable and necessary for healthy child development, it does help illustrate the differences. Women, on the other hand, are more personal and expressive. Mothers talk and relate with baby.

Sue and John are young, bright, and educated. They are devoted to each other, reading the latest books to help their marriage and to prepare them for parenthood. Taking care of their beautiful, new son, Johnny, occupies their energies. John is trying hard to be a sensitive, liberated husband and father. Yet the transition to modern fatherhood revealed some blind spots for John. He and Sue sought help from a counselor.

In the counselor's office, Sue expressed her frustrations to her husband. "John, you rarely take care of Johnny alone. I need some time away, out with friends."

John threw up his hands. "How can you say that, Sue? Why, just last night, I babysat Johnny while you went shopping."

The counselor and Sue could not contain their smiles. Finally Sue said, "John, when was the last time I *babysat* Johnny? We're his *parents*, John. There's a big difference between babysitting and parenting. Parenting is the kind of full-time commitment I hope we've both made to our son; babysitting is something you do for a few hours each week to earn money for pizza and a movie."

John woke up.

Children are sponges soaking up praise and affirmation. Their souls feed on the messages they receive from their parents. If you are a parent, this applies to your children and what they need or needed from you as a father. It also applies to your own childhood, and what you needed from your parents as you were growing up.

The most powerful messages you received during childhood had to do with who you were as a person. Chances are, your mother may have provided more of this kind of affirmation than your father. After all, women tend to express more positive messages about relationships and personhood (*being*), while men tend to evaluate performance (*doing*).

Boys are capable of learning tenderness and touch, nurturing and kindness. Yet most boys mimic the emotional landscape they see in their fathers, not their mothers.

Toddler boys have learned from their mothers that it is okay to express their feelings. Around three, however, they may begin picking up on different messages from Dad. Dad may not be expressive emotionally, but he's a lot of fun as the source of physical play and roughhousing.

Although a boy learns how "to be" from his mother, he soon begins to observe the differences between women and men and tries to identify with the men. To do this, he must "shed" his "femaleness" learned from Mom. "Male," to a child of this age, can be interpreted as the opposite of "female." Contrast this with little girls who learn from their mothers how "to be," and then continue learning from their mothers how to be female. Their earliest bonding begins a less interrupted learning process as they continue learning from Mom what it means to be a woman.

A preschool boy, however, is faced with a more traumatic transition. He still needs and wants the approval of his mother, but suddenly he wants to please Dad, too. And, as we've noted before, Mom and Dad have very different perceptions and expectations when it comes to emotions. A little boy may learn to repress a number of vulnerable emotions in order to please Dad. Mother, on the other hand, recognizes and rewards an entirely different set of emotions. Under pressure, a small child might "act out" or explode. Parents wonder what is wrong with little Johnny, suddenly "out of control," not seeing the impossible emotional dilemma they have unwittingly laid on him.

Fathering

Somewhere between the ages of three to five, little boys are "discovered" by their fathers. To put it crudely, at that age, children begin to "function" better. Most men know better what to do with children when they function. Now that a little boy plays more productively, a father can step in and begin to teach him to "do" some things.

About this time, a little boy also discovers his father. He recognizes a kinship with his father in sexual identity. He learns to discriminate male from female, and begins to form an identity as a male.

Samuel Osherson, in his book *Finding Our Fathers*, says that somewhere "between the ages of three and five boys begin to withdraw from mothers and femininity, becoming quite stereotyped and dichotomized in their thinking about what it means to be 'like Daddy' and 'like Mommy.' Little boys begin to segregate by sex, to focus on rules rather than relationships and to emphasize games of power, strength and achievement. Eventually they repress their wishes to be held, taken care of, and cuddled."[4]

What does a little boy get from his father?

Our fathers teach us how to work. Daddy spends most of his time working. He spends a lot of time at work; he may even bring work home with him. When he is home, he has plenty of work to do—yard work, things to make, things to fix. Dads are busy.

Our fathers show us how to do things together. Watch the Dodgers play ball on television. Do yard work together. Fix things. Play catch.

Our fathers teach us to take risks. To venture out. To make things happen. To have courage.

All of these are great lessons. And if you were one of a fortunate few, perhaps your father was also tender and nurturing. He said, "I'm sorry. I was wrong," after hollering at you. He affirmed your base-hit or piano recital without adding, " . . . but you could have done better." He asked how you felt about losing your new watch without screaming at you or "fixing" it by quickly buying you a new one. His affirmations helped your self-confidence to grow strong. You gained competence in social skills and problem-solving.

But if your father was emotionally remote, your self-confidence suffered. You may have become remote and/or aggressive. Even today, you might still work hard to earn self-esteem. The bottom line is this: if your father did not model emotional skills for you, the little boy in you could be stalled in his emotional development.

In most families, little boys do not get much verbal expression from their fathers. What they do get has more to do with functional things as they hear comments like:

- "Good shot!"
- "Try it this way."
- "That's no good."

- "That's right!"

Some boys get emotional expressions that are anything but constructive. Instead, they get powerful negative messages:

- "You throw the ball like a girl!"
- "Lose some weight. You're fat—get some muscle!"
- "Fight like a man!"
- "With grades like this, you'll amount to nothing!"

Sometimes they get silence on sensitive life subjects. This can be just as hurtful. For example, few fathers know how to speak comfortably with their sons about sexuality. The silence can be deafening! A father's awkwardness can be turned to an advantage if he can admit that he is still growing and learning as well. But that takes vulnerability.

Once a boy has distanced himself from his mother, if he does not find comparable emotional closeness and fulfillment from his father, loneliness can root itself in his growing personality. This loneliness sets up a "hunger" for approval from his father. His ego begins to measure how "good" or "bad" he is by his estimation of what his father thinks about him. He begins to measure himself by what he does right or wrong—according to Dad's standards.

Osherson calls this "one of the great underestimated tragedies of our time."[5] He writes: "The sense of loss extends into adulthood, as many sons try to resolve their guilt, shame, and anger at their fathers in silent, hidden, ambivalent ways. . . . And, too, many sons' relationships with fathers shape in subtle ways how they respond to their wives and children."[6]

Little boys never have the chance to "grieve over the loss of mother." They also experience grief over their absent or rejecting fathers. The result is that "men carry around as adults a burden of vulnerability, dependency, or emptiness within themselves, still grieving."[7]

Men? Grieving? Therein lies another problem. Men don't grieve very well. Grief, after all, is not an "acceptable" male emotion. Grief hurts. Grief reveals us as vulnerable people.

And so many men are unaware that they still grieve for the emotional closeness they longed for, but never received, from their fathers. They are unaware that they are grieving for their mothers, whom they rejected. Finally, many men are unaware that they also grieve the rejection of their own "feminine" sides—their vulnerable emotions that, experienced in the early, naive days of childhood, have been lost for a very long time.

RESPONDING TO THE MISTAKES OF OUR PARENTS

There are no perfect parents, only persistent parents. Most parents know they are imperfect. Most have general goals to help guide their parenting, but a good portion of parenting is a knee-jerk reaction to a child's latest behavior or provocation. Parents often can do no more than simply try to hang on for the ride!

Some of us discovered that our parents were imperfect back when we were three. Some of us learned when we were twenty-one. Still others of us have yet to figure this out. Do you still need your parents to be semi-gods or perfect beings? Or can you see them as normal people? Can you imagine them as people apart from being your "parents"?

For some men, the realization that "all parents are imperfect" might have a relatively small impact on their day-to-day lives. For others, the impact can be a profound relief as they realize, "Wow! My parents are just people. I guess I have choices regarding how to relate to them!"

For still others, "releasing" their fathers and mothers from being "perfect parents" seems terrifying, if not devastating. Those who continue to idealize—even idolize—their parents must either deny or be devastated by their parents' frailties and mistakes. Many of these men still have a need to be parented. Some become bitter.

Parental Consistency

Consistency is of the factors that may have determined how wounded you became as a result of the mistakes of your parents. Children, after all, can be quite resilient. They survive their parents, and can do quite well as adults if their parents *were consistent* in their parenting, especially if that parenting was constructive, but even if it was remiss. By consistent, I mean that the parents tried to be steady or patterned—or at least were predictable—in their behaviors, ideas, and feelings.

And what about troubled parents? There are, indeed, demonic parents. There are abusers or neglecters. There are parents addicted to chemicals or work or sex or religion or greed or whatever, to such a degree that their child becomes a pawn to the addiction. A child in situations like these virtually loses his or her childhood. Yet even in these grim scenarios, there is hope. If parents are predictable in their patterns—even though the patterns were destructive—a child can learn predictable coping styles. Sometimes a child from this kind of home life will duplicate some of his parents' craziness (who doesn't!) but later in life, as an adult, he may well be able to change those crazy patterns for healthy ones.

Jed, for example, grew up with two impoverished but steadily working alcoholic parents. In a twisted way, his parents bonded through their drinking. They were drinking buddies. They neglected Jed more than they abused him. Jed was buying groceries and cooking meals by the time he was seven years old. He put himself to bed when he began to fall asleep from exhaustion. He helped raise his brother and sister. His father died when Jed was ten.

As an adult, Jed mourns the loss of his childhood. He was the father in the family. Yet his parents were predictable in their craziness and Jed learned to compensate, surviving his childhood and his adolescence. As an adult, he has worked hard to make choices different from those of his parents. And to his parents' credit, they never viciously attacked Jed's self-esteem. Jed has the chance to live his own life. Today, with his sons, he is learning to play and laugh for the first time.

The adults who seem to be in the most severe pain from their childhood are the men and women who lament, "I never knew what to expect. Sometimes my mother said she loved me; then she hated me. She was happy; then she was depressed. They said I was good; then they said I was bad. What I did in public was cute, but I got punished in private for the same behavior. There was no rhyme or reason to my parents' punishments or behavior."

Children need consistency. As children, we can cope with what is predictable—even if we hate it!

Looking back on your years in your family of origin, what were your parents like? Were they predictable? Did you understand the rules in your home, or were they always changing? Did you know what to expect each day when you came home from school? Did you feel relatively safe?

Assessing your answers to questions like these can help you get a better understanding of the degree of hurt or fear that may well be fueling your anger and rage!

HOW WE EXPRESS OUR ANGER

Jack Balswick, in his book *The Inexpressive Male* confirms what we have already examined in this chapter and what many of us know from firsthand experience: women are more expressive of love, happiness, and sadness than men.[8] These, in fact, are the very emotions a man rejects in order to feel masculine, since our fathers tended to be less consistent in their emotional expression.

Yet Balswick contends that for any young man to have a chance to grow up emotionally whole, he must have an expressive mother "and a highly expressive father" to root confidence and skills to counter the power of social hostility.[9]

Furthermore, he warns that any man who manages to learn how to be emotionally expressive may well be setting himself up for regular misunderstanding and resistance from society. A man seeking to be emotionally well must not only get well, he must also handle social and personal opposition. Tragically, society tends to reward men for staying emotionally deficient!

What this boils down to is the fact that it is not easy to be an expressive male. We are socialized from childhood to steer clear of emotional expressiveness. And should we decide to incorporate this trait in our lives in our pursuit of peace, we may feel opposed or at least misunderstood by those around us.

As you strive to recognize—and express—the hurts and fears that drive your anger, you may very well feel that you are going "against the grain" of what society expects and demands from you as an American man. Yet I believe that with the help of other like-minded men, we can sustain such an effort!

Look in the mirror. What do you see? It's time to face yourself—your fears and hurts—and to stop running away from the pain. Life has limits. There is no such thing as absolute power. There is no fantasy of being and doing it all.

But what there is—well, is enough:

- learning to be responsible . . .
- learning to express hurt and fear . . .
- learning to defuse the anger . . .
- learning to live again.

In return for taking responsibility for your anger, you get the power to make peaceful choices. Of course, no choice will be perfect, and each choice has it's own cost and sacrifice. But you have *choices!* The choice to stop the craziness. The choice to change, to be different. The choice to listen to the "still, small voice" whispering in your soul. The choice to go against the grain, buck the system, and learn to be more expressive—and to teach your sons to be emotionally expressive too!

When you feel your anger crossing the threshold into rage, take a time-out. Go for a walk. Burn off some energy. Ask yourself, "What is truly bothering me?" "What is the root of this anger?" "Am I hurt?" "Am I afraid?"

We can make it, you know—with the help of God and each other.

7

Step 3: I Am Responsible for My Anguish

MY STORY: ANGUISH IN CHILDHOOD

I did well in school. I got good grades. I won awards. To the casual eye, I was a regular, well-adjusted kid.

The truth was that school was a battleground for me. Each test threatened me like an oversized bully. I was driven, miserably so, toward success. I *had* to succeed. I *had* to do well to fight off failure. Yet each good grade only raised my expectations and standards for the next time. I couldn't rest. Anxiety drove me forward.

As a boy, I struggled with bouts of "feeling down." There was nothing dramatic—the adults who knew me said I was just "serious" for my age. Few noticed my depression, since I was not clinically depressed and did not exhibit the more tell-tale signs. Besides, what did I have to be depressed about? I was too good to be a "troubled kid." I was not an abused child. I had no wicked school teachers. My family was stable. And I had lots and lots of potential.

In a strange way, potential was my curse. It dared me to perform well . . . even better than well. My potential ran hand in hand with the fear of failure, and together they jumped out at me—taunting and haunting—from around every corner. I had ability, so the grownups in my life told me, and that ability terrorized me with opportunities. I should/ought/must do well—and I did—yet every success added another monkey on my back. Each success only made it more imperative that I achieve even more the next time. I lacked the confidence to seize opportunities with pleasure, without performance anxiety.

Perhaps confidence can compensate for lesser ability. But ability without confidence was a terrorizing combination—it made me feel consciously inadequate. Fear and anxiety stalked me.

Second Grade

Friday mornings meant share time. I hated sharing aloud so I never volunteered. I felt nervous just considering the prospect. Then one day my teacher informed me she wanted Chuckie Oliver and me to sing a duet the following Friday during share time. All that week I prayed she would forget. My prayers fell on deaf ears (where is God when you need Him?).

Friday morning came. She called my name. I slithered forward, my heart pounding. My face was hot with embarrassment and fear. I was sweating profusely. I stood next to Chuckie, gasping for air. Suddenly I heard, "Ready . . . sing!"

I opened my mouth, and my shrill voice managed to falsetto these few words: "My country 'tis of thee . . ."

Then I froze. Chuckie dutifully bellowed on while I stood trembling, every eye glued on me. When the song ended, the class roared with laughter. I stumbled to my seat, broken and humiliated. My heart hid for weeks!

Third Grade

By the third grade, I began some Monday mornings waking up sick with anxiety. I could not handle the pressure to do well.

My mother took me to see a doctor, who prescribed mild tranquilizers. I feared failing but, even worse, I was unable to explain my internal pain to anyone. I could not articulate the throbs of anxiety. I could not control my fear.

Most adults knew me as a "good" boy who was "quiet and shy." But I knew better. I was struggling. Anxiety gripped its steely hands around my confidence, which was soft like putty in the grasp of my tormenting fears. Under the slightest pressure I began to shut down, paralyzed.

Fifth Grade

New math was the rage. Our teacher, Mr. Kok, wanted to prove to us that the new method was faster. I was chosen to use long division in a contest against Mr. Kok, who would be using the new, short method. What would be the reward if I won? An extra recess for my entire class! What an opportunity! But right about then, my old friend—performance anxiety— awoke from its slumber. This contest was no longer a benign opportunity—it was a performance-phobic's nightmare.

Heart racing madly, I strode to the chalkboard, the frenzied cheers of my fellow warriors in my ears. This was war! Friends slapped me on the back as I passed their desks. For the moment, I was their leader. I carried student dignity on my shoulders.

Everyone watched intently. The designated keeper of the stopwatch, a fellow student, said slowly, "On your mark . . . Get set . . . GO!"

"C'mon Dick!"

"Get it right!"

"Faster, faster!"

I solved the first equation, then the second. My opponent and I were neck and neck when suddenly . . . Mr. Kok got stuck! The warriors screamed madly, sensing victory. I felt their roaring, hot breath on my neck. Victory was within grasp— when suddenly I blanked out. MY MIND WENT TOTALLY BLANK! Anxiety wrapped it's steely fingers around my throat and squeezed tightly!

For the next thirty seconds, I could not remember why I was at the blackboard! I didn't know which way was up. I couldn't find my hand. I forgot what chalk was. What was my name? I was getting dizzy. The room began to spin. Victory and honor at my fingertips, panic squeezed all blood from my brain.

Mr. Kok won. I had let my fellow warriors down. It was a bitter defeat. I had failed miserably. Again.

Sixth Grade

"Shy" Dick Klaver had been chosen to narrate the Spring Play—the Great All-School Spring Play. My teacher said I had a good voice. That I projected. All I knew was that in a week, all our parents and relatives would gather in the huge, monstrous, wooden auditorium. The auditorium was an echo chamber of horrors, where young boy narrators were rumored to have died of fright. Dads and moms, students and teachers would be there. There was no escape! I was bound to lose my place. I would mess up the whole play.

Everyone would see me sweating. I would be the topic of post-program coffee-time criticism: "Did you see that Klaver boy sweat tonight? Glasses fell right off his nose. Had to stop the program while he tried to find them on the floor. Messed up the whole program. What a disaster!"

The week before the play, I prayed for measles. And when the big day arrived, believe it or not, I had itchy spots everywhere—probably psychosomatic! Still, my mother tried to talk me into going to the play. I refused, believing I had worked hard enough to get this illness, I was determined to enjoy it. I never went to the play. The next day, home from school, I suffered from an even worse case of guilt.

Eighth Grade

Nominated for student body president, I told everyone to vote against me. My campaign theme said it all: "Don't Make Me Stand Up in Front for Assembly!"

Assembly. Everyone stares and snickers at the student body president. What if I got the hiccups before I had to give a speech? What if I had to run to the restroom right before I was supposed to lead assembly? What if I couldn't hold it?!

On election day, I lost the vote in a runoff. In public, I expressed relief. But I could tell that my friends were disgusted with me. Privately, I was disgusted with myself.

Adolescence taunted and mocked me. Skinny and gangling, "four-eyed" with a blemished face, my body seemed drained of all coordination. Afraid of girls, feeling ugly, I lost what little confidence I had in myself. I went out for basketball, but I was not good enough to play much. This increased the pressure I felt to succeed academically.

Growing up, sometimes, I cried alone in the night.

I am willing to tell these stories to make a point. I know I am not alone with private and painful childhood memories. I have worked hard in my adult life to resurrect the feelings and meanings of these and other painful memories because these old wounds have haunted me.

As an adult, I always knew these memories were there. I sensed my life being controlled or limited by fear and hurts—but in the beginning I had a hard time attaching my fears clearly to previous experiences.

I know men who faced the same struggle. Feeling the wounds, somewhere, they have been puzzled about the origin of their pain: "I was never abused," they tell me. "I was never locked in a closet or beaten. My parents weren't alcoholics and I had plenty to eat and a nice place to stay. So why do I feel this way?"

Other men have memories of profound abuse. They can pinpoint the precise moments when the damage was done to their hearts and souls.

Whether our hurts and fears come from recognizable "abuse" or from less dramatic childhood traumas such as mine, it is a fact that the hurts and fears of little boys—when ignored, repressed or denied—can fuel the depression, anger or rage of full-grown men.

Please understand that dredging up the past "just to do it" is not our purpose. Our goal is to face the present. Yet in facing the present, we must be prepared to deal with any painful memories that might surface. The little child in you wishes to speak. Listen to him. He will remind you of deeply buried hurts and fears that, left uncovered, will continue to sabotage your efforts to live at peace.

Neither is our quest to pick on our parents, or anyone else in our past. On the contrary, the quest for personal peace begins by facing ourselves squarely, eye-to-eye. We might be reminded of how others have hurt us, but today those hurts are our responsibility. We are about the business of finding healing for ourselves. We can, and will, say aloud: "I am responsible for my anguish." We are willing to face the attitudes, moods, choices, and actions which have contributed to our chaos.

If you are one of the many brothers who have suffered profoundly, you may be wondering if "looking back" can help. After all, while some of us are looking back on bruises and scars, some brothers have endured deep wounds. For them, returning to the hurts and fears of childhood means confronting open wounds. It might hurt to look back. You might even think you are too old to look back. The past is past and, besides, it happened so very long ago . . .

Unfortunately, avoidance, in the long run, hurts more.

Today, your healing begins.

HOW FEAR AND HURT BECOME ANGUISH, DEPRESSION AND DESPAIR

Like anger, the word anguish is derived from the Old English word *ange* which, we learned in Chapter Six, means "to narrow or to tighten."

On a hilly, forested English countryside, around the year 1700, a middle-aged man with a full and greying beard walked slowly, body bent, pulling his cart down a dusty road. In a nearby cottage, a young woman, Sally Johnson, peered from her cottage window, observed the broken-looking man, and made the following comment to her husband: "The elder Longfellow walks with a stiff burden. His crops are bad. His wife is ill and bedridden. He seems to bear the ange."

A man "bearing the ange" feels distress. He feels a tightening of his heart and a pain in his soul. And these feelings always begin with hurt or fear.

Other words that seem well-connected with anguish are the following: dread, worry, grief, agony, torment, distress, heartache, anxiety, uncertainty or fear. Anguish is, indeed, the flip side of anger. Anger is the externalization of our emotional pain; anguish is the internalization of the same kind of pain.

Anguish is a Legitimate Emotion

Anguish, like anger, is a legitimate emotion. Anguish occurs when we feel significant grief. We can feel anguish for others when we see them suffering, physically or emotionally. Anguish can motivate us to act compassionately toward others.

More often, though, we suffer anguish for ourselves as we experience hurts and/or fear in our lives. We feel anguish when we have seasons of quarreling with someone we love. We feel anguish when we must choose between two wonderful jobs. We feel anguish when we see our child heading for trouble despite our best parenting and our consistent warnings.

Anguish allows us to feel loss and pain, and to grieve. Feeling anguish is, in fact, a necessary part of grieving. Through anguish, we can expend pain, and thus save ourselves the long-term problems that occur when we repress that pain and thus become locked in its power.

Men and Depression/Despair

Anger becomes harmful when it becomes aggressive and crosses the line into rage.

Anguish becomes harmful when it becomes passive and crosses the line into depression.

In the service of passivity, men slide from anguish into depression. When we resign ourselves to our anguish and hopelessness, depression takes over. It envelopes us. It paralyzes us. It begins to control us. If the depression persists, we lose all hope and slide into clinical depression. Untreated or unchecked, depression becomes despair. A despairing man feels no hope. Life itself seems drained from his spirit. Sometimes he begins to panic that the light will never return. Without help, he might contemplate releasing his depression through some form of violence, even suicide, if his self-hate or dread feels overwhelming.

Some people describe depression as the fear or dread of having to feel any more pain. The "fear of fear" becomes a life of terror. What's worse, the pain that we fear so much can come from one of two places: It can come from without if we feel that people or events are causing us pain or stress. It can also come from within our own dark, anguished and hopeless souls. There is no safe place. The skies of our mind are deeply dark and cloudy. Storms are brewing.

Some people describe depression as internalized rage. Rage can also be described as externalized depression. I believe both of these statements are true. In depression, rage turns inward to create shame or guilt or self-hate.

This relationship between rage and depression can sometimes be seen in men who have bouts of violence. These men feel "down" much of the time, experiencing anguish, depression and despair. They tend to be passive in taking care of themselves, particularly their emotional lives. This surprises people who see only the violent side and interpret the quiet side as just "the lull before the storm." Many men have bottled-up anger or rage towards themselves. They are wounded with guilt or shame, and they try to control themselves and others with punishing actions.

We are saying that anger and anguish are closely related. They are emotions of the same heritage, just expressions of a different nature. Anger and anguish are two sides of the same coin. The anguish men feel fuels their anger. Anger, in turn, fuels anguish. The bottom line is that men feel helpless.

We do not know how to live with our daily *ange*.

DENIAL OF HURT AND ANGUISH

We suffer when we lose someone we love and care about. Not only do we feel gut-wrenching *ange* but we are incredibly helpless in knowing how to handle our powerful, agonizing emotions!

Some men have powerful denial mechanisms. They survive funerals with exterior calm and sunglasses. Often I find these men—days, weeks or months following the death of someone they cared about—quite full of rage, depressed or sick. *Yet many of them still refuse to connect their feelings or illness to their profound loss and grief.* Grief then finds a pathway by wearing through the body, much like rivers running over and through piles of rocks.

Many men suffer modest depression most of their lives. Others suffer profound anguish. When unresolved anguish boils and blows out, that "steam" is rage.

Are you aware of your *ange*? What causes your *ange*? Do you respond more often with anger, or with anguish?

There is no escaping the fact that each day brings trials and pains. Some days, weeks or months bring massive trials and pains. How do you handle these? What is the present quality of your life? Are you living in peace with yourself and with others?

Often a man will find himself feeling lonely or bored. Sometimes he just feels anxious or restless. Ask him how he is doing and he will say, "Great! Couldn't be better!" If you followed him you might see him acting compulsively or obsessively in some way (exploding in rage, moping, complaining, drinking or doing drugs, watching lots of television, eating, perfecting his landscaping, overworking, etc.).

One man I know has tried desperately to find a medical basis for his depression and fits of rage. He endlessly searches for "the cause." Maybe it is allergies or epilepsy or tumors or body chemistry. If he can find "the cause," then a doctor can fix it. By all means, have these possibilities checked by a physician if you think you have a medical problem. Depression can have biochemical origins. But when the doctor says, "Mr. Smith, there's nothing physically wrong with you," then it's time to look inside at the emotional wounds of your heart.

Another man I know, seventy-seven years old, was diagnosed as "anorexic." This is a strange diagnosis for an old man. Anorexia is considered a young woman's disease. Yet is it so strange after all? How many elderly people lack the self-esteem to live? Who cares about them? We think they are dying merely of "old age," yet how many of them "will" their own deaths? Today, this man lies semi-comatose, near death in a hospital.

He was once a pastor. He believed in high moral standards—standards he feels he has been unable to live up to. Guilt and shame are killing him! In particular, he feels guilty about leaving his first wife and children many years ago. His children have disowned him, he told me before lapsing into his coma.

"What happened?" I asked him.

"I just couldn't handle the responsibility of being a husband and father," he admitted weakly. "Guess I had a mid-life crisis. But no one called it that in those days. I was just a 'bum.'"

"Wow. Is that how you feel about yourself?"

"Yeah, I guess so."

"Can you forgive yourself?" I asked.

"I don't know how. I try, but it doesn't seem to work."

"How would you know if it worked?"

He thought a moment. "I guess I would feel better."

I had one more question for my friend. "What do you want to live for, today?"

There was a long pause. "I don't know. I don't know that I want to live at all."

I held his hand.

This is a man with lots of skills and abilities. Death, in the form of despair, has taken hold of him. He lies alone in his sterile, white room, pale and gaunt, with tubes down his nose. He is little more than skin and bones, forced to live by pale white fluids dripping through IV tubes.

The doctors tried shock therapy, but my friend's depressed body could not take the full treatment. He developed pneumonia. Now he lies semi-comatose, not recognizing even his wife.

I fear his chance is over.

Many of us deny our emotions so savagely we have become a bit crazy. Yet most men only admit crazy things happen *to* them, not *in* them.

A crazy man says, "Your mother is upset!" when he is the one who is upset. Of course, he can't admit that he's upset.

A crazy man says, "Why didn't you clean up the bedroom?" after tripping over his own dirty laundry on the floor.

A crazy man says, "You spent *how* much on that dress?" as he smokes a pack of cigarettes and heads out the door to buy a round of drinks for his friends.

Crazy talk is not taking responsibility. A crazy man is a child in a big body.

MEN AND MID-LIFE

Many men suffer a kind of emotional unleashing in their mid-life years. Let's call mid-life the early forties to late fifties. Some men find themselves crying for reasons they don't fully understand. They cry at small impulses. Their eyes well up at inopportune times. They wonder if they are going crazy. In mid-life, many men are no longer able to handcuff their emotions.

What evokes these "new" emotions?

Perhaps it is the joy at the birth of a grandchild.

Another man feels deep sorrow when his son divorces a partner they all loved and adopted as part of the family. He grieves the loss and worries about his son, daughter-in-law, and the grandchildren.

Someone else reads the story of a high school soccer star who contracts leukemia and dies after a brave struggle. After putting down the book, he sobs with deep heaving sobs.

Another man watches the movie *Dead Poet's Society* and sees himself in the young poets. He feels things he does not fully understand. Tears slide down his cheeks as he remembers being fearful as a youth. He secretly wonders, *What is this all about? I thought all this was in the past . . .*

A brother sees *Good Morning Vietnam* and cries out of pent-up, excruciating pain flowing from the insanity, chaos and torment remembered from his own tour of duty.

Yet another man recalls how much he longed for his father to say that he loved him. This man's unexpressed tears have nearly fermented with age. Now there is no holding them back.

Someone else goes to a high school reunion. He sees how much everyone has aged. Some have died. Time has moved on. He visits the family grave site. There lies his father. On the plane ride home, he stares out the window at the endless plains and feels very small in a big world. He feels alone. He hides these feelings even from his wife.

We can hold back our emotions only so long. One day our defenses wear thin. Either our emotions erupt or our body erupts with an illness or disease quite possibly encouraged by feelings held back.

What causes this emotional flow? In Paul Ciotti's article "How Fathers Figure," Ken Druck, a Del Mar, California psychologist who works with men, explains it this way: "I see many men walking around in mid-life with a sense of yearning for things that they can't get from their wives and can't get from their jobs and can't pull from inside themselves . . . I'm convinced that what the men are missing is a sense of their own identity: a very primitive and very deep sense of validation that passes from father to son."[1] And I might add, "and from mother to son."

In *Resurrection* by Leo Tolstoy, Nekhludov, a Russian prince, sought to recover from past sins. He recalled his days of youthful innocence:

> Then he had been free, fearing nothing, a man with endless possibilities before him; whereas now he felt entangled in the meshes of a vapid, insignificant, and purposeless life from which he could see no way of escape—and he was not even sure that he cared to find one. He remembered how proud he had always been of his straightforwardness, how he had made it a rule always to speak the truth and had indeed been truthful; now he was living a lie, a fearful lie, and everyone who knew him accepted this lie as if it were the truth. And there was no way out of it, or if there was, he didn't know how to find it. He had been so long in the mire that he was accustomed to it and enjoyed it. . . .

> Then suddenly it dawned on him that the disgust he had been feeling that day for everything and everybody . . . was really disgust for himself. It is surprising that the recognition of one's own baseness should be accompanied by a sense of relief, and yet Nekhludov, for all his distress, felt comforted.

> More than once in his life he had undertaken what he called "the cleansing of the soul." This was the name he gave to certain mental exercises to which he subjected himself at intervals on discovering the slothfulness and wickedness of his inner life:

he would work to clear away rubbish that encumbered his soul and hindered all proper action.

After such an awakening Nekhludov would make rules, fully intending to observe them; he would keep a diary and begin a new life which, he hoped, was to go on forever. This he called (using the English phrase) "turning over a new leaf." But time after time the temptations of the world ensnared him and, before he knew it he had fallen—sometimes lower even than before.

Thus he had several seasons of awakening and purification. . . .

[Then one day,] he folded his hands on his breast as he used to do when he was a child, raised his eyes, and said: "Help me. O Lord! Teach me, abide in me and deliver me from all this abomination!"

He prayed, asking God to enter into him and purify him; and while he was thus praying, it came to pass . . . [2]

Or so Nekhludov thought. He set about a life of "righteousness" seeking to pay for past sins. He did this by trying to marry Katusha, a woman he had raped years before. He did this by fighting injustices in the Russian prison systems where innocent persons suffered atrocities.

In the end, his system of self-purification did not work. His system of doing good deeds to earn "righteousness" did not work. Katusha did not want to marry him; the evils in prison continued. In the end, he found that his motive for fighting evil was selfish. He was no different than those he tried to "save." He learned the grace of God cannot be earned.

We can become shapers of our own emotions, but it will not happen through moral purging. First, we begin to tame our volatile or depressed emotions by becoming more responsible for our behaviors. To do this, we need encouragement from others.

Second, we start to discover the roots of our hurts and fears. Willfully, we begin to work responsibly toward changing our emotional reactions.

Yet even these worthwhile efforts can accomplish less than we might have hoped for if we undertake this task without accepting what cannot be earned: the grace of God. It is a gift, free for the asking. In fact, it is this gift of grace, coupled with God's boundless love, that can make the difference between self-help strategies attempted in vain, and a process that leads to—finally—becoming men at peace.

MEN AS VICTIMS: ROOTS OF ANGUISH

A superficial vision of the American male is that he is simply tight, angry, often enraged or violent. One might wonder if men are born this way. Yet a deeper look reveals something different. A clearer picture of American men shows that American men, despite the facade, are fearful and hurting.

The following two stories illustrate the male dilemma:

Tom's Hidden Pain

Tom came to the Men at Peace group for more than a year. He made tremendous progress, learning to take "Time-Outs" to stop the escalation of his anger. He ventured into his feelings and discovered ways to articulate feelings beneath his anger. Tom freed himself to express thoughts, feelings, and needs rather than rage. He felt pride in his progress.

Then Tom faced a new barrier.

It is difficult for any of us to see weaker aspects of ourselves as clearly as others see them. Once we see them clearly, it is even more difficult to change what we see. We are used to who we are—why change what "works"? Change, even "good" change, is difficult.

So it was for Tom. One day, he and his wife, Mal, had a modest disagreement. Tom was handling himself well, using his newly developed communication skills. Suddenly Mal said tersely, "Tom, you are getting angry and that makes me nervous!"

"No, I'm not."

"Yes, Tom, you are."

"I am not!"

"You are too!"

Tom paused in thought for a moment. Then he said, "Mal, how can you say that? How can you judge what I feel? I'm handling my anger better than ever before. I think you're trying to manipulate me and I resent that!"

There was a long pause before Mal responded. "I appreciate what you've been learning, Tom. But I am looking at your face. That flushed, tense look on your face looks like anger to me. Look at yourself in the mirror."

Tom went to a mirror and stared. He saw the tight jaw, the furrowed forehead, the sharp eyes. He saw his flushed face. He saw anger. Tom's heart sunk. After all his hard work and perceived progress, at that moment he wondered if he had made much progress at all. What Tom didn't recognize was that only great progress had allowed Tom to accept Mal's constructive criticism and handle this new level of growth!

Most men stay in a men's group for only one or two weeks. Men look for a quick fix. After all, we can fix cars, appliances, computers, furniture. We certainly should be able to fix problems.

When the wife or kids share their problems with us, we listen briefly, then tell them how to "fix" their problem. When they don't like what we tell them, we get frustrated. After all, we're Fix-It-Experts! It's our God-given right, isn't it?

Some men try to fix their wives—until she walks out the door. Then these brothers feel anxious, sometimes enraged, sometimes depressed. Even then, one of the most common reactions—once the initial shock has worn off—that I hear from men in this situation is another version of "How can I fix this situation?" Of course, that's not what it sounds like when it leaves their mouths. What they actually say is, "What can I do to get her to come home?" But the implication is the same.

A brother in this situation may then launch into a program to fix himself. Guilt and a flash of remorse drives him to ask us, "What do I do to fix this? Just tell me what to do!"

A few weeks or months later, when the quick fix program has failed to rebuild the marriage, often a man will throw up his hands and say, "Forget her, then! Forget the whole thing!"

This kind of thinking is a fantasy. It is part of our illness.

Tom, however, was courageous. He did not quit. He did not give up. As he looked at himself through the mirror of his consciousness, he discovered a deeper, hidden truth: his broken heart.

Later he told us: "The reason I felt so badly so often was that, inside, I felt so broken! I had been denying it. I had talked a lot about being 'positive' and for a time in my life, that seemed to work. But all that time, I was not listening to my insides. I was not seeing myself as I really was. And how could I have? I was doing everything I could to survive, to keep my defenses up and running.

"Mal helped me look at myself. She was right. I was still angry. Not because I was mad in my heart, but because I'm hurting. My face and body showed anger—but when I finally dared to look and . . . well, *feel* on a deeper level, I found something I have been hiding most of my life: I'm depressed! I just didn't see it.

"I'm tired of it. Tired of the pain, tired of the fear, the hurt, the struggle, the chest pains, the denial, even the anger. I don't want to hurt anymore."

Tom's courage led him to see how alone he felt. He had worked so hard to succeed—to compete and win, in sports and in business. Why? On one hand, he liked it. He liked the thrill and rush of competition. On the other hand, he hated it. He was tired of performing to make others happy. Tom found the roots of his conflicting feelings in his childhood.

As a boy, Tom longed to please his father. But Dad never gave Tom significant affirmation and acceptance. Of course, the reasons for that aren't too hard to see. Dad, still living, never got affirmation and acceptance from *his* dad. Plus, Tom's dad lived in a survival generation. On the farm, there was one relevant question: Will there be a good crop at harvest time? Feelings seemed less relevant then; today, however, we expect and demand feelings. During his growing-up years, it became apparent that Tom's dad would never be the father Tom longed for him to be. So the unspoken issue for Tom became clear: how to find the affirmation and acceptance he longed to have.

At the same time, another issue surfaced for Tom. He had never felt particularly attractive or sexually adequate. Boys' earliest evaluations of their attractiveness come through their mothers' responses to them. The words, "Wow, you are a handsome young man. If I were a young girl I would snatch you in a minute" go a long way in establishing a young man's blossoming self-esteem. Yet Tom's mother never praised his sexuality. Instead, she repressed physical affection and expressions, except for criticism such as, "You smell! Go take a bath," or "Your pimples are getting worse." As a result, Tom feared women because he felt unattractive.

One of the ways that men compensate for feeling unattractive is by fantasizing about sexual conquests. Thus, women are reduced from people who have the power to frighten or reject us to becoming mere objects. We fear women's rejection, yet we long for their affirmation. In our confusion, we turn them into conquests.

Reaching deep into his soul, for the first time in his life, Tom heaved a sigh of relief. He cried a lot. He released a lot of pain and anxiety. In the process, Tom learned to rest his soul. He learned to slow down to enjoy new pleasures—a good cup of coffee, a walk in the park, a new class at the church. Today, Tom is a man at peace.

Tom was also fortunate that Mal was doing some growing of her own. Mal realized that she was conditioned to look for Tom's anger even when it did not exist. After all her years of knowing Tom, it was not easy to let him change. She had been hurt. And she was afraid. She wondered, "If I become more vulnerable to Tom, will he hurt me again some day? Is it worth letting my guard down?"

Mal chose to take the risk. In time, Mal and Tom began to trust the new persons they were each becoming. The change took time but the rewards were fantastic!

Men are victims, too.

We are all victims, and yet each of us is still responsible for our own path to peace. This fact may not seem fair, and it's not always easy to hear. But it is nevertheless profoundly true, and the sooner we apply it to our lives, the sooner we will find the peace we are so desperately seeking.

Marlin: A Battered Child

I met Marlin because he had battered his wife, Ellen, several times over the course of a few years. Ellen finally called the police. Marlin had crossed her line of tolerance.

Her line had not been that he had come home drunk. Her line was not that he had thrown her to the living room floor. Her line was not that he kicked her in the ribs, cracking one. Her line was not that his fist busted her lip and blackened her eye. Her line was that he threatened to harm the children. Little, helpless kids.

Marlin resisted the police. He screamed through his intoxicated rage, "I don't have to leave! She has to leave. I'm sick and tired of that woman nagging me! You get that woman out of MY house!"

With that they hauled him to jail.

The next morning, Marlin woke up. His head spun on the ceiling from his hangover and his heart bled on the floor from his dizzy memory of the night before. He longed to call Ellen. He vaguely recalled pushing her. He wondered what else he had done. He remembered the police knocking on the door and hauling him away. What else had he done? For a sickening second, he wondered if he had severely hurt Ellen. Were the children safe?

Marlin was charged with third-degree assault. His sentence was deferred if he agreed to attend our men's group. He did so.

Do you feel disgust toward Marlin? You might even feel rage! But remember, Marlin was once a little boy. He was not born with the instincts and desire to batter. He learned violence—from his dad.

As a young boy, Marlin longed to please his Daddy. His father, however, was hard to please. In fact, his father did not want to be pleased. Dad preferred rage to pleasure.

One day, Dad asked eight-year-old Marlin to steady the end of a heavy eight-foot two-by-four so that he could make a perfectly straight cut with his table saw. As Marlin began to recall this story aloud for our group, he began to weep convulsively. Marlin, now thirty-five, still wonders what he did wrong on that long-ago day. He will never know. He assumes that he did not hold the board straight enough. All he knows for sure is that suddenly his father was using the two-by-four to beat his son. The little boy curled into a ball on the garage floor to survive the beating. Marlin's body was severely bruised. His heart was shattered.

This was just one of the memories which Marlin began to uncover. Little Marlin's body and/or soul were beaten on several occasions. There was no safe place for his fear and hurt. In essence, Marlin was beaten into the raging and violent man he had become. This is not an excuse; it is reality. The group told Marlin that he could never hit his wife again. Violence could simply not be an option for Marlin. At the same time, we tenderly helped Marlin to bare and cleanse the wounds that had been inflicted on him over the years.

There are millions of Marlins in this nation—with lesser and greater wounds. Some boys were not hit. They just were not loved. Their fathers were stone cold. Having learned well, the sons have become stone cold fathers themselves. Who will stop the craziness?

The Origins of Our Fears and Hurts

Men fear. Men hurt.

Each day of our lives, we face the challenge of fear and hurt. Each day, we awaken to new life dramas; each drama unfolds with new scripts, new settings, new casts of characters. Yet the basic emotions behind the scenes stay the same: fear and hurt. How we face the challenge of our fears and hurts determines the quality of our lives, from the womb to the tomb.

Fear and hurt are feelings of the soul. They pulsate from our deepest reaches, our innermost parts. They are powerful because they can cause us to react or respond as few emotions can. They can dominate us, pushing us toward destructive habits or choices. Or they can serve us, helping us to make wise choices and to sense the breadth and depth—the beauty and color—of life.

Fear and hurt are our greatest emotional assets, our most useful emotional tools. Fear warns us, saving us from harm. Hurt tells us to slow down and listen: we have lost something. Having fear of God "is the beginning of wisdom," said King

Solomon, a man of legendary wisdom (Ps. 111:10). If we can tame these twin tigers—fear and hurt—we can put them to good use. We might even befriend them! But, of course, this takes courage and hard work.

Thoreau wrote in *Walden* that "The mass of men lead lives of quiet desperation." Our quiet desperation is exposed by fits of rage or depression. By these fits, we submerge or block our most basic vulnerable emotions: fear and hurt.

Our quiet desperation is our spiritual bondage to obsessive drives and hedonistic goals.

It is seeing too many choices in life as black-and-white, all-or-nothing. And whatever we decide, it had better be the "right" choice (as if such a thing exists!).

It is attaching ourselves to disloyal people and/or idyllic dreams which draw our attention away from becoming the persons we were meant to be.

Children, for example, often choose to gratify their desires without thought. Imagine a little boy with no parents and fistfuls of money at an eternal carnival. When a little boy sees cotton candy, he knows what to do: eat it! Not a little, but a lot! He will eat cotton candy until his tummy aches badly. But he will not believe that the cotton candy hurt him. Left to himself, as soon as his tummy feels better, he will gorge some more. He might survive the first day, maybe two. But by about the third day, he feels sick. On day four, the boy becomes seriously ill, suffering malnutrition, diarrhea, headaches, and rotting teeth. Somehow this child must learn to manage his impulses and delay some of his desires!

Life is lived best within limits. Fear and hurt are wonderful teachers of the limits of life.

Fear and hurt, in fact, are not the cause of our problems. It is the decision to ignore, fight, repress, or deny our fear and hurt that send us squarely down the path to rage or depression. However, if we take the time to learn the purposes of fear and hurt, and teach ourselves how to handle these potent emotions, then we will find them powerful aids in understanding ourselves and others. We can learn to trust our hurts and fears. We can befriend our pain and live better lives as the result.

Walk toward your pain, lest you become imprisoned by rage or depression. This is a truth that takes time to learn.

And what do we get from learning to embrace our hurts and fears? Two things:

Learning to simply feel our fears and/or hurts bears its own reward. There is a confidence which comes from facing these feelings rather than fearing them. And feeling these emotions opens doors! Most of us have learned to respond to emotional pain by avoiding or "fixing" something or somebody. By habit, at the slightest feeling of hurt or fear, we mask these feelings with anxiety which pressures us into aggressiveness (rage) or passivity (depression). Yet by facing these feelings, you will soon learn that neither rage nor depression is necessary. As you identify your anxiety, you will learn to hear and see and feel the primary emotion *causing* the anxiety. Feeling hurts and fears means getting in touch with your primary emotions. And until that happens—until you love yourself enough to feel your deepest emotions genuinely, without facades—you will never have the freedom to make the kinds of peaceful choices you long to make.

Once we tap into our deeper, primary emotions of fear and hurt, we begin to have more honest choices and responses. Suddenly the dissonance in our souls is gone. We feel less drive to prove something to ourselves and to others. We are more in control of our choices. We can choose to act, think, or just feel what we feel without intimidation, inhibition, or the need to compete. Superficial success becomes much less important; personal peace becomes more important.

At this point in the journey, your willpower is about to be exercised and strengthened. This process requires you to do emotional, psychological, and spiritual exercises, and the same truths work here that apply in the gym: No pain, no gain! But don't let that stop you.

From this point on, you will encounter various challenges and trials demanding nothing short of great stamina, strength, and courage. What you are about to discover, as you embark on this journey within, is that, quite honestly, it's a jungle in there!

You might need to clear the brush of neck-high emotional pain. A dense growth of emotional defense may need to be cut away with the machete of honesty. For a time, while on this path, you may have doubts that you are getting anywhere at all! Consulting trusted friends who are experienced in relational matters can be very helpful. With courage, you *will* clear a path.

THE PSYCHO-SPIRITUAL ORIGINS OF FEAR AND HURT: WHERE DID IT ALL BEGIN?

". . . the LORD God formed man of the dust of the ground and breathed into his nostrils the breath of life, and man became a living being" (Gen. 2:7).

Being a creature of God gives us dignity—but even being created by God did not keep the first human from becoming lonely. Even friendship with God was not enough! Loneliness is not evil; it's part of being human. Loneliness is the space where love makes its home.

"Now the LORD God had planted a garden eastward, in Eden; and there he put the man whom he had formed. Out of the ground the LORD God made every tree grow that is pleasant to the sight and good for food" (Gen. 2:8-9a).

The garden of trees was pleasing. Pleasure is not evil. The garden of trees provided food; man, after all, needed nourishment. And man worked the garden. Work is not evil, either. But none of these things—pleasure, food, or work—satisfied the loneliness of the man.

Then "The LORD God said, 'It is not good for the man to be alone. I will make a helper comparable to him'" (Gen. 2:18).

Loneliness. Our first and greatest hurt. Imagine what it feels like to be completely alone and lonely; empty. What if nobody knew you? Nobody cared? No one thought about you or paid you a bit of attention! Your existence denied, refused and ignored, you would be lost. Alone. Abandoned.

It is one thing to spend time alone if you are secure in someone's love and care. It is quite another to *be* alone.

Elie Wiesel survived the horrors of German concentration camps. According to Wiesel, the greatest form of torture came when, alone with his thoughts, it occurred to him that no one might know that he was still alive; that no one cared anymore. That, he admits, was like hell.

"Out of the ground the LORD God formed every beast of the field and every bird of the air, and brought them to Adam to see what he would call them. . . . But for Adam there was not a helper comparable to him" (Gen. 2:19-20).

God created creatures; He let Adam create their names. But neither God, the creatures, nor the creative work of naming the creatures was enough. The hole in Adam's heart continued to hurt.

"Then the rib which the LORD God had taken from man, He made into a woman, and He brought her to the man. And Adam said: This is now bone of my bone, flesh of my flesh; and she shall be called woman because she was taken out of man" (Gen. 2:22-23).

Whether you take the Bible to be God's word or mythology, this is a story that—literally and/or figuratively—speaks volumes about the origin of man and his humanness.

Woman, or the "of-man" being, was God's best answer to male aloneness. Was this the cure? Was this enough?

"And they were both naked, the man and his wife, and they were not ashamed" (Gen. 2:25). They belonged! They fit! They needed no cover; they would never hide again! They felt no shame: not physically, not sexually, not psychologically, not emotionally, not spiritually. Would they live happily ever after?

Unfortunately, about that time a crafty serpent convinced the woman to eat fruit from the one tree God told them not to touch. The serpent said, "For God knows that in the day you eat of it your eyes will be opened, and you will be like God, knowing good and evil" (Gen. 3:5). The man ate the fruit, too. "Then the eyes of both of them were opened and they knew that they were naked; and they sewed fig leaves together and made themselves coverings" (Gen. 3:7).

Fear. The innocence and beauty of "belonging" was shattered by too much knowledge—a knowledge they were not equipped to handle. Adam and Eve suddenly needed coverings. Defenses. They felt shame. They felt fear. They felt alienation.

"And they heard the sound of the LORD God walking in the garden in the cool of the day, and Adam and his wife hid themselves from the presence of the LORD God among the trees of the garden. Then the LORD God called to Adam and said to him, 'Where are you?'" (Gen. 3:8-9).

Not what are you doing, or what have you done . . . but where are you? What an interesting question, pregnant with nuance and meaning. Where are you? Do you know where you are? Are you in the open or are you in hiding? Why can't I see you?

They were hiding. They were *afraid* to belong!

Adam answered, "I heard your voice in the garden, and I was *afraid* because I was naked; and I hid myself" (Gen. 3:10, emphasis mine). Afraid of what? Afraid of being vulnerable. Afraid of being found out. Afraid to belong. Afraid to belong even to God.

Our greatest fear and hurt is to be alone. Our second greatest fear and hurt is to belong! This is one of the great paradoxes of life!

Fear. Hurt. How are we to deal with these emotions?

God asked Adam if he had eaten from the forbidden tree. And "the man said, 'The woman whom you gave me to be with me, she gave me of the tree, and I ate'" (Gen. 3:12).

Doesn't that sound just like a man! Adam was the very first to use the "victim" technique—the great escape from responsibility! First, the man blamed God. A few days ago, she was "bone of my bone and flesh of my flesh." Now she's that "woman *you* put here, God!"

This is our first layer of defense. We hide from God. Then we blame women!

Well, women can play at this game too! After all, Eve's excuse to God was that "The serpent deceived me, and I ate" (Gen. 3:13).

Blame, blame, blame!

The hurt and fear of being alone. The hurt and fear of belonging.

Fear and hurt.

Alone and belonging.

This is our incredible human dilemma.

How you deal with this dilemma determines the quality of your life!

Step 4: I Am Responsible for My Fear

Jon was tall and angular, well-dressed and groomed. But his deep eyes shadowed a blank stare.

"What were you afraid of, Jon?" I asked.

"Nothing," he said in monotone. "I was just angry."

Jon was telling his story to the group. He and his wife verbally sparred a lot. His wife had heard about Men at Peace and suggested Jon "get some help from those people." Jon was skeptical.

The previous night, they had an argument and in the heat of the moment, she tried to walk out the front door. Jon had blocked her path, refusing to let her go.

I repeated my question: "I know you were angry at your wife, but something deeper than anger led you to block her path. Jon, what if she left? Why did you block her? What were you afraid of?" Jon looked confused, half-irritated at my persistence, half wondering what he did not know about himself.

About three months later, after about twelve Men at Peace sessions, Jon awakened past his macho defenses and began to get in touch with his fears. He feared that his wife might leave him forever. Abandonment, at any moment, always lurked in the back of his mind. He felt deeply inadequate. He had felt rejection at times from his mother and grandmother. He was rarely held or touched by his mother. He knew that women, especially his wife, could hurt him by rejection. Blocking his wife's path to the door was an attempt to control her, to force her to stay in his presence. Jon grew to recognize his fear. As he became acquainted with his fear—with help—he could face it.

THE PURPOSE OF FEAR

"Fear is the first experience of the fetus in the womb," wrote the late Joseph Campbell in *The Power of Myth*. "Fear is the first thing, the thing that says 'I.' Then comes the traumatic event of being born."[1]

Before birth, a baby feels rhythmic contractions preparing for his birth. What does an unborn baby know about life outside the comfort of the womb? He must sense an impending struggle and experience primitive fear at the awareness.

Birth. Our senses are bombarded with stimuli and pain. Dramatically, our consciousness "jumpstarts" into being. Yanked or squeezed into the world, flung upside down, helplessly we cry out: "I am here! What more do you want?" Then those grown-ups to whom we were born begin to holler with delight. We sob. Barbaric!

Our identity starts with fear. Then we feel hurt and pain. Perhaps this becomes our earliest subconscious memory.

Clearly fear, at its very root, is not bad. Fear gives us a sense of ourselves. Our feelings, awakened by fear, help us to learn to respond to our world. Our first response is the Big Ouch! Shock! Hurt! Sob! Fear is essential to know ourselves in relation to our surroundings.

Fear warns and protects us. I peer over the jagged edge of a Grand Canyon cliff—I fear falling thousands of feet to my death! I feel the heat of a cracking fire—I fear the sharp pain of sizzling skin. I come into contact with poison—I fear choking off my air from within. These fears are learned from experience and wisdom passed along by words and by discipline. I feel safe because I trust and respond to my fears.

FEAR OF PROBLEMS

Some fears warn or protect us—yet we can choose to override these fears for personal growth or gain. I feared tearing up my knees as I began riding a two-wheeled bicycle. Raw knees only proved that my fears were well-founded! Yet I had a greater need—to face those fears and hurts, and in so doing, to gain personal freedom. Bike riding gave me fun, comradery, self-esteem—not to mention mobility! The fear was true and reasonable but my will overrode that fear.

We fear making conversation with that pretty woman we've had our eye on. She might reject us. We fear beginning exercise programs, diets, painting classes, college courses, new careers, writing projects. I fear beginning because I might fail. If I fail, I fear becoming disappointed and let down. When I am disappointed, I become discouraged. When I am discouraged, I may feel emotionally paralyzed. What's the answer?

Let's not make any plans! Let's not do anything with risks! Let's protect ourselves at all costs! Then we can avoid fear. Or can we?

It is fear that pushes us to avoid fear. By never taking risks, we live in a cul-de-sac of fear, traveling in circles, never going anywhere, experiencing dead-end living and *still* surrounded by fear: the fear of trying. Real living can only be experienced as we face our fears. The greatest failure, after all, is never to risk failure.

Each hurt we feel from then on becomes just another dagger in our collapsing soul: another bitter proof of our victimization. Our souls bleed to death. We convince doctors to medicate us so we feel even less. We tell friends that life is horrible and that nobody understands us (at best, a self-fulfilling prophecy). At some point we confront a clear choice: we can revive our life by facing our fears, or we can die a self-proclaimed "righteous" death.

FEAR OF ABANDONMENT: OUR GREATEST FEAR

Our most profound fear is the fear of being abandoned. Rejected. Left. Fear of being permanently, absolutely left alone. Fear of being unable to connect to anyone in any way, helpless to save ourselves.

Campbell says that fear begins in the womb. *Clearly, fear is one of our earliest emotions, and fear of abandonment is one of our earliest and most profound fears.* These fears never completely go away. You and I deal with the impact of such fears daily.

There are two subtle and powerful forms of abandonment that we face constantly: abandoned trust and abandoned self-esteem.

Abandoned Trust

I fear diving into water. Why? Perhaps because we did not go swimming when I was little. Or, perhaps, because one Saturday my father took me on an air raft onto Lake Michigan. I was six years old. I was scared.

The sun beat down. People all around me were screaming, yelling and splashing, having fun. The chaos frightened me.

But even more so, the waves—small though they might have been—frightened me.

I remember screaming at my father, "No! Let me go back! I don't want to go!" But he wanted me to learn to brave the water.

Slowly we moved into deeper and deeper waters. The waves bounced my raft up and down. I had no control. I kept screaming "No!" as I fought hysteria. I had no choices. We were in too deep, and I was trapped on the raft with my fear!

Suddenly, a big wave crashed onto the raft, flipping us into the swirling waters. I went under, thrashing wildly. Which way is up when you're drowning? Lost and terrified, for a few seconds no one touched me. I vividly remember the horror. Horror! My thoughts raced madly. My lungs felt like they were exploding. There was water in my mouth. I was choking.

Suddenly a hand gripped my arm and yanked me up and above the water. Gasping, sputtering, gagging, spitting up water . . . then sobbing.

My trust in Dad as a god-person was shattered at that moment. I had said "No!" because of my deep fear. For whatever reason, I wasn't ready to brave the water that day. I love my father. He is a wonderful, sensitive man. And that day I learned he was human.

It happens. We are hurt.

Sometimes deeply.

Trust is tender. That trust broken, I felt alone and abandoned.

Can you remember such an experience? How did you feel? If you cannot remember such an experience but still know what it's like to fear instead of trust, don't worry. As we show you how to work on present fears, you can deal with the power of past fears even if you cannot clearly identify the details surrounding those past fears.

Abandoned Self-Esteem

Children need affirmation as much as their growing bodies need food. Self-esteem is confidence in ourselves; belief in our abilities; a sense of well-being about ourselves; and hope for the future.

How do we build self-discipline? Some child-rearing literature, particularly that of the past, focused on teaching children by saying "no." Do not touch a hot stove. Do not take candy from strangers. Just say "No!" to drugs. But today we realize that discipline, especially self-discipline, also requires saying "Yes."

My oldest son, Matthew, when he was nine, ran an elevator at our church, the Crystal Cathedral in Garden Grove,

California. One Sunday, my wife Kriste said to our son on his way to "work," "Do a good job, Matthew!"

Matthew frowned. "Mom, have faith. I always do a good job."

What was Matthew telling us? What did he mean by "faith"? Obviously, he was asking us to quit bugging him with our standards. He has a good idea what we expect of him; he was asking us to believe in him, to believe that he will do the good, the right, and the best—at least to the best of his ability.

By whose standards? Our standards for Matthew? Or Matthew's standards for himself?

Experience tells us that our standards are often different from Matthew's. Our expectations are high. Being legalistic, Matthew does not merit our unconditional "faith." Matthew can let us down, at least according to our perfect standards. So shouldn't we mold this kid to function better? Shouldn't we keep telling him to do good? Shouldn't we continue reminding him of our expectations for his life?

Matthew is more than an extension of our ideas of the good and the right. This child of mine is a separate, unique person. That is scary! The risk—no, the reality—of hurt and pain for Matthew and for us, as parents, is tremendous.

And yet Matthew is saying to us, "Mom and Dad, have faith in me so that I can have faith in myself." And the flip side is just as true: "If you don't have faith in me, I can't have faith in myself either!"

It is hard to have faith in each other and in ourselves. But it is imperative, too.

How, then, are we to handle the pain when people let us down?

Kriste reminds me that God must have faith in people. God has faith even though He must suffer tremendous loss, hurt, pain, frustration and disappointment. He has faith despite solid evidence that He *shouldn't* trust us. He allows an awful lot of evil, chaos, and hostility towards Himself, and yet—if the Bible is to believed—He has a plan. His plan is to bring us the best possible good in our apparent chaos.

What is God's motive? The Book says simply "love."

What kind of faith is this, that God trusts us against all odds? Certainly He can't have the faith that we will do the good and the right in all circumstances of our lives—we've already proven that impossible. It appears that God's faith in us is that He trusts us to do the best we can most of the time. And it's a good thing He has this kind of faith in us too! It seems that His faith is the very thing that gives us the courage to do anything at all that's good or right! God's faith is encouraging, esteeming faith. Obviously God, if you believe in Him, is not a perfectionist. God esteems! Kriste thought further: Why would anyone believe in such a God? How can we trust God for anything? Sometimes we wonder if God is a poor judge of character.

Which leads us back to Matthew, my son. Matthew needs us to affirm his potential to do good and right so that he can choose the good and the right as he determines it, not as we do. He has learned a lot about our sense of what's right. He has internalized our standards. Increasingly, he is driven by his own determinations, not ours. We see it is time to let him fly. Not entirely on his own at first, but with increasing independence. And this is exactly what God does for us.

Constantly forcing behaviors, even the right behaviors, on a child violates his dignity. Expecting the worst—and letting our extreme precautions advertise the fact that we expect the worst—virtually guarantees it! Such does not prepare a child to live. It only prepares a parent to be disappointed in his child. At the child's expense, the parent creates a bitter cycle of negative expectations and prophetic disappointments. Everyone loses.

Free your child as he or she is ready to fly.

Free yourself!

This thought may well lead to some memories—some painful, others joyful—from your childhood. As you were growing up:

- Who believed in you?
- Who had faith in you?
- Who gave you permission to believe in yourself?
- Who encouraged you to "fly"?
- How is this impacting your life today?
- Who believes in you today?

• Do you believe in you?

SELF-ESTEEM AND YOUR PARENTS

Each parent contributes something unique to a child's developing self-esteem. A boy needs particular gifts of esteem from each parent. Dad gives him something Mom cannot easily give. Mom gives him something Dad cannot easily bestow.

Fathers and Self-Esteem: Learning Skills

Traditionally, fathers give us the skills we need to be men. They teach us how to be male. They teach us the following:

• What clothes to wear
• How to groom (hairstyle and shaving)
• Language (how to be polite; how to be aggressive)
• Sports (how to play; how to understand the rules)
• How to use tools (fixing or building things)
• House upkeep (yard work, painting, plumbing)
• How and what to think about girls/work/jokes/ sports, etc.
• What we believe regarding politics/religion/ economics, etc.
• How to relate to and treat women
• How to relate to other men

Most boys do not get much quality time with their fathers. Particularly, they do not get much time to *talk* with their fathers—especially about feelings and dreams and fantasies and wonders. Traditionally, fathers have taught us how to *do* and how to *think* but not how to *feel*.

And yet feeling competent as a male is critical to our whole self-esteem. If Father was hyper-critical and harsh, we might have learned skills but gained little confidence in ourselves. Dad was never pleased, never satisfied. If Dad did not give us time—time to learn, patiently, these basic skills—we can add feeling inferior to the toxic mix described above. Our self-esteem suffers even more. We feel loss and hurt.

Men born between 1925 and 1938 are children of the Great Depression. Many reached adolescence during World War II. These were days of fear, loss, and deprivation for the nation. When these men became young fathers, they vowed to give their children "what I never had." Their children are part of the present "boomer" generation.

Baby boomers, myself included, were raised on the American dream. Our fathers worked hard to make a better life. They did not necessarily learn great nurturing and parenting skills. They did not necessarily develop sterling relational or communication skills, nor did they spend large quantities of time with us. They are not always willing mentors in business. They do not "turn over the controls" easily.

Most men, of all ages, suffer the absence of good communication with their fathers. Some had occasions to talk, but then felt rejected by their fathers. Their ideas were judged as being "dumb" or "silly." They learned to fear talking with their dads, feeling incompetent in their eyes. And that hurts. It really hurts.

Mothers and Self-Esteem: Sexuality

Mother has great power to determine how desirable we feel to women—whether we perceive ourselves as physically and sexually attractive. Whether we can hope to be a prize—someone the girls will gaze at longingly—or second fiddle is determined primarily by our relationships with our mothers.

How do our mothers do this? By their language. Think back to when you were a kid. As you climbed into your swimming trunks, what did Mom have to say about your body? Anything? Nothing? Most boys interpret silence as a negative. Little boys will not ask for positive comments—they just wish for them, even though they *act* disdainful when they get one!

Did Mom say you needed to change your body? Did she say you needed to "lose weight" or "put some weight on those bones"? If so, you probably felt embarrassed and powerless. If these were the primary kinds of messages you got about your body, your self-esteem couldn't help but suffer.

When you got all dressed up for the prom, did you hear, "What a handsome young man! Your date is a lucky young lady to be going to the dance with you!" Boys need to hear these kinds of comments from their moms.

Perhaps even more than words, touch is also critical to our self-esteem. Boys need to be touched by their mothers. How? Hugs. Shoulder rubs. Kisses. Occasional hair-mussings. Of course, all touching from Mom needs to be honest touching, that is, without inappropriate sexual overtones. Dishonest touching is worse than no touching; it disturbs the personality, violating fundamental boundaries and shattering trust.

If we did not get affirmations—both verbal and physical— from our mothers, we can suffer insecurities about our sexuality. Sexual self-esteem is basic to our whole self-esteem.

I have seen men with handsome features emanate ugliness. I have seen men with modest features radiate genuine, calm confidence. I wonder how they developed such images of themselves? Look at your relationship with Mom. What do *you* remember? Do your memories provide any clues about your life today?

Both Parents and Self-Esteem

A significant truth is that each child is unique and will respond to parents differently. Each child must be treated with respect. Parents must work to understand each child and to see "what works" with each child.

Further, cross-contribution is important, too. Father can help mold a boy's sexual self-esteem and mothers can have input on a boy's skills esteem. Yet the fact remains that the primary gifts of esteem from each parent to their son is as we have outlined. These patterns—sexual self esteem from our mothers and skill esteem from our fathers—are most critical to our emotional development.

DIVORCE AND SELF-ESTEEM

Judith Wallerstein has documented the impact of divorce on sixty families in her book *Second Chances: Men, Women & Children A Decade After Divorce.* Commonly, she found that young men of divorced families developed "aimlessness." She explains: "The aimlessness of young men is related to low self-esteem and to their feelings of being rejected by one or both parents. . . . Young men fear not being loved."[2]

JEALOUSY: THE SEXUAL FEAR

Jealousy begins with low self-esteem. When one feels inferior, he is set up to feel jealous.

Jealousy toward our partner is a fear that she will give what "belongs to us" to another. Studies indicate that women fear their husbands will fall in love with another woman. "Do you love her?" is the question a wife will ask her adulterous husband. Men, however, focus on a different fear. We will ask, "Did you have sex with him?" This is another indication of our relational-emotional frailty. We focus on the "act" of sex.

We can be jealous that our wife gives a lot of time to the children, her job, her successes, her girlfriends, or swooning at Paul Newman. These types of things we can often resolve by sharing our feelings and trying to understand our partners' needs. We might even find enough maturity within ourselves to be able to share in her joy without giving rein to our jealousy.

When we suspect, however, that another man—a competitor—might have some inside experience with our wives or girlfriends, then we feel rage. This threatens the core of our male self-confidence.

Many men don't need much evidence to be jealous. A shred of evidence coupled with a strong mental fantasy leads to painful fear and hurt. I have heard it all: a cigarette butt in the car; extra miles on the odometer; a busy signal when we tried to call home; an incoming phone call at home during which we are greeted with silence when we say hello; we come home to an empty house and aren't sure where she's gone; an odd look from her, or even sexual aloofness. The possibilities are endless; the result is that men can become fearful, anxious, even paranoid about the perceived unfaithfulness of their wives.

Why? Because the bottom line is that we have serious doubts we are worth her fidelity. Beneath male bravado lurks severe sexual inferiority complexes.

Fantasy fuels jealousy. We do not ask questions or seek clarification, we just burn. Our minds imagine what we do not see—and very likely what never even occurred. Our hearts palpitate with feelings of betrayal, of being made a fool, of rage, and perhaps even of violence.

And what do we do when our jealous fears are true?

Phil

"But she really did it!" Phil screamed in group, jumping off the couch. This was Phil's first night. Medium height and build with curly hair, his body was pent-up with rage.

"I didn't imagine it. She was with him! What are you telling me to do? Be stupid? Naive? Just let it happen? She was sleeping with my best friend. I will *never* be made a fool of again!"

One of the leaders in our group asked, "What would you do differently if you could do things over again?"

Phil raged. "I would lock her up. I'd make her report everything she did all day long."

"Oh? And what would that accomplish?" the other man asked.

"She wouldn't get away with this!"

"You would spend the rest of your life being a zookeeper. And she would still find a way—"

"So you're telling me I'm wrong? That I should just let her do whatever she wants? That it's okay for her to hurt me?"

"No."

"Then what *are* you saying?"

"Your solution means you'd have to watch her twenty-four hours a day. It's impossible. It wouldn't work."

"You think what she did was okay," Phil spat the words.

"Not at all. But she chose what she wanted. She chose to lie to you and sleep with your friend. We cannot force our wives to be truthful, to love us, to treat us with respect. We can't force anyone to do anything, really! That's scary, I know."

"But I deserve better. I deserve respect."

"Absolutely."

Phil stared at the floor for a while in silence. It was important not to interrupt his thoughts. Then he said, "I should never have married her."

Our friend in group said, "What do you mean?"

"It wasn't right. I didn't love her. I just liked how she made me feel," he admitted. "I felt good with her."

"How did you feel without her?"

"Mostly like . . . nuthin'."

Phil began to see that he married to possess his wife, like a trophy. He liked to show her off. It gave him a sense of pride that he might be good enough for her. But to get her, he had sold his soul. He strained himself to make her happy, because the moment she became unhappy, he was afraid. He was afraid she might leave.

Showing her off also made Phil afraid because he saw other men as threats. He saw how men looked at her. And she loved the attention. He knew her commitment to him was fickle. He had hoped marriage would "tie the knot." He could not, however, keep the knot tied. He hated her for that.

Over time, Phil realized that he had sold his soul for a trophy. Being honest about this new insight brought relief. "I'm done selling myself," Phil resolved. "I want to find out who I am so that I can begin to be myself."

Yet even with this insight, Phil's fragile self-esteem feared being without her and having to go on with his life alone.

Phil gathered the courage to stop pampering his wife. He told her about his fears. He told her he wanted to spend more time with her. He wanted to make their marriage work—for real this time. She responded by leaving him for a guy with a Porsche.

At first, Phil felt anger towards the group. "I shouldn't have listened to your stupid advice!" he blamed. "You guys messed up my marriage." Weeks later, Phil apologized, admitting his hurt and loss.

Phil's second instinct was to hunt quickly for a new woman to relieve his pain and loneliness. He hit the bars, had a few dumpy relationships and then "fell in love" again. This woman was, he assured us, "totally different." But Phil was, in fact, moving toward unwittingly duplicating his first marriage! His weak self-esteem fell in love with a beautiful face. After some bitter arguments they broke up. Now, with the help of the group, Phil learned to live "within" himself. He faced his loneliness by talking more about it. It did not scare him anymore. "I will survive!" he said. "I can make it by myself!"

Phil made new friends, went to various groups, and sometimes enjoyed just being alone. Two years after his divorce, Phil remarried. He and his wife are doing well.

Phil learned that he could find peaceful feelings in himself. No woman could do that for him. He had to learn to like and trust himself. He also found relief from his jealous feelings. He no longer saw every other man as competition. Learning to like and accept himself, he had found reprieve from his fears of rejection and abandonment. And the paradox is that as Phil became less jealous, suspicious, and hostile, he became even more attractive to his wife.

ANGE AND ANXIETY

Even before its English usage, the Latin origins of *ange* related it to *anxiety*. The Latin usage compared it to the idea of strangling. When anxious, one feels strangled. Our breathing becomes short and shallow. Our chests feel constricted. Suddenly our hearts and minds and lungs are left gasping. There is panic, and fear. What's worse, our very response can make us feel even more *ange* and anxiety!

The cycle is vicious and self-propelling. Unresolved, the ultimate end of *ange* can be angina, which is spasmodic heart pain.

Separation Anxiety

Babies attach to the persons who give them comfort and security. A child depends on these sources of nurture. When a child senses that his nurturing presence is absent, he can experience what psychology calls "separation anxiety."

We all feel separation anxiety at various times, to various degrees, and for various reasons throughout our lives. Usually, the consistent presence of significant persons during the first year-and-a-half of life can secure for each of us a greater ability to handle security absences in later years. It's a snowball effect, really, as security—or lack of security—can build in intensity as life progresses. The snowball effect can be for better or for worse, depending on our earliest experiences.

Have you experienced "separation anxiety" in your adult life? If so . . .

- Who (or what) left you?
- What did you feel?
- How have you handled this?

General Anxiety

Anxiety can be understood as a form of fear. It is unconnected fear. You may have had anxiety or panic attacks. These are very real, not "just in your head," as some say. An attack can occur while driving a car, being in a certain place or around certain persons, when you're alone or in a crowd. There are many triggers for anxiety attacks, and many symptoms. You might feel hot flashes, cold flashes, fear, a sense of dread, shaky, light-headed, sweaty, tight in the chest or head, short of breath, or unable to function.

Anxiety is submerged fear which surfaces at unannounced times. It operates like a submarine of pain surfacing in our emotional seas without warning. Anxiety is fear disconnected from its original cause, surfacing when triggered by something that reminds us—often subconsciously—of that original cause.

In other words, we feared something and never faced that fear. The fear has gone into hiding in our subconscious depths.

Juan was waiting for a green light so that he could make a left turn in a busy intersection. Suddenly, he felt a flash of heat and began sweating profusely, his heart racing madly. He felt dizzy. He began to shake. His breathing became labored; he gasped for air. In the space of twenty seconds, he had lost control. He managed to make the turn, though how he did remains a mystery to him still today. Immediately, he pulled the car over to the side of the road and climbed out, fearing he might black out.

At first, Juan thought he had a heart attack. Later he learned, after several more incidents, that these were panic attacks. A therapist helped him to identify the stresses lurking within.

Juan grew up in poverty. As a father and husband, he felt tremendous pressure to make enough money to pay his family's over-extended budget. He had not dared tell his wife about his anxieties, fearing her reaction if "I can't cut it." Juan felt a "real man" should be able to handle his responsibilities and certainly his fears.

Once Juan identified his primary source of anxiety, he made some significant changes in his lifestyle to lessen these stresses. He also learned about the load of anxiety he had carried as an impoverished child.

Phobias

If anxieties are repressed fears, then phobias are repressed anxieties. A phobia is a condition of anxiety, even further removed from the original, unresolved fears. Phobias can relate to heights, crowds, foods, people, etc.

Paranoia

If phobias are conditions of repressed anxieties, then paranoias are repressed phobias. Paranoia is a major condition or lifestyle of fear disconnected from reality. One can have paranoid *ideas* ("They're after me!" "The Communists are putting things in our water!") and may still be able to function in life. In some cases, though, one can be in a *state* of paranoia that inhibits day-to-day living.

FEAR OF BELONGING: THE FLIP SIDE OF FEAR OF ABANDONMENT

This is a great human paradox. It is part of our complex emotional makeup. One moment, we fear abandonment. Logic would dictate that belonging to another person would alleviate that fear.

Not always.

A recent wave of books and articles are highlighting our fear of intimacy. Many fear feeling close to another person. We ask ourselves: What happens if she really knows me? What if she uncovers my secret fears and hurts? She might reject me! Do I dare belong? What is worse—the pain of my loneliness or my fear of belonging?

The fact is, these fears are not mutually exclusive. We can feel both of these fears at the same time.

How can this be? Let's consider the origins of these fears. We have already discussed separation anxiety which pushes us to want to cling to someone. But there is another, major infant anxiety which can confront us from another angle. It is called "stranger anxiety."

Stranger Anxiety

An infant may experience anxiety when a significant person leaves his presence. That same infant can also experience anxiety when *a strange person enters his presence.* The child perceives the stranger with fear because this stranger is not within the infant's frame of reference. Why should an infant trust that which he does not know? His instincts toward self-protection and security are working properly.

Stop for a moment and think. We experience this fear nearly every day in more sophisticated ways. How can I know whom to trust? How can I know when to trust? People hurt us. We feel fear of others as a way to protect ourselves. Yet if our defenses function too rigidly, too tightly, we may never trust anyone at all.

Fear of Women

The most potent fear of belonging that men suffer is fear of intimacy with a woman. As a result, men can appear aloof and cold—even downright uncaring! The most common statement women say to me, in various forms, in marriage therapy is, "My husband is so insensitive to me! I just don't know what he's feeling."

When a woman tells me this, I know what is fueling her dilemma: her husband is fearful and dependent! Yet I can make you a guarantee. If you ask a man directly if he is fearful or concerned about his dependence on his wife, he will say the thought never occurred to him. In fact, I have heard some men get hilariously ridiculous about this, practically denying they have ever even heard of the words "fear" or "dependence." The absurdity of their denials betrays the truth of their fear.

Many men are afraid to fear.

Salvatore and Susan walked into my therapy room quiet and somber for their first session of therapy. She was fidgeting; he sat firmly cross-legged and cross-armed, filling up the corner of the couch. They were in their late forties, early fifties. Sal was balding, had puffy eyes and a touch of alcohol abuse in his face. He sells pharmaceuticals. Susan had dark hair neatly styled. Her thin face belied her weight problem.

"What brings you here?" I was the first to break the silence.

Sal nodded. "You go first, dear." He said this with a patronizing, quirky smile. Susan, watching his every move, caught the innuendo and immediately reacted to it with a stare and a huff. Their game was so powerful, they could not even see it, much less break it. They were stuck in the actor-reactor game. Both sold personal power to play the game. Sal had quickly established his power as the first actor. He got her, temporarily, on his turf. She reacted. That was what he wanted. It protected him from his fear of what might happen in therapy.

When Susan huffed, Sal played the victim. "Well, you *are* the one who set this up," he said innocently. He nodded toward me. "The man wants us to tell him the problem. I think you know it better."

This was Sal's way of staying aloof to "the problem"—notice he didn't say "our" problem. "The problem" was his relationship with Susan, which he had managed to depersonalize through his choice of words. Sal secretly hoped a male therapist would team up with him to teach Susan that she was the one with the problem. Sal thinly covered his patronizing attitude by throwing in a "nice" statement about Susan: ". . . you know [the problem] better."

When Susan spoke, she did so bluntly. "I've been married to Sal for twenty-three years. The children are raised and gone, except for Susie. She's finishing her last year in high school. We're basically done with parenting. It's just Sal and me. And I'm lonely.

"He goes to work," she added. "He plays golf with the boys. He putters around the house or takes care of the yard. But when it's just the two of us in the house, he does one of three things. He watches TV, especially sports. He reads the paper. Or he goes to sleep."

"That's not true!" Sal interjected, smiling through a hint of discomfort. "We talk. Why just last night—"

Susan had begun the session by trying to outline her loneliness and feelings of rejection. Now Sal retorted with a litany of experiences which he called "talking." She longed for Sal to understand her feelings. But Sal didn't get it. He responded to her deep hurts with statements of "fact" designed to prove her wrong, to verify his point of view. Obviously, they were not communicating.

Why do men do this? What is at the root of the way men relate to women?

When Sal was a toddler, like most boys, his mother was his primary parent. Daddy was off at work. Mommy ran his life. And guess what? He learned a lot about how to be like Mommy! He learned about sensitivity and feelings and touching and nurturing—Mommy stuff.

Somewhere around three, Sal's Daddy decided that he could relate to his more "functional" little boy. He bought little Sal a mitt and ball. Sal could play in the yard as Daddy mowed the lawn. Daddy could tackle and tumble and tease his little boy.

Sal learned, now, about what it meant to be a boy: Daddy taught him. Of course, some of this conflicted with what Mommy taught him, so little Sal started making choices. To please Daddy, he had to reject some of Mommy's way. In fact, sometimes he figured out how to be a boy by being the opposite of Mommy.

Working so hard to be masculine, a little boy "finds himself pressed to reject so powerful an inner presence as mother has been in his early life. It's a fear so great that he can live with it only by taking away her power—by convincing himself that she is, after all, a weak and puny creature," says Lillian B. Rubin in *Intimate Strangers: Men and Women Together*.[3]

Sal grew up with powerful defenses toward women. He longs for Susan's love but fears it. So his treatment of her is aloof. He wants to give her love, but fears he will depend on her as he once depended on his mother. He longs to embrace and fears embracing all at the same time! The intensity of his aloofness is an accurate measure of his disease. He denies his deepest longings—he shuts down his feelings, and in the process, shuts down Susan's feelings as well.

As men, we need to admit this fear. Face it. Tame it. Even go as far as to share it with the women we love.

Fear of belonging is a natural and basic fear. It is a protective fear. But we must tame this fear lest we cut ourselves off from all powerful love and tenderness.

OTHER FEARS

Our two most profound fears are fear of abandonment and fear of belonging. All our fears ultimately relate to these, though they may show themselves with many different faces.

Fear of Failure

A man who works twelve-hour days, drives a car with a phone, and is "on call" even in his free time is doing one of two things—he either "plays" via his job, or is he obsessed with fear. Perhaps both.

If he is fearful, what is he afraid of? That he will fail to have success? To have prestige? To have enough money? To satisfy a parent, spouse or boss? Fear is a great source of energy. It generates adrenaline. Channeled positively, fear-driven people can produce great things. Fear of failure can also eat us alive.

Fear of Success

I have a friend who was quite successful in his profession. He was a pastor, and I believe he cared about his congregation and his ministry. Yet once he told me, "If a book were written about the family I was raised in, it would be titled *Snatching Failure from the Jaws of Success*. My family feared success!"

I laughed at the possibility of that ever becoming *his* story.

My friend was prophetic. Shortly after he spoke those words, he suffered from tragic choices. He lost his family and his profession for a season. Perhaps he had compensated for fear by believing too desperately in his own success. After all, when one feels—or convinces himself that he feels—invincible, he is doomed to fail in character, even though he may succeed for a time in amassing raw power.

For others, the responsibility, prestige, and awesome choices that come with success can cause them to avoid it like the plague. Sometimes we sabotage true success to feel safely nestled in failure.

Fear of Disapproval

This is the fear that others will not like something I said, something I did, or even the fact that I exist! It can also translate into always feeling like a foolish child in a world controlled by adults. It's feeling that your ideas, fantasies, and dreams are silly, stupid or evil. Often this fear begins by not living up to the expectations of a parent. But soon it becomes a way of life; part of our personality. You *can* break free—with help. Stay tuned!

Fear of Impotence

Male enjoyment of sexuality is wound up in our sense of performance. Studies show that, for men, sex is more genitally focused than it is for women. Women, on the other hand, orient more toward relationship- and whole body-pleasure. How we perform physically becomes our measure of "good sex." Though male and female physiology differ (and is partly the reason for this) I believe men can mature in experiencing the wholeness of sex. We are whole bodies and whole people—sometimes, non-intercourse sex (massaging, simple touching) can be great.

Fear of impotence means we feel "sexless" if our sex organ does not perform to our expectations. We feel we have lost "power." Wow! What a loaded fear for a man! Yet it need not be that way. Give yourself the freedom to explore other parts of your body! Are there other areas of your body that respond to a touch or massage? What feels good? Tell your partner!

Fear of Feelings

Most men fear their feelings to some degree. Perhaps the great fear is that we might cry when someone is watching. As a result, we practice being dull to our feelings. After all, big boys don't cry—do they?

For most of us, there is a dammed-up torrent of feelings waiting to gush out. If you have been in denial of your feelings for so long that you can't agree with this statement, think again. The only men who really *don't* have feelings are psychopaths! They end up in prison because they have no feelings to help them discern the moral life. In other words, they hurt or kill without remorse. They don't fit into society.

You, of course, are not psychopathic. But you are dammed-up! And if you're like most men, you fear the dam. You're afraid that if a trickle of emotions is released, the whole dam might burst! If you know you are afraid of the dam, you are ahead of many brothers—at least you know the dam exists! If you, however, don't know what I'm talking about, then you may be protecting yourself with denial or repression. How deep is your hurt?

Fear is a natural, common emotion. Most of us are also frightened of fear. Facing our fears takes courage: the courage to see our defenses and the courage to explore and admit our fears. Knowing our fears frees us to enjoy an emotional life that is whole. Emotions give life zest and zeal.

What are *your* fears? Speak about them.

Step 5: I Am Responsible for My Hurt

Fears are anticipations of hurts; hurts are fears realized. Hurts are fears which happen. Hurts are violations of the body or soul.

Some hurts are necessary. Can you imagine life without hurt? "Yes!" you're probably thinking, "I could do without it!" But think again. Without hurt, your body would be unaware of injury. Jagged glass could rip through the flesh of your foot—you would feel nothing. You could bleed to death without pain. For persons who have suffered nerve damage this is more than a concept—it's a real life challenge. Hurt warns us; it can protect us.

In this chapter, we examine emotional and relational hurts. These hurts can be necessary too. They point us toward areas that we need to work on. One couple, for example, might argue constantly about their finances. Their hurt communicates an area of opportunity: they need help in this area of their relationship. Perhaps they lack good communication skills and can find help through a seminar. Perhaps their understanding and empathy are immature and they need counseling. Perhaps the husband is insecure about money because the memories of childhood poverty continue to haunt him: he needs some therapy.

Too many marriages try to exist on fantasy or romantic love alone. Then boom! When the first real hurt hits, one or both partners bail out. The emotional high crashes. Yet, contrary to what it might feel like, the first marital crisis can be an opportunity to begin building a quality marriage, "for better or worse, as long we both shall live!" It can be a chance to break through superficial love.

Still, it makes sense that we try to avoid hurt. Hurt scares us. Hurt can paralyze us. Emotional hurt even causes our bodies to ache—in our heads, hearts, stomachs, muscles, everywhere. Hurt hurts! Sometimes for a moment, sometimes for years.

Hurts come in many sizes:

Smaller hurts. The rudeness of a stranger. No birthday card from a good friend. No appreciation for a hard day's work. We have all experienced these small hurts at times. They make us sigh. Perhaps our stomach tightens a little. Still, we are able to lift our heads and go on with our lives.

Modest hurts. A poor job review. A sharp word from a lover. No money in the checkbook and there's another week before payday. These tighten our jaws, temples, shoulders, necks or chests. I usually feel the tension in my stomach. Others get headaches or feel fatigued. We are temporarily stunned but we get back up, hesitate, and then try again.

Larger hurts. The death of a parent or loved one. Being fired. A divorce. These shock us. Our body slows down. We might feel dizzy, shaky, numb, hot or cold, tight, tense, or exhausted. We might even get sick. Or angry. Or we might have a rush of anxiety. We've got to do something to stop the hurt!

Hurts come in many sizes. But regardless of the size, we must face each and every one. If we don't, we run the risk of becoming paralyzed from living.

WHAT MAKES US HURT EMOTIONALLY AND RELATIONALLY?

Emotional and relational hurt occurs whenever we feel small (belittled, intimidated, put down, treated like a child), vulnerable (lost, weak, endangered), or wounded (betrayed or abandoned). Do you remember being a small child, peering up at a big person, and being pummeled by humiliating words from that big person's angry face? What did that feel like?

Perhaps your father became angry when you made a mistake. He bellowed, "You didn't do it right!" Think about what you didn't do "right." What was his message to you? What names were you called that made you feel small or vulnerable? What did Mom say to you?

Perhaps your childhood was not unlike that of the little boy who, on his first day in kindergarten was approached by his new teacher. When she asked him for his name, the boy smiled. What an easy question! After all, he heard the answer often enough at home. He answered immediately: "Dangit George."

Hurt occurs whenever we feel loss of any sort. This is because any loss can lead us to feel empty. Our emotional cup is drained. There seems to be nothing within—nothing to draw from, nothing to give. We feel hollow. We feel grief.

Hurt is likely to occur whenever we feel insecure. We find ourselves wondering, "How will life assault me next?" We justify our feelings with a report card of all the recent injustices: "The kids drive me up the wall." "The boss gets on my case." "The wife knows just which buttons to push." "My marriage is on the rocks." We feel loss of control over a situation, or even of life in general. Our business fails after all our hard work. One of our children is seriously injured. These are profound hurts.

THE HURT OF LONELINESS

We fear abandonment. When the abandonment that we fear actually happens, we hurt and loneliness sets in. This is one of our greatest, most basic hurts. Loneliness is the loss of belonging. Loneliness is the heart's longing that it might be found.

Loneliness comes in three forms: environmental loneliness; emotional loneliness, and existential loneliness.

1. Environmental Loneliness

Environmental loneliness is caused by changes or stresses in our surroundings or circumstances. It is a temporary form of loneliness as long as we begin to reach out to others around us and develop and enjoy meaningful relationships.

This kind of loneliness, for example, can be brought on by moving. A new house. New streets. New stores. After a move, I drive around the new turf imagining places I will "hang out": parks, libraries, discount stores, ice cream shops. There will be so many new people! Who will become my friends? Bob? John? Sally? Ann?

A young fellow in high school fell in love. She was his first true love. She loved him too. He tasted the fruit of belonging, of being found, of being loved. Then his dad got transferred and his family had to move. He and his girlfriend broke up. Longings for her covered his heart like a thick fog. He grieved for months.

Sometimes we miss personal, caring support. The absence of committed, accepting friends. Spouses cannot fill our entire capacity for such friendships. Living far away from true friends or family members—far from their physical presence—leaves us hollow. Aching, even.

On the other hand, being near people we love does not always work, either! Once I lived near my parents. Rarely did I call. Writing seemed out of place. We saw each other only occasionally. I missed them even though they were nearby.

Then Kriste and I moved 2400 miles away. I called. I wrote. I planned a trip to visit them. The physical distance awakened my sense of our emotional distance. Then I worked at our relationship.

There are other kinds of environmental loneliness. Women who spend most of their time in the home, handling most of the child rearing, can feel terribly lonely. I have known young women who were supposedly satisfied with homemaking to have sudden "nervous breakdowns," fueled by the isolation in their lives! Such loneliness is difficult to admit for women (or men) who think they should be experiencing nothing short of marital or family bliss. The "perfect" marriage or family are myths. Whether she is employed or not, every woman must have some kind of life outside the home. It contributes to her as a person, and also enables her to be a better wife and mother!

Children are wonderful. Homes are nice. But they do not fill that empty spot—the need for adult conversation, significant friendships, personal accomplishments, loving touches, and time and space to be alone.

Even going away to college can be painfully lonely. Leaving home sounds like fun until you realize that, suddenly, everything in your life depends on you and you alone. The first days of class can generate a fear of failing. Competition for grades can be fierce. Pleasing the professor or teaching assistant pulls out the best and worst in you. The pretensions of some peer friendships can leave you exhausted. Is all this image-making really worth it? You might even begin to wonder how much you resemble the "person" you are presenting to those around you. Who *are* you?

My freshman year at UCLA, I remember studying in the dark quiet hours at Rieber Hall. It was two or three in the morning. Only my desk lamp fought back the darkness, boredom, and sleep. My mind drifted as my half-shut eyes gazed into the night beyond my dorm window. Suddenly the booming voice of an unknown fellow student echoed distinctly across the ravine from Sproul Hall. "What is reality?" he bellowed into the darkness. "What is truth?"

I smiled, then laughed aloud for my lonely-hearted friend. For a moment, we shared our situational purposelessness. He loudly, I quietly, yet both of us feeling temporarily disconnected and alone. Five minutes later I—and perhaps my friend, as well—was back in the groove, cramming madly to pass an early morning exam.

2. Emotional Loneliness

The second form of loneliness is emotional loneliness. There are two sources of this kind of loneliness: crises and development deficiencies.

Crises

Crises are emotional bombshells, gashing holes or gaps into our emotional landscape. Crises often hit us blind-sided with little warning. The consequences of a crisis can become the preoccupation of our lives.

Divorce is one such bombshell. One person described divorce as "a death with no body." No one intends to divorce. When the decision to divorce is being made, there are usually more than enough feelings of guilt and hurt to go around. Few people make the decision lightly. And yet I wonder if many people fully consider the long-term implications.

Judith Wallerstein's study (cited in the previous chapter) peels away our denial and avoidance of the emotional consequences of divorce. We used to hope that the effects of divorce on children were limited to grief after the first years of a divorce. But now we know that divorce impacts children the rest of their lives.

Wallerstein has said about her study: "We were able to see clearly that we weren't dealing simply with the routine angst of young people going through transition but rather that, for most of them, divorce was the single most important cause of enduring pain and anomie in their lives."[1]

Divorce is a ripping experience. There is no such thing as an easy divorce. Our identities as husband and wife intertwine— if we separate, we might pull apart slowly, but the heart still gets torn in the process.

Too often parents recognize the intensity of their love (or need) for their child(ren) as the divorce becomes final, and they may launch a brutal fight for custody (a word, by the way, often associated with prisoners).

Divorced adults re-enter the "single" world, sometimes after many years of marriage. They ask, "Who am I now? With whom do I share myself?" The mechanics of dating—such as where to meet potential dating partners—are difficult enough without having to deal with the fact that, suddenly, trust terrifies and loneliness agonizes.

This is reality. No amount of moralizing, justification or denial can mend the pain from a broken marriage. Are there consequences of a divorce in your life? Are you the child of a broken marriage? Is your partner? Are you married to someone with a broken marriage in *her* past? Is there one in yours? How have you healed from this?

Another powerful crisis of loneliness hits us when someone we love dies. If divorce rips, death tears. Death tears someone away from us. There is no way to replace the torn cloth; in time the tear can mend, but it never disappears.

I know of a thirty-year-old electrician who went to work yesterday. Probably he hugged his wife and two young children goodbye. Late in the day, perhaps rushing to finish and head home, he stood on a ladder and touched two live cables. Electricity surged through his body, burning his hands. He stumbled down the ladder. He spoke these words to a coworker: "I made a mistake." Then he died. Alive and vibrant one minute—dead in a flash. Too often death gives no warning.

Developmental Deficiencies

As we race through our lives, we face critical stages of emotional development:

Birth
Entering school
Puberty and sexual awareness
Entering college or work
Dating and/or developing friendships
Marriage, or remaining single
Having your first child, or not having children
Experiencing mid-life issues
Watching your children leave home, aging
Retirement

Where are you in this maze of stages? What memories do you have of each of these stages in your life? How have you been impacted by events surrounding each stage? Which stage has been the most difficult for you. Why?

Each developmental change leaves its mark on us. Perhaps the most profound change occurs at puberty. Our bodies go through obvious remoldings. Our emotions dramatically remold at the same time. Adolescents balance on an emotional fence. One side of the fence stands for their need for dependence: acceptance, affirmation, love, and security. On the other side, we see their need for independence. When a parent tries to pull the teenager back onto the "dependence" side of the fence, the young man or woman is bound to jump (or fall) to the side of independence. Pressure doesn't work. Usually, it is the parents' job to be available, while not clutching at the youth too hard or too obviously. Being an adolescent— and parenting one—is hard work.

Each developmental stage demands that certain emotional requirements be met. These include our most constant, basic emotional needs:

- **Love.** This is the feeling that we are accepted unconditionally and touched with wholesome affection.
- **Affirmation.** We are regularly given support, encouragement and praise.
- **Discipline.** Having the structure and guidelines which teach us respect for life, and limits which provide for our greater freedom.

A crisis such as divorce, illness, neglect, or death, can slow our emotional maturity in a particular stage. We can become deficient in social skills or develop inhibition toward attaching to others. For example, many adult-aged children of divorced parents face obstacles to forging committed relationships. Whether we like it or not, we have to grow past the models our parents gave us.

We do not have to remain trapped by our deficiencies. We can learn and change. The pain experienced as a child can force us to face questions of trust and commitment with greater maturity. It's possible to learn to be more flexible and resilient in relationships because of the things witnessed and experienced in the past.

3. Existential Loneliness

For others, life feels dull, depressing, aimless or hopeless. Existence itself is marred with a deep-seated loneliness. The heart aches most of the time.

What are the origins of profound life loneliness? Deficiency of love and care in childhood may have turned the soil for this particular strain of loneliness. Perhaps Dad provided shelter and food but no emotional affection or closeness. Perhaps Mom made the meals and laundered our clothes but was emotionally remote. They did not intend to be that way—they gave what they knew to give. They were wounded children too.

Dr. Craig Ellison described a well-known study in this manner: "Psychiatrist Rene Spitz (1945) first showed that satisfactory physical care of human infants was not enough. Infants placed in an institutional situation with adequate physical provisions and cuddling by their mothers developed normally. Those placed in a second institution with superior physical care but no opportunity for adequate maternal or nurse cuddling never learned to speak, walk or feed themselves. Most tragically, by the end of two years, *37 percent of the second group died of marasmus or lack of love.*" (Emphasis mine.)[2]

Ellison summarized a second study which showed that any disruption of the bonds of attachment (ten days or longer) between a baby and his parent(s) can cause a kind of "grief" in the baby. The child mourns the loss of his loved ones.

Furthermore, when the child is reunited with Mom or Dad, he is not necessarily quick to return to them. His defenses warn him not to reattach too quickly to people who disappear without warning! The child has learned to fear belonging!

The hurt of loneliness operates under the same conditions as the fear of abandonment: loneliness occurs with breach of trust (abuse), and the absence of acceptance, affirmation, love, and comfort from nurturing persons (neglect).

THE HURT OF POOR COMMUNICATION

William: The Demands and Rewards of Honest Communication

William came to the Men at Peace group depressed. His brown eyes were rimmed with red. He was unshaven and his hair was tussled. His tailored suit was disheveled. William was in agony.

"No one understands," he began. "I'm not a violent person. I'm trying to get my business going, I've got two kids . . . she doesn't give me a break."

"Who is *she*?" we asked.

"My wife," William answered.

"What is her name?"

"Ellen."

"Thank you."

(We often go through this routine with first-timers in the group when they begin by referring to their wives as "that woman," "my old lady," or just "she." We help men by not participating in the habit of using demeaning language to depersonalize women and other persons. Using first names creates more respect.)

"William, what do you mean by 'Ellen doesn't give me a break'?"

"Ellen doesn't understand how tough it is out there. She wants lots of things. . . . I try to buy her things."

"What things?"

"A new sports car."

"So she wants a new sports car?"

"Yeah," he nodded. "She's been talking about it for a long time. It makes me uptight when she talks about it. I want her to have it, but what will she be like when she gets it? We've got kids, you know. I can't have her racing around town! She might do something crazy!"

"Crazy? Like what?" we all wanted to know.

"Oh, I don't know. I haven't thought much about it. Maybe go out too much. Fly around with her girlfriends while I'm at work. Flirt with some guys. Neglect the kids maybe."

Obviously, William had thought about this quite a bit. He was scared. The loaded words were "flirt with some guys." We decided to begin by asking him about Ellen as a mother.

"You mentioned neglecting the kids. Has Ellen ever neglected the kids before?"

"No, well, sometimes when I come home the house looks like a dump."

"How does that make you feel?"

"I don't like it."

"Yes, that's what you think. But what do you *feel*?"

He thought a minute. This was a new one. "Ticked, I guess. Angry. I mean, she's home all day. Why can't she do her part?"

"Her part?"

"Yeah. Keeping the house clean and the kids clean."

"Orderly, clean . . . no chaos. William, does Ellen ever truly neglect or hurt the children?"

"Well, no, she's a good mother. But she does need to stop bugging me about buying her stuff."

"Aha! What's that about?"

"She doesn't know how hard it is for me. The pressure at work . . . there's no end. I can line up extra jobs, but then I won't be home as much. She doesn't know what I go through out there. It's a lot of pressure."

"William, what do you want from Ellen?"

"Some peace . . . some support."

"So, what would peace be for you, William? What could Ellen do that would create peace in your life?"

"That's easy. Take care of the house and listen to me."

"Listen to you?"

"Yeah. I want to talk about how I feel!"

This was a great breakthrough for William, so we talked for a while about this. He recognized that he wanted to talk with Ellen about his feelings. It was a beginning. Yet he had a long way to go to learn how feelings can be communicated and understood. In particular, William needed to learn empathy—that is, how to share and understand the feelings of another person.

We began to probe again. "William," one of the group facilitators asked, "How do you suppose Ellen feels at the end of a day?"

"Tired, I guess."

"You guess? You aren't sure?"

"Okay, yeah, she's tired."

"So she's tired too. What might make her tired?"

"She's been home with little kids all day. That's probably what does it."

"I would guess so! I wonder if she needs rest about that time? But even more, if I've listened at all to the wives that have talked to me in counseling, she needs adult conversation. She needs to be listened to, too! That must be a tense time when you get home. You're tired and she's tired. Your needs clash. What can you do about that?"

For awhile we helped William figure out ways to be more direct with Ellen about his needs for rest and communication. We also considered how he might help Ellen handle her needs. Yet William had something even deeper on his heart—something even he was not aware he was ready to express.

"Yeah, well . . ." William paused. "I suppose this will help. But I just can't stand women being demanding. My mother used to do that. I hated it. Sometimes I wished Dad would can her."

"That's some powerful stuff."

"Yeah, women at work do that to me too. I hate it. Women pushing me."

"So what do you want from women?"

"Respect. Some respect."

"Respect? What does that mean to you?"

William shrugged. "Just to listen. Listen to what I have to say. You know, I really want Ellen to have what she wants. But I don't know if she cares about me. *Me.* It scares me."

"Wow. So that's what you mean by *listen.*"

"Yeah. Does she really give a rip about me? Does she really love *me*?"

Not many men can open up this quickly. We could see William repressing tears, yet he wanted to talk. He had a lot of courage to allow other men to help him face these fears and hurts in his life. Yet what he was describing is a common fear for men. We feel vulnerable with women, especially our wives.

"Do you want to ask her?" the facilitator asked. "Do you want to ask her if she loves you?"

"Yeah, sure, but what if she says no? You don't know my wife. She's hard."

"Okay, you're right. I don't know her. So I'll take your word for it. You married a cold, hard woman."

"I didn't mean that."

"But you're afraid to ask her if she loves you."

"Yeah."

"So how will you find out?"

"I don't know. You're the big expert, you tell me. What if she says 'no'?"

"That's a risk. I guess you'll hurt and have some tough decisions to make. Can you think of any way to find out besides asking and talking with her about this?"

"No." He sighed.

"And here's a tough question, William. Do you love her?"

"Sure."

"Do you tell her that you love her?"

"I bought her the car, didn't I?"

The group broke into guffaws thinking about how often men buy things to avoid saying and doing simple loving things. William wanted to be understood. But he perpetuated the very problem which hurt him. He didn't say what he felt.

"William, Ellen might wonder what you wonder. She might, this very moment, be thinking, 'I wonder if he really loves me.' Tell her! Tell her today!"

"She ought to know that I love her," William argued.

"No, William. She might not know. She deserves to hear you say, 'I love you.' She may not know a lot of things. She may not know how much you hate her screaming and why you hate it. Or how much you love her. Or how hard you're working for her and the kids. Or even about your fears that she—"

"But sometimes I don't want to talk at all," he protested. "She just comes at me sometimes, the minute I open the door."

"She's frustrated. Tired. She needs a break too, remember? And what is your typical response to her needs? What do you do to relax?"

William smiled. "Have a couple of beers?"

The guys laughed. William was teasing us since we had already determined he didn't have a drinking problem. When the laughter died, William shrugged. "Okay, okay, I know I should handle it differently—talk to her and all that. But I don't know if any of this will work. She's pretty tough."

The guys laughed again. They had heard it all before. The mood had lightened. William was clearly feeling hopeful.

"Maybe she's tough. But maybe you're not clear enough with her about your needs, your feelings, your fears . . . or even about how you really care about what she feels and thinks after being home all day with screaming kids."

William became a success story. He and Ellen struggled with a lot of immature, impulsive moods and sloppy communication. Yet over time, they made progress. I met Ellen once with William in a grocery store. I could tell she felt awkward meeting "the men's group guy," but she also seemed thankful. After William was in group for a year, he and Ellen decided to get help from a marriage therapist for a time.

Most success stories occur when a man commits himself to work patiently at the "little things," like asking honest questions and giving honest answers. These are miracles—miracles wrought from patience and hard work. They are crafted with practiced skills and gracious attitudes.

William learned to allow the men in the group to be his understanding friends. He continued to be vulnerable in group—sharing his fears, hurts, strengths, and successes.

He learned that Ellen did love him, loved being his wife and raising the children well. They worked out a realistic budget. They struggled with tenderness, but they learned the basics of communicating with love. The behavior of their children even reflected the positive change as the tension in the home diminished.

Some men are lonely because they feel no one understands. Any sort of change—in us or in our partners—causes us to fear. Yet we don't talk about these fears. We get into the pattern of feeling hurt and afraid in isolation. Change is scary! And yet we fall into the misconception that it is unmanly to talk about feelings that actually are familiar to all!

What do you need to talk about? For many men, it is feeling confused, deeply lonely or just plain afraid that a partner no longer cares. Don't give up. And don't clam up! Talk to your partner. Be clear about your needs—and listen well to *her* needs too.

And don't forget to tell the truth! Being understood requires honesty. How often do you tell half-truths? What are you trying to avoid or cover up? Think about your responses. Can you see why this approach would make it difficult for your partner to understand you? Others can tell when we are not telling the whole truth. Sometimes we even give ourselves away by saying things that are inappropriate: sometimes jokes or crude language are avoidance techniques. No wonder people avoid or leave us!

How do you respond to anger? Rather than getting defensive and angry, try responding calmly with something like, "I see that you're angry. Tell me more." And then stay calm and listen. This might shock your partner! She may be used to more volatile reactions. Be genuine. Hear her clearly and ask about her feelings. Show her respect and care. Remember, underneath her anger is fear and/or hurt. Listen to her!

If you suspect she may be angry but you're not sure, ask her. You might try saying, "I'm wondering if you're angry. If so, what is that about?" Then listen to what she has to say, even if she is angry at you! *You don't need to react.* Listen carefully without reacting. This is a great skill that takes time to learn well. Reacting, on the other hand, shows our immaturity and insecurity. Responding calmly shows strength! Remember:

- Be the first to listen.
- Listen well.
- Then ask for time to express your feelings too.

THE HURT OF PROFOUND ISOLATION

Loneliness is intrinsic to our human condition. Its gnawing on our souls reminds us that we need God. Once we know God, it reminds us "that this world is not our home"—or at least not our only home. Loneliness pushes us to dream, imagine, create—transcending our limitations in space and time. Loneliness dares us to reach for another's hand even in the midst of our fear. We learn to persevere in seeking, so that we might be found.

"Fixing" our loneliness is futile. Fixes can even produce pain worse than the loneliness itself. Loneliness is not our greatest enemy. Isolation, or worse, polarization are greater threats.

Loneliness, unchecked, can become a wildfire. We enter moods of isolation. Fear begins to dominate our thoughts of conversing with others. Polarization is a white-hot fire. It is a fire fueled by the ache of hurt.

In the article previously cited, Craig Ellison vividly described how our technocratic urban society, for all its comforts, can turn its back on us: "The individual has become a means to an end or a production tool whose worth is seen in commodity terms, i.e., wages. . . . People increasingly tend to be attached to objects as sources of security and self-validation, rather than to relationships. . . . When efficiency and convenience or comfort have been internalized as guiding values, relationships inevitably become more superficial and shallow, and people experience loneliness."3

Henry Nouwen, an American Catholic priest and theologian, warns: "The growing competition and rivalry which pervade our lives from birth have created in us an acute awareness of our isolation."4

Nouwen sees men hoping to find ". . . the man who really understands our experiences, the woman who will bring peace to our restless life, the job where we can fulfill our potentials, the book which will explain everything, and the place where we can feel at home. Such false hopes lead us to make exhausting demands and prepare us for bitterness and dangerous hostility when we start discovering that nobody, and nothing, can live up to our absolutistic expectations."5

Isolation and polarization drive us to confront our hurt with power. That is, we hide our hurt behind the illusory world of performance success. We use people, and they use us. At times, this seems the only alternative in a world of alienation.

Yet a higher way calls us to be "forgivers" rather than "takers." This way seems foolish to the taker because it requires honesty and vulnerability—two dynamics that signal disaster to power's manipulative style. Desperately, the power broker tries to avoid vulnerability. Forgiveness is a threat as well.

The paradox is that *forgiving is the more powerful way!* True forgiveness is disarming. It's disarming because it does the unexpected: it does not force justice, and it looks bitterness and revenge in the face and says, "I will not respond with bitterness; I will not fight."

Forgiveness says, "You are free from any obligation to me. You owe me nothing. I might not forget, but let us be at peace. Further, in the future, I wish you the best." The Forgiven One is free from bondage. The Forgiver is free from hate. He has, in fact, transcended human kindness; he has stepped into the realm of spiritual strength. This is the lifestyle that Jesus Christ modeled for us: nothing is more powerful than that!

Robert Bellah and others, in *Habits of the Heart: Individualism and Commitment in American Society*, identify another cause of isolation among Americans. Strangely enough, it is often touted as one of our strengths as well: individualism. Bellah and his colleagues remind us that Alexis deTocqueville in *Democracy in America* (written in the 1830s) warned that:

> Some aspects of our character—what [deTocqueville] was one of the first to call "individualism"—might eventually isolate Americans one from another and thereby undermine the conditions of freedom. . . .

> We are concerned that this individualism may have grown cancerous . . . that it may be threatening the survival of freedom itself. [6]

The authors interviewed Marra James, born in West Virginia, then living in Southern California, who lamented, "Many people feel empty and don't know why they feel empty." Marra longed for a sense of community in America but she doubted it could happen. "Most people have been sold a bill of goods by our system. I call it the Three C's: cash, convenience, consumerism. It's getting worse. The reason you don't feel part of it is that nobody is a part of it. Loneliness is a national feeling." [7]

Are we becoming a society of loners? What are our values and morals? Under the guise of being accepting ("Do your own thing as long as it doesn't bother me!") have we actually become an amoral—even immoral—society? Flag-waving and patriotic talk cannot hide our loss of spirit as a nation. Do we have any sense of our need for community? If so, what are we, as individuals, doing to rekindle community in our own lives? If not, what implications does this have for our personal and corporate futures?

We talk a lot, for example, about stopping drug pushers. Meanwhile, many American adults imbibe mind-altering alcohol, nicotine cigarettes, painkillers, tranquilizers, uppers, downers—all legal—in record quantities. Our children are not naive. They sense the glaring double standards. We grown-ups simply don't mean what we say.

We're outraged by the violence of Crips and Bloods and other local gangs. We pass laws making gang membership a crime. We declare "war" on the gangs. Power against power. Still, we are losing the war. Why?

Is it possible that gangs are simply seeking many of our society's explicit values? Most gangs are nothing more than hard-nosed "capitalist" organizations. True, some use "wild west" and guerilla warfare tactics—much like the television movies we glorify. The problem is that they do it in real life in our neighborhoods!

Bill Moyers, the PBS journalist, interviewed Joseph Campbell who, until his death in 1987, was the world's foremost authority on the social implications of mythology. Savor these profound and prophetic insights in light of our isolation: isolation from our very own feelings, isolation from those around us, and even isolation from the concepts—in this case, myths—that help weave the very fabric of our society:

Campbell: Man should not be in the service of society, society should be in the service of man. When man is in the service of society, you have a monster state, and that's what is threatening the world at this minute. . . . young people [no longer know] how to behave in a civilized society.

Moyers: Society has provided them no rituals by which they become members of the tribe, of the community. . . . Where do the kids growing up in the city today—on 125th and Broadway, for example—where do these kids get their myths today?

Campbell: They make them up themselves. This is why we have graffiti all over the city. These kids have their own gangs and their own initiation and their own morality, and they're doing the best they can. But they're dangerous because their own laws are not those of the city. They have not been initiated into our society.

Moyers: Rollo May says there is so much violence in American society today because there are no great myths to help young men and women relate to the world or to understand that world beyond what is seen.

Campbell: Yes, but another reason for the high level of violence here is that America has no ethos. . . . [Ethos is] an unstated mythology, you might say. "This is the way we use a fork and knife." "This is the way we deal with people," and so forth. It's not all written down in books. . . . law has become very important in this country. Lawyers and law are what hold us together. There is no ethos. Do you see what I mean?

[Mythologies] are stories about the wisdom of life; they really are. What we're learning in our schools is not the wisdom of life. We're learning technologies, we're getting information. There's a curious reluctance on the part of faculties to indicate the life values of their subjects.[8]

Have we reduced life to the "values-free" quantitative judgments of science and technology? Is this our new religion? We seem to have an agenda against mythology and classical religion. The essence of being human and living in community has been lost. Qualities of character—dignity, honor, loyalty, commitment, integrity, love—are sentimentally dismissed as bygones. We modern men (and women) glorify production and quantity.

In the words of Flannery O'Connor: "Not long ago a teacher told me that her best students felt it no longer necessary to write anything. She said they think that everything can be done with figures now, and that what can't be done with figures isn't worth doing. I think this is a natural belief for a generation that has been made to feel that the aim of learning is to eliminate mystery."[9]

Quiet desperation. Our antidote has been bold aggressive competition in the hostile urban environment. Life becomes a game. And our goal—perhaps even our god—is to win. The rule is: Each man for himself.

Men play games. We long for true love and belonging. We're running on the hamster's treadmill. Is there a way out? What do you value? How much time and energy, how much of yourself, do you give to your highest values?

11

The Antidote to Fear and Hurt: Forgiving Yourself; Reconciling with Others

FORGIVING YOURSELF

Forgiving yourself is a necessary step toward peace. Forgiveness means to pardon or free without exacting punishment or penalty; to release from guilt or shame; to wipe the slate clean. Forgiveness is a form of rest.

Freeing yourself from guilt or shame, in fact, must go hand-in-hand with all the responsibilities we've been examining in the preceding chapters. When we say, "I am responsible for _____!" it's critical to realize that we are not just taking on responsibilities, we are also letting some go. Chances are, in the course of your lifetime you have taken on some emotional responsibilities that are only hurting you. We've all done it! Now is the time, however, to begin releasing

168 MEN AT PEACE

ourselves from these impossible burdens if we hope to experience peace-living.

Having worked hard on your responsibilities through Step Five, you might feel too responsible at this point! You might be taking on too much of the burden of your recovery. You might be too hard on yourself, thinking that you are not recovering fast enough. What might be lacking is for you to declare yourself *free*. Declaring yourself free celebrates the transition from releasing the past to living in the present, free at last! Begin to live your freedom!

Free from What?

What exactly are you declaring yourself free *from*? How about these, for starters:

- Free from suffering for mistakes of the past.
- Free from lingering guilt or shame.
- Free from emotional chains inhibiting new choices.
- Free from relationships that are only destructive.
- Free from having to do everything "right."

Can you free yourself from your past mistakes? Can you forgive yourself for having flaws? You will continue to have flaws. This is part of being human. Can you give yourself the gift of imperfection? Can you answer with a simple, clear yes?

Many have responded to these questions with a resounding "Yes, but . . ." If this describes you, why are you still punishing yourself? What will it take to set you free?

Free for What?

Declaring yourself "free" does not free you from everything in your past. For example, you may still have to cope with difficult circumstances that remain from your past mistakes. Yet declaring yourself free can enable you to begin living a new life, creating positive consequences in the future for healthy choices made in the present. Declare yourself forgiven and free to:

- Start a new life.

- Begin a new style of living—with contentment, purpose, and joy.
- Develop new friendships.
- Seek help and community without fear of weakness or dependence.

What Forgiveness is Not

Forgiving is not forgetting. We forget what does not matter. Lewis Smedes wrote that to forget, "all you need is a bad memory, or maybe a fear of reality so intense that you stuff the ugly pain of the past into the dark pit of your unconscious."[1]

Forgiving is not excusing. There is a time and a place for excusing the wrongs we have done or the wrongs done to us. Excusing means tolerating. It enables us to accept human quirks; it understands reasons for modest misbehavior; it frowns but does not get deeply wounded from unintentional hurts; it shrugs its shoulders at human foibles. Excusing is okay for daily minor emotional abrasions *but not for deeds crying out for forgiveness.* When forgiveness is necessary, settling for "excusing" only postpones the pain. Forgiving—not excusing—is needed for lingering wounds.

What Forgiving Is

Again, taking concepts from the writings of Lewis Smedes:

Forgiving is the creation of a new beginning. Forgiving invites us to try again. It says, "In spite of everything that has happened, I want to try again." We *choose* to stop the bitterness and to make a fresh start. The hurt may not go away quickly—even though, in time, the pain will heal—and yet despite the lingering discomfort we are still willing to forge a new start.

Forgiving is seeing the past through new eyes. Through forgiveness, we create a tolerance, if not an understanding of, our woundedness. We become, in a sense, our own priest. We pronounce our absolution because *God has already absolved us*—if we have asked Him to do so, and if we believe that He is able. Do *you* believe?

Forgiving allows us to remember the past but frees us from the "imprisonment" of our wounded feelings. When we hate, we are enchained to bitterness. We are controlled by hate. It makes little difference if the bitterness and the hate are directed at ourselves for our bad choices, or at someone else whose choices hurt us. But by freeing ourselves, we do what we can to be free of the power of bitterness.[2]

Declaring Your Emotional Pardon

Write down your flaws, mistakes, choices—even downright evil deeds—that you consider the most difficult to forgive. What makes this flaw, or deed, so difficult to pardon?

If you aren't sure, ask yourself what you gain by continuing to punish yourself. And don't allow yourself to answer this question with "Nothing!" We are asking you to think deeply and uncover whatever reward you are gaining by continuing to punish yourself. For example, sometimes being "bad" covers our fear of taking positive responsibility. Being a "mess-up" lets us feel as though we don't have to be accountable; we can pretend we're still children! These are nasty games we play. Are *you* playing any games?

Share your answers with a confidant or with your group. Let them help you carry your load. Ask yourself how your friend or group members can help you to forgive and free yourself. Share your answers with them.

Perhaps your barrier is not a matter of forgiving, but of mourning. What loss do you feel as you think about pardoning yourself? Of what will you have to let go if you make the choice to let go of your guilt and shame? What needs to be re-born in you? In Chapter Twelve, we'll be taking a closer look at grief and mourning. But for now, why not approach God in meditation with the following prayer of pardon:

> God, I accept your pardon.
> I am free by your grace.
> Grant me the joy of new life.
> I live by your love.
> I move in your peace.
> > Amen.

RECONCILING WITH OTHERS

Having begun to forgive yourself, you are ready to begin building peace with others. Reconciliation has a powerful definition. It means: restoring harmony or communion to a friendship or creating peace in a relationship.

For those of us who need to be forgiven—not by ourselves this time, but by someone we may have wounded—we cannot demand forgiveness. Neither can we demand that our wrongs be forgotten. We can hope that others will not throw past mistakes back in our faces, but to be honest, they might. If they do, we need not re-accept the power or pain of guilt or shame. We need not respond to their anger. The pain is theirs, not ours, even though we may empathize with them. We can remind them that we are sorry—but allowing ourselves to wallow in punishment or self-blame does neither party any good! If we have pardoned ourselves, then we can hear our accusers with understanding ears and hearts—but we do not need to devalue ourselves.

If they can't let go, and they demand that we grovel or suffer, then we do not force reconciliation at that time. We might feel sad. We might grieve. We might need to take a "time out" to let go of any frustration we feel over the fact that this friend or partner is not ready to forgive us.

Requesting Forgiveness

When, in the process of reconciling a relationship, it becomes necessary for us to ask forgiveness for something we've done, it's important to keep in mind these truths.

First, we do not ask forgiveness so that we can gain eternal freedom from guilt or shame. That is too much to ask of the person who forgives us. The forgiving person cannot free us unless we accept forgiveness in the spiritual realm as well, from God. Only with God's help can we be washed with the cleansing waters of everlasting pardon.

Second, we must ask to be forgiven for specific deeds. We ask directly and calmly. We do not grovel or launch into a defense. We look the person in the eyes, with dignity, and say, "I made a mistake. As I see it, this is what I did wrong. I am sorry."

The person from whom we are seeking forgiveness might need time to think about our request. They might need time because they are taking us and/or the situation seriously. We might be ready to be forgiven—but they might not be ready to dispense forgiveness. Meanwhile, both parties can't help but feel the pain of sorting out uncomfortable feelings.

There are no guarantees. There are no requirements that the other person must forgive us. Forgiveness cannot be forced. It is a free gift.

Yet there is power simply in our heart-felt confession of wrong. We, at least, with our request have set the stage for the miracle of pardon. Our humility and honesty opens the door for reconciliation. And we can hold up our heads, knowing we've done the right thing, regardless of whether or not the wounded party has the power or ability to forgive.

Once again what we can do is to say: "I am sorry. As I see it, this is what I did wrong."

Then the ball is out of our courts. However, when our friends or partners respond to our request, we let it go. We try to honor their response.

Here is a partial list of the kinds of hurts we might have inflicted on others:

- Broken promises: Covering our shiftiness with lies. Using another's trust to manipulate them for our advantage.
- Embarrassing behaviors: Becoming boisterous, losing control, getting angry or depressed in public; making insensitive comments toward others and then justifying ourselves.
- Violence: Physical, sexual, psychological or even property.
- Hostility or rebellion: Fighting or opposing just to create turmoil or chaos or to hurt another.

- Intolerance: Being prejudiced or racist, demeaning or degrading others, being proud or boastful. Impatience.
- Dishonesty: Telling lies to deceive, confuse, manipulate, or to cover our wrongs.
- Selfishness: Having little concern for others while thinking a good deal about ourselves. Greediness.
- Immaturity: Reacting childishly to others; getting angry easily, pouting, leaving, punishing, not talking.
- Denial: Refusing to admit our weaknesses, wrongs, or harm toward others.
- Procrastination: Waiting until the last minute to make a decision, or not making a decision, especially when the delay has impacted or hurt others.
- Self-pity: Feeling sorry for ourselves.

When making plans to approach someone with whom you hope to reconcile, be clear about what you want to confess. If necessary, write down the details of what you want to say so you will not become distracted. When possible, speak face-to-face, although some persons may need to be contacted by phone and others by letter.

If the person you hurt is deceased, write him or her a letter anyway. Find a quiet place and read your letter aloud, imagining that you are expressing these thoughts face-to-face. This can help you resolve the matter in your own heart and allow you to live free of any guilt or shame attached to that relationship.

Forgiving Others

Perhaps, in order for a relationship to be reconciled, you are the one who needs to forgive. But what should you do if the person who hurt you is not acknowledging their action or asking for your forgiveness?

Above all, avoid beginning a conversation by saying, "I forgive you"—especially if your friend, parent, relative or partner is not convinced they did anything inappropriate or hurtful! Instead, begin by saying, "I would like to talk with you about a situation. Do you remember the time . . . "Go ahead and be as precise as possible without sounding accusatory. Conclude by saying, "This is how I felt about the situation. I felt—" and then clarify your emotions.

If the offender is able to show understanding and empathy toward your hurt, you have an open door to express forgiveness. Are you ready to do that? It's possible that you need to wait until your motives, reactions and feelings are clearer before proceeding with the reconciliation attempt.

When we forgive those who have injured us, our eyes may be opened to the fact that they are imperfect people—just like us! This might be difficult to accept, especially if we unfairly expected or needed them to be something more. We often need parents to be semi-gods. We want our friends to be caretakers. We prefer siblings to be invisible except when we need them to support us or give us something. In forgiving, we discover that the people in our lives are ordinary men and women. Perhaps we've been too demanding with our expectations. We might even have cause to *seek* forgiveness as well as *grant* it.

In forgiving, we release the intensity of our emotional feelings. We make room for new memories and new emotions regarding the reconciled relationship. Our relationship begins anew with fewer expectations and greater simplicity.

Reconciliation is a courageous step. It might create strong feelings within you. In the process, friends, family or partners might say things or respond in such a way that you experience relief . . . or even pain. Go back and read again the section on "Forgiving Yourself" to make sure you understand clearly what forgiving involves. Let your group know what you are doing so that they can support you during your hard work.

We are not God. Sometimes we need to recognize our inability or unwillingness to forgive a major hurt in our lives. Yet this very admission can begin us on the path to forgiveness. Sometimes we need to recognize and experience the depth of our need for God's forgiveness to gain a humble perspective from which to forgive. Jesus of Nazareth was, if anything, a fleshing out of divine forgiveness (Matthew 6:7-15, 7:1-5, 18:21-35; Luke 23:26-47).

Bless you for your courage. Be at peace!

Step 6: I Am Responsible for My Grief and Gratitude

You might wonder why we speak of grief and gratitude in the same breath. Grief and gratitude seem to be opposites. Grief is an emotion of loss; gratitude is an emotion of gain. Grief expresses emotional poverty; gratitude, riches. Actually, grief and gratitude are two sides of the same coin. Perhaps an even better illustration would be to see grief and gratitude as two connecting ends of a circular "emotional continuum."

Loss, after all, creates opportunity for gain; gain creates the opportunity for loss. These ebbs and flows are inescapable in our lives, and how we handle them impacts our sanity and our peace. Both grief and gratitude are powerful emotions, tapping into our deepest reaches, calling us into deeper awareness of the divine. If we can learn to freely explore and express grief and gratitude—emotions that men tend to avoid because they make us feel vulnerable—then we can learn to explore and express many other emotions.

GRIEF AND MOURNING

Life brings grief. Daily we confront hurt and loss, pain and anguish. Yet we treat grief as an aversion, something to "get over." The truth is that we must welcome grief. Our souls grieve to expend the pain of loss, and so it is natural for us to grieve. Grief is not evil. In the book of Genesis, Adam grieved the absence of human relationship in his life *before* he fell into sin. He grieved an absence, not a loss, since he had not yet experienced a relationship with a woman.

Grieving is as necessary to our souls as breathing is to our bodies. To try *not* to grieve is like trying not to breathe. You can only hold your breath so long! When we fight grief, we fight our own life—and certainly the peace in our lives—because that which we cannot grieve, we cannot move beyond.

Grief. We know it best as an intense, enveloping ache. A heaviness. A soul so parched that no drink can quench the thirst. The wrenching away of a part of our very souls by the termination of a person, place, thing, or a quality in our lives.

We associate grief, primarily, with death. Actually, degrees of grief result from *each meaningful loss in our lives.* The feelings we have from any loss are, in fact, grief.

Mourning is the path of behaviors, feelings, and thoughts we take to deal with our grief. To handle our grief, mourning must be conscious and intentional. We mourn in order to process our grief.

To know God, a person must learn to mourn well. The Psalmist, for example, often mourned the injustices of life, and God's apparent inaction in response. The Psalmist lamented and cried out in pain. In one song he wrote:

> Truly God is good to Israel,
>   to such as are pure in heart.
> But as for me, my feet had almost stumbled.
>   My steps had nearly slipped.
> For I was envious of the boastful,
>   when I saw the prosperity of the wicked.
> For there are no pangs in their death,

> But their strength is firm.
> They are not in trouble as other men,
>   nor are they plagued like other men. . . .
> Behold these are the ungodly,
>   who are always at ease; They increase in riches.
> Surely I have cleansed my heart in vain,
>   and washed my hands in innocence.
> For all day long I have been plagued,
>   And chastened every morning.
>
> Ps. 73:1-5, 12-14

There are sacrifices to know, love, and serve God. We give up "securities" such as a materialistic life, power and ego trips, selfish satisfaction. We are enticed by others who seem to enjoy the world's benefits. What we gain, however, is the God who claims to "bear our griefs and carry our sorrows." We gain, not an escape from life, but a life full of real pain and joy. We gain an entrance into the hope of eternal bliss with God. Yet we are not rescued wholly—not yet—and so we grieve!

Jeremiah had his own portion of griefs and complaints. He wrote: "Righteous you are O LORD, when I plead with you; yet let me talk with you about your judgements. Why does the way of the wicked prosper? Why are those happy who deal so treacherously?" (Jer. 12:1).

And again, after Jeremiah suffered derision and violence from his own people and family, he cried out, "Cursed be the day in which I was born! / May the day my mother bore me not be blessed! / Cursed be the man who brought news to my father . . ." (Jer. 20:14-15a).

Some of us feel like Jeremiah! We suffer and we wonder what good is God? What good is life? Why suffer any more? How are we to bear this pain? We cry out to God to hear us!

We spend a great deal of our lives in grief and the practice of mourning—or the practice of repressing our grief and trying *not* to mourn! Perhaps this never occurred to you before. I had never given it much thought until I began working with men who were emotionally "stuck." We thought we were just a "little down" or "feeling stuck" at times. But in reality, there was much more to it than that! Dealing with grief, and mourning over the many irritations, aggravations, and desperations of our lives has a direct impact on the quality of peace that we live.

Irritations

Irritations are often minor losses:

- You lose the car keys. Frustration!
- The refrigerator goes on the blink. Annoyance!
- Your wife looks at the painting job you just completed and asks, "Honey, don't you need to do another coat?" You are bugged.

These are minor losses—of order, time, pride. And yes, they hurt. But usually not for long.

Minor losses can be nearly invisible. An irritation? We often dismiss it. Frustration? We stuff it!

"Our two boys are always fighting," said a tired, discouraged father. "When one gets hurt, he tells on the other. We separate the kids. Sometimes one or both get privileges taken away. But that doesn't stop it. The whining never ends! It drives me nuts!"

Kids grieve by whining! We think kids whine just because they are selfish. In fact, kids whine because they grieve their powerlessness to get what they want "on demand." Yet if we choose the alternative—giving in to their every whim—we do our children a great disservice. We teach them selfishness and greed. Children need to grieve! It's their choice of how they mourn that needs to be redirected.

"Give me some soda!" little five-year-old Jimmy demanded.

"I didn't hear the magic word," his mother corrected.

"Give me some soda, PLEASE!" Jimmy screamed impatiently, barely crossing the line of graciousness.

Frustrated, his mother opened the refrigerator door only to find that all the soda was gone. For Jimmy, this was a monumental tragedy! He wailed and whined. He fell prostrate on the floor. He rolled around the house, bellowing agony. It was an Academy Award performance. What's a parent to do?

Children need to learn to handle their losses without endless whining. They must learn to delay gratification of their wants—without hysteria. This is called "impulse control."

These skills are difficult to learn, but necessary for survival in the world.

How do we teach them this important lesson?

1. By teaching them to live with a significant goal, a plan, a purpose, a direction. Too often, even as adults, we live by impulse and by reaction. Children need to learn impulse control over time because if they do not, their adult lives might become filled with chaotic choices, addictive behaviors, and/or unending pain.

"Just do what you feel" does not work as a life philosophy. It might be a temporary counterbalance to a functional, workaholic lifestyle, but it is not a well-balanced, thoughtful way of life. Impulses are to be listened to, but only in the context of a purposeful life. Living by emotional whim exhausts our souls.

2. Parents must model—openly and intentionally—impulse control. We must express our emotions purposefully and appropriately with our small children, not to get our deeper needs met and not to manipulate them—but to teach them how to feel and express a range of feelings.

3. We must appropriately say "no" to some of our children's demands and learn to say "yes" to some of their wiser choices. Simply, this means we must be active parents, not just a theoretical, absent parent, and not just a buddy or friend.

4. We must learn and model the skill of having and expressing honest emotions without crossing the line into emotionalism or whining.

It's one thing to have and express emotions. It's quite another to *be* emotional. Whining is being emotionally out of control. It's allowing yourself to be emotionally sloppy. Whining is emotionalism. Having honest emotions—without crossing the line into emotionalism—means we must learn to discriminate emotions.

There are two reasons why discerning emotions is a critical skill. First, it keeps us, as adults, from using the childish technique of whining to handle our grief over the daily losses and irritations we experience. Second, it also prepares us to teach our children to do the same.

Discriminating our emotions begins by asking questions. *What am I feeling?* is an important initial question that helps us to explore our feelings.

Once we know what we are feeling, a second question to ask is, *With whom can I share these feelings?* Shall I keep them to myself or tell them to someone? Who would care? Whom do I trust? Will they honor my feelings? In sharing my feelings, will it help me to release them?

This may sound like a rather complex and contrived pattern, but it usually happens quite naturally. We do this mostly by intuition. Yet even intuition needs training in order to handle this well. Unfortunately, some of us have not yet trained our intuition. We are too busy *being* controlled by our emotions to simply allow ourselves to have and experience our emotions.

The next time one of your children whines or becomes hysterical, sit him down. Do this calmly—don't allow yourself to become involved in the power and manipulation of your child's emotionalism. Perhaps hold his or her hands and look calmly into your child's eyes. When he or she is sufficiently calm, ask, "What are you feeling?"

Since this may be a new and shocking, even abstract, question, you might need to help. Be patient, not pushy. Ask questions like, "Do you feel frustrated? Angry? Sad?" Give options. Or ask questions that include metaphors such as, "What do you feel like? Like no one cares? Like you are stuck in a hole and can't get out? Like a cloudy day?" When your child begins to speak, don't correct him. Just accept what he has to say.

Some adults have not learned to do this—for themselves, and certainly not with their children! You may need to start by asking yourself these same questions! This could be the beginning of a whole new way of looking at your feelings! I can promise that when you begin to master this, you will feel powerful and in control of yourself. Enjoy what you find in yourself!

Aggravations

- A job termination.

- The failure of a major business deal.
- A wicked storm destroys part of your home.
- Your back acts up.
- A son gets into trouble with the law.

Aggravations are daily irritations—with a punch. They are modest losses. Like irritations, aggravations demand to be grieved and mourned.

In our culture, we associate grief primarily with death. Perhaps this is because our culture permits a *limited* time to grieve a death: the grief is expected to be intense . . . and then we are expected to move on with our lives. Maybe it's our pioneer spirit: pioneers had little time to grieve before it was time to get back to the work of survival. Or perhaps our competitive spirit has something to do with it. After all, you can't hold up the corporate system or the factory if you are grieving—your cog in the wheel is too important! When someone dies, we have social permission to mourn. But not for too long!

Why are we so awkward with grief? First, we suffer grief so poorly because we have so little experience at identifying our minor and modest losses. Life is rushing by so quickly, we don't give ourselves permission to "stop and feel the feelings." We describe our minor and modest losses as "out there"—"I lost my job," "The car died," "The landlord raised the rent," "My business trip went longer than expected, and I missed my daughter's school play." We don't admit that each "out there" incident creates feelings and loss "in here!" We don't admit this, and therefore we don't identify—or grieve—the feelings. They begin to accumulate. Before long, we are feeling restless, anxious, sad or angry—and we have no idea why!

Second, we rarely practice mourning. When we are hit with a death, some of us suffer long-term emotional or functional paralysis precisely because we have little skill at mourning! We have few skills and little practice in expressing our grief; no time to indulge in a behavior or ritual devoted exclusively to grief (how inefficient!).

Irritations pile up and become aggravations. Some minor or modest losses are fuzzy, hard to see or understand. You know only your depression or ache. Where did it come from? What caused it?

You and a friend quietly compete. You play wicked tennis games. You compare business successes. You compare the successes of your wives and children. The competition is not open, but subtle. Then suddenly you experience a sticky conflict with your friend. Neither of you understands, really, the problem—all you know is that intense feelings dig deeply. Attempts at resolving the discord leave you bewildered and shaken. Bitterness raises its ugly head. You are stuck. The friendship wanes. You suffer loss.

Or imagine another scenario. You make good money, but your job lacks meaning. Your wife is a wonderful, attractive woman whose success has become a bit of a threat to your fragile ego. Your kids are good kids, but the rascals test you with their crazy behaviors. Even worse, they seem to pass your level of maturity or success in some ways. Maybe you drink or eat a little more than you should. Stare at the tube more than you used to. You are stuck. Anxious. Moody. Jealous. You suffer loss.

Has anyone ever told you that you are grieving? Perhaps you are grieving the loss of a friendship. You feel the loss of hopes and dreams. Your marriage isn't what you had imagined. Your sexual fantasies are not all going to happen. Young turks are passing you on the career ladder. Your stomach bulges. Your hair is thinning. This is the stuff of grief. Modest losses require alert mourning.

Desperations

Men, fearing emotional pain in general, have difficulty permitting themselves to mourn when someone dies. Even then, we are primitive in our practices of mourning. Perhaps men are crying more openly these days. Still, recently I experienced something like this:

We join the VanderVan family on a sad day. Jane VanderVan has died of cancer. She is survived by her husband, Jim, and two children, Jim Jr. and Alice. Her casket is closed at the funeral.

Thomas, a sensitive fellow and close friend of the family, approaches them with his sympathy. "Well, Jim, Jimmy, and Alice, my love to you. We will all miss Jane."

Jim Sr. shakes his head. "Perhaps it's just as well she's gone . . . she doesn't have to suffer now. We didn't want a viewing—I didn't want to see her like that. No point to it. I tried to keep the funeral quiet, but I'm glad you're here. Thanks for coming."

"Thanks, Jim. I really wanted to come." Thomas looks at Alice, who is sobbing. "Alice, I know how you feel. Your mother was a wonderful woman." He breaks down and hugs Alice.

Jim Sr. and Jim Jr. fidget.

A moment later, Jim Jr. pulls Thomas aside. In a low voice he confides, "We're a little concerned about Alice. She's been crying a lot since Mom went into the coma last Friday."

"What are you concerned about?"

"Her crying. When will she stop? I mean, we don't know what to do for her. We wonder if maybe she shouldn't have gone in to see Mom's body. That probably shook her up. Maybe she should see a doctor. Get some medication or something."

Thomas tries to tell Jim Jr. and Sr. that he thinks Alice is okay—in fact, her grief seems appropriate to the circumstances. Jim Sr. seems bothered by Thomas's words, though he says he appreciates the thoughts.

In the months following the funeral, Jim Sr. found himself feeling great anguish, but he couldn't talk about it openly. He remarried eight months later. He rarely talks about Jane or visits her grave, though they were married for forty years.

Jim Jr. began having trouble with high blood pressure. He decided to change jobs and move to another state. Father and son had only awkward snippets of conversation about Jane. They deeply missed her, but they did not know how to talk about their love and grief.

Alice joined a support group for six months. She still mourns her mother deeply and visits her grave once a month. Alice is doing well.

Many of us struggle with letting go of loved ones. We are rational people, but we can become emotionally stuck. An acquaintance of mine, for example, can talk about his father's death, but he cannot "accept it."

"I don't *want* to accept it," he told me. What were his feelings? Anger. Abandonment. Fear of letting go. Hurt. The loss hurts so deeply that it cannot be. *It just can't be!* But it is.

This same friend once admitted, "I'm tired of crying myself to sleep. I'm tired of being numb inside."

Divorce can produce the same sort of grief. Divorce, like death, requires active mourning.

Desperate loss shocks our whole system. It occurs when we depend on a person—or place, thing, quality of life—to be there. Consistently. Forever. We depended on him/her/it to be an anchor in unpredictable seas, to give us security in a haphazard and unfair world. Perhaps, in the case of a relationship, we depended on that person to be someone to disagree with—to have safe, though heated differences! Maybe we even needed someone to dislike—even hate—at times. Then there are the relationships we counted on for trust or purpose. For joy, inspiration or affirmation. A death or divorce or other profound loss tears apart our very sense of self.

The image of that lost person or object still lives in you! He or she remains "alive" because you still care. When people die, their image only fades. Their images live longer than they do. These images are branded into the subconscious of the survivors, the people—like us—who are left behind, grieving in the wake of death or loss.

It is common to create a mythology of the people we have lost, through death or even divorce. Their images grow very large. We see them as god-like or, in some cases, demon-like.

Sometimes the pain of letting go can be too much. You think to yourself, "But I *can't* let go! I'm not done with this relationship yet! There are things I need to say, things I still need to do. Don't you understand? I just can't let go . . ."

Other questions soon follow:

- What will happen if I let go?
- Can I reconstruct a self without him/her?
- Is life worth continuing . . . alone?
- If I let go, will I lose myself?
- Will I go crazy?

- Can I survive the pain of absence?

Letting go can even feel like disloyalty. It can seem, somehow, like a betrayal of what we shared together.

HOW LONG DOES GRIEF AND MOURNING LAST?

Elisabeth Kübler-Ross has outlined the "stages" of grief. They are: denial, anger, bargaining, depression, acceptance. Other authors have outlined different stages. In either case, knowing that stages exist, and having names for the stages, helps us identify what is happening within ourselves.

"Stages" of grief, however, are misunderstood if we think to ourselves: "Once I get through these stages, I can stop grieving." Grief does not run the same pattern through each person. Grief does not follow a direct or consistent path. Grief takes a variety of paths, and you will travel a path that is unique to you, yet similar enough to the experience of others so that they can offer care and understanding.

"When will I stop hurting?" is a legitimate question.

- How many more sleepless nights?
- How long must my heart ache?
- How long will I endure this tortuous emptiness?
- Will it ever go away?

Ask these questions. Scream them if you wish!

You have the right to expect that the pain will become bearable. You will even re-experience hope, in time, as you share your feelings with others. Studies show that talking about your feelings is important to releasing the pain and getting on with life. Your feelings include how you plan to live without the person you have lost. In time, you can expect to function "normally" again.

But when will you stop grieving?

Never. Not completely, anyway.

Grief and mourning are a part of life.

This sounds discouraging, but in reality it is a statement of hope! This is because the false hope that life will return to "normal" traps us in grief. It trips us up. "Normal," after all, died with our loss.

If we are truly courageous, we learn that to bear our griefs, we must be re-born to a new life. We must define new parameters of "normal." When we have suffered a great loss, life will *never* return to what it was. Things will always be different. Yet life can still be good.

Even physical birth involves grief, as we described earlier. A baby mourns the loss of the womb: "Leave me in the brine!" he cries.

A child bonds to nurturing parents. They are not always there at the child's beck and call. The child grieves.

The first day of pre-school or kindergarten, we grieve.

Adolescence. We grieve.

From then on, grief is a regular part of life, so we had better learn to mourn well. And part of grieving well means learning that significant grief requires re-birth. Not the fundamentalist version. Not a "New Age" mystical transcendent version. It's something else entirely.

To be re-born through our grief means accepting the end of one era and moving into the next. Little deaths occur often. Big deaths occur occasionally.

A woman lost her beloved husband. She felt pain. Displacement. Several months later, she actually knew joy again. How had she found it? She went to real estate school, received her license, and became a successful agent. She was not the same woman. She found a new sense of self. She rediscovered her dignity. She was re-born.

When I asked my wife-to-be, Kriste, if she would marry me, she said yes. Immediately, I felt acutely depressed.

Depression was definitely not in my plans. If it was disconcerting to me, it was even less comforting to Kriste!

I had worked hard figuring out the pros and cons of becoming engaged to this woman. But now, having done it, the bottom dropped out! I realized I was losing ownership of my whims, wants, and desires. I was committing myself . . . for life! Rigorous analysis had satisfied my mind that engagement—and particularly engagement to Kriste—was right and good! But I had not anticipated the emotions I would feel once I was, in actuality, facing marriage. These feelings could only be known, and experienced, once I was engaged. The fears hit me full force.

After a few months of wrestling, my joy returned. How? I spoke with others long and hard. I allowed myself to *feel*, rather than *fight*, my feelings. I thought about what I would be losing. I recognized that loss. I also awakened to what I was gaining. My joy continues to this day.

Grief is not man's favorite emotion, and mourning is not our strong suit. So when a man experiences a loss—of a job, marriage, pet, home, long-held belief, health, youth, a car, a friend who moves away, power, prestige, salary, memory, dexterity, hair, teeth, 20/20 vision, security, a wife who mothered him but now goes to work, a child leaving for college, a toy, a career, or even a sacred set of golf clubs—he will grieve, but not without a fight!

GRIEVING IN HAPPY TIMES

Let me tell you a well-kept secret: we also grieve in happy times.

Weddings are happy times, yet there is a great deal of grief at weddings. Think of the losses for the blissful couple! They lose their "singleness." They lose individual freedom and rights, their childhood, a certain youthful innocence. They even lose their excuse for irresponsible behavior!

Not only do we feel loss at our weddings, we are taught to publicly deny our feelings of these losses! Sadness is not permitted during happy times! It just seems wrong. Inappropriate. No one would understand anyway. Usually at weddings, a bride or groom may admit to being nervous or comment on their anxiety with phrases like, "Gee, it's hot in here!" Certainly, some of that is genuine nervousness about the public ceremony—or genuine discomfort in a room that is too warm! But beneath the nervousness, for most brides and grooms, lurk some fear, loss and grief.

Think with me a moment. What would happen if we could deal more openly and honestly with our grief prior to—and after—the wedding? For one thing, we might do better in our marriages! Instead, we stuff feelings of loss, insecurity or depression and blame our spouses for our unhappiness.

Parents cry at weddings because they are losing a child. Parents grieve the fact that they will no longer play a significant role in the life of their adult child. They are, in effect, "losing" a person they loved and have invested in. It's simply not true that a married son or daughter is "still my baby!" It will never be quite the same. Those days are done. People can be happy and sad at the same time.

Whenever we attend a wedding, we face our own marriages. If our marriage is troubled, we weep openly or in secret. Grief.

Recently, I performed the wedding of a young woman whose father had raised her by himself. His wife—her mother—left them when the daughter was about five years old. At the wedding, he was weeping with joy and loss. He walked around mumbling, "I did it! I raised her alone!" He had, indeed, succeeded in raising a wonderful young woman, and I felt joy for him.

Weddings, and other major family events as well, recall lots of memories. Memories of deaths. Memories of divorces. Memories of our weddings and marriages. Memories of good and bad.

Retirement is another happy time that can bring grief. We send people off with parties. But when do we allow time to grieve? Grief is not as inappropriate as it may sound: we are losing a trusted worker or friend. The retiree is losing a major preoccupation in his life and perhaps even a significant source of self-esteem. If he has not built, or is not able to build, other purposes in life, he may become depressed or ill or even die.

Retirement, too, requires constructive mourning.

Other happy times which require mourning:

- When leaving an old job and starting a new one.
- When being promoted.
- When moving.
- When your child is born.
- When you reach a goal or have personal success.

Have you learned to admit grief?
Can you give yourself permission to mourn?

GRATITUDE AND GIVING THANKS

Life is good to us. Daily we experience pleasures, relief, appreciation, thankfulness, freedom, and joy. Yet men tend to either pridefully gloat over successes or demean achievements ("It was nothing!"). Few men are skilled at graciously giving thanks. Yet just as grieving is necessary to our souls, gratitude is necessary too. Remember the analogy of breathing? Grief and gratitude are breathing to our souls. This is why we need to learn to live gratefully.

Gratitude

We know gratitude best as being thankful for something given to us. Unfortunately, since we cannot "do gratitude," gifts can make us feel vulnerable and even obligated to return the favor. There is no better way to extinguish the joy of receiving a gift than by thinking in terms of "debts": "Now what do I owe this person?" "How am I going to return the favor?" We need to remember that the word "gift" means something given without compensation.

We can also undermine the purpose of a gift by valuing the object or favor, but neglecting to express our appreciation to—and for—the giver of the gift. The joy of a gift is knowing that someone cared enough to think of you; that they knew what you liked, found it, arranged for it with their money or time, and gave it to you in a way and at a time to affirm you! The true gift is the love expressed. The true gift is the relationship.

Giving thanks is what we do to show our feelings and thoughts in response to a gift. Giving thanks is the gift we give back to the giver of the gift.

Gratitude should play a role in any significant relationship, but perhaps nowhere more so than in our relationship with God. We would do well to follow the advice of the Psalmist:

> Enter into His gates with thanksgiving
> and into His courts with praise;

Be thankful to Him;
   and bless His name.
For the Lord is good; His mercy is everlasting,
   and His truth endures to all generations.
Ps. 100:4-5

GRATITUDE IN GRIEF

Just as we grieve during happy times, we can also feel gratitude in times of grief. To frame this in your mind, you must first accept that we can feel diverse, seemingly contradictory emotions at the same time.

Perhaps gratitude in grief has been a well-kept secret!

Funerals are sad. Yet relief can be a form of gratitude. If the one we loved suffered long, we might feel grateful that their pain is over. Others feel comfort at funerals as they remember funny stories and events about a person, or wonderful events in a person's life story. We can feel grateful for having known and loved this person, and grateful for the time and experiences we had together. If we believe in life after death, we can feel grateful that our loved one has entered eternal bliss. Some funerals are, in fact, celebrations as much as they are mourning events. There is joy in touching the transcendent, even in mourning.

There is yet another, even less understood form of gratitude in grief. We feel loss at the death of a spouse, for example, and yet I have heard widows and widowers describe "the new life" they gained following the death of their partner. This is not to say they wanted their partner to die, but having faced death, they found a life which was not possible during their marriage. They feel gratitude for opportunity, even though that opportunity was created by a death.

Survivors can arrive at this kind of gratitude through a variety of experiences. For example, people may experience great intimacy and satisfaction while serving a spouse who is handicapped or limited in other ways. Service and selflessness can be a source of tremendous peace and happiness. Yet after years of self-sacrifice, the death of a partner may create an opportunity for a new kind of life.

There are also spouses who find new life when their partner dies because they feared grasping life boldly while married. It is tragic, but some people put aside their personal growth because they fear opposition from their spouses. Whatever the reason, the loss of the marriage relationship triggers an opportunity to try anew.

Of course, it is no secret that life is filled with death—and not every death has to do with the demise of an individual. Marriages die. Careers die. Sometimes, in these deaths and others, new life is born.

One young fellow I know spent much of his twenties trying to build a professional baseball career. It was his father's dream first, and then his own. He had just enough skill to justify the attempt but not enough to "make the big leagues." Meanwhile, he ignored his passion and ability for carpentry. When his ball club finally released him, he grieved. But he also felt strangely unleashed from his confinement to playing ball and the accompanying stresses. He found joy in his new career as a carpenter.

At the same time, he realized how little he had enjoyed playing ball because his goal had been the big leagues. He turned to semi-pro baseball and enjoyed playing more than ever before. This time, he played with love for the game.

Life is always born of death. It's the cycle of the ages. Biblical literature describes "death" as a requirement for being "re-born." We die to ourselves—our old drives, needs, expectations—and we are born to a new life, complete with new drives, needs, and expectations.

When fires ravaged the hills of Oakland, California, in October, 1991, victims of the fire grieved tremendously. Most victims felt tremendous loss and uncertainty. Some people expressed anger with God. Others felt grateful to God for the gift of life despite their material loss and seemingly hopeless situation. Simply being alive takes on fresh meaning and zeal after great loss or near-death experiences.

Some people get stuck in their grief because they don't allow themselves to feel gratitude! The problem is not being mired down in grief, but being uninvolved in joy! A key to grief recovery is this: we cannot fight grief, but we can incorporate gratitude into our lives. This, in turn, helps the power of grief to fade over time.

Others get stuck in "joy"—or more accurately, pseudo-joy. This is positive-thinking gone hay-wire. It's a kind of mania. Such joy is forced and actually based in fear, not gratitude. It is not rooted in free-response and peaceful choices. Persons caught in pseudo-joy cannot allow healthy grieving since everything must always be "wonderful." Tragically, by not allowing themselves to grieve and mourn appropriately, they also rob themselves of the ability to experience true joy.

We all need gratitude and joy—even grief and mourning—paced throughout our lives, in good times and in bad.

Joy

> Weeping may endure for a night,
> but joy comes in the morning.
> Ps. 30:5

Men may have trouble with grief—but they loathe joy. Oh, we have pseudo-joys: the flush of sexual arousal without love. The mood swell of "getting high." The rush of the big sell. While these might be pleasurable flashes, they do not comprise joy. They lack spiritual sustenance; food for the soul.

Real joy spices life with tantalizing flavors. A walk becomes a mystery tour of nature's colors, shapes, sounds, and smells. A gaze into your lover's eyes becomes an adventure into her soul as you sense her fears and hurts, her love for your children, even the way she cherishes your quirks. Looking at the stars becomes a moment with the Almighty. When done in the presence of joy, even breathing can become a transcendent experience as you feel the flow of air into your lungs, one of the rhythms the body uses to sustain life.

Mourning is letting go. Joy is creation, newness of life, the refreshment of being re-born.

Grief and joy are melody and harmony, evening and morning. Grief without joy starves the soul. Joy without grief is tasteless.

Many of us are spiritual drifters—drifting through life with temporal goals. To attain these goals, we use things and we use people. Anything outside of self becomes an object to use toward the accomplishment of our goals. We are users.

True spirituality is found in the exploration and expression of grief and joy. Spirituality is the turf of joy because joy requires emotions of eminence, such as awe, tenderness, and tranquility. Joy is felt in one's whole being. It demands to be savored. It calls us to empathize. It inspires as little else can. Joy sees ambiguities not as problems to resolve, but as mysteries to relish.

Joy is one of the ways we know that we belong in this universe, in this time and place. In the quiet, alone, joy prompts us to sing, to wonder at our place between our ancestors and generations yet to come; to savor our value and the value of others.

Re-birth is made possible when we can bear grief while being renewed by joy; washing in its soothing, sparkling waters, allowing our souls to be held in God's firm but tender hands.

Joy frees us from the burdens of grief, better enabling us to do the work of grieving. Joy is play. It can be scary to play, to be playful. What, after all, does it accomplish? What will others say? Yet without this play, our joy muscles atrophy from so little use. It takes practice and regular exercise. Joy is not earned. It is a gift to be practiced.

There is a magnificent passage in the Bible about the Messiah, the one who would come to save the people. I have paraphrased it below:

> He is despised and rejected by men
> > a Man of sorrows, and acquainted with grief.
> And we hid, as it were, our faces from Him,
> > He was despised,
> and we did not esteem Him.
> > Surely He has bourne our griefs
> and carried our sorrows;
> > Yet we esteemed Him stricken,
> smitten by God, and afflicted.
> > But He was wounded for our transgressions,
> He was bruised for our iniquities
> > the chastisement for our peace
> was upon Him,

And by His wounds we are healed.
Isa. 53:3-5

And why would the Messiah suffer such grief for men and women then and yet to come? So that they—so that you and I—might have room for joy!

> For you shall go out with joy
>   and be led out with peace
> the mountains and hills
>   shall break forth with singing before you,
> And all the trees of the field
>   shall clap their hands.
> Instead of the thorn shall come up the cypress tree
>   and instead of brier shall come up the myrtle tree;
> And it shall be to the Lord for a name,
>   for an everlasting sign
> That shall not be cut off.
>
> Isa. 55:12-13

Daily I feel grief from present or past losses. I cannot always bear these easily. Among the Messiah's graces are that He carries our griefs and sorrows. Because He is well acquainted with grief, you and I can feel joy. Because of His wounds, you and I are healed!

Peace is more than the absence of conflict, more than the absence of anger or anguish. Peace is a way of living with joy and with grief—sometimes at the same time!

Peace is knowing we are safe in the arms of God. Peace is the sense, to borrow from Lewis Smedes, that "it is all right with us even when everything seems all wrong."

Step 7: I Am Responsible for My Passions:
Our Passions for Women

Most men hear the word passion and think of sex. And most men, when they think of sex, think of intercourse. This is a prescription for dissatisfaction and abuse.

Our passions, in the broadest sense, are those emotions and drives which empower, excite and motivate us. Passions can drive us like ravaging lions, or they can allure us to objects or persons like powerful electromagnets. Whether by push or pull, our passions pulsate powerfully. The emotionally skilled and seasoned person can channel passions into focused drives to accomplish great things.

In the New Testament, Paul of Tarsus warned us about passions. In Colossians, chapter three, he gave instructions about two of the attractions for our passions: women and work. The beauty of purposeful love for a woman can be made fraudulent by pornography. The satisfaction of vocational accomplishments can degenerate into scandalous desires when infected by greed.

Let us begin by considering our sexual passions.

THE SOUND OF MUSIC AND SEXUALITY

"The hills are alive with the sound of music. . . ."

Friday night, December 30, 1988 I watched *The Sound of Music* on local television. Kids in bed, Kriste cuddled beside me, the lights dimmed, I settled onto the couch for a night of distant yet enticing memories. Indeed, old feelings percolated—but not the feelings I expected!

As a young boy, my family's religious convictions prohibited movie watching. We had never seen a movie until *The Sound of Music* hit the silver screens. I suspect that movie broke the movie barrier for a whole generation of virgin eyes! I must have been about ten years old. We broke our bondage by bundling up one winter's night to drive to a magnificent Hollywood theater. Ornate architecture! Heavenward spires! Plush carpets! I was breathless. Setting foot in a hall of decadence didn't seem so bad. Little did I know what I was about to experience!

Privately, I wondered if the movie would show naked people. That is, after all, what I had heard movies were about. I was rather excited about the prospect, though I dared not reveal it. I also wondered what had happened to my parents: had they lost their minds? What if Jesus came back while we were watching the movie? Could we bail out of this one if God asked what we were doing in there?

The movie began. And there she was, sweet, innocent, glowing, singing joyously against the bright blue sky, into the crisp, cold air atop a majestic Austrian mountaintop. Maria! My heart was pounding. Why? I was too young for a heart attack . . . what was this?

Shortly, we met the von Trapp children. They lived with their father, called the Captain (remember how he would blow a whistle and the children would line up in sailors' suits?). Their father was strict, solemn, and disciplined.

Yet my heart also felt for the Captain, who was proper, proud, but so alone. Being just a kid, it might seem odd that I would empathize with the character of the father. Yet, somehow, I knew how he felt as he tried to hold life together. I was ten, but I was intense. I knew people's pain. This man looked like my destiny!

I watched the children awaken to life through Maria. Her innocent charm and grace, her passion, honesty and freedom drew me like a magnet. This nun-turned-mother awakened deep longings in my heart. She was tender, simple, beautiful, effusive in love, safe and kind. I found myself crying quiet tears. I longed to be held in her arms. Close.

All this, I remembered again on that winter's night not so long ago, as my charged affections exploded from the dim recesses of my soul. Suddenly there was an interruption: a commercial break during which soup, cars and fast food took over the screen. As my mind drifted, I was suddenly struck with a sense of horror! What was I feeling? I had the strong sense of secret, adolescent feelings . . . but of and for what? What had I felt so many years ago? Had I been feeling secret urges for a mother . . . or a lover?

And what did that mean, anyway? What was "a lover" for a kid who was only ten? At ten, I had only vague, playground-fostered notions of love and sex. Yet my body had pulsated with feelings. Why? Had these been the early sex wishes of an unchristened boy? Were they evil impulses? Or were they good? All I knew is that, at the time, they felt awfully good.

I remember longing to be held, safe and secure, close to her warmth and tenderness. There was a physical component to these feelings, of course, on the same continuum that includes sexual intercourse. But this was not an urge for intercourse. *That* part of sex was still vague and fuzzy to me. Instead, these were impulses of passion which filled my whole being.

Freud, you did us wrong. You reacted too much to "the sex act" and thought too little about the whole of our sexual identity. Our longings are greater than for sexual intercourse. Men need tenderness and touch too.

My five-year-old wants to "marry Mommy" when he grows up. This is not rooted in genital flames burning for his mother. He is not waging war with Daddy for Mom's affections. He just knows a good woman! He feels loved by her. She nurtures him. (My son also says he wants to "give Daddy money when I grow up so we can stay together." I'm not sure what this means exactly. I'm rechecking my messages to him about money, but at least he doesn't want to marry me! We must be doing something right.)

Freud interpreted the wonder of sexual passion in a dark way. He tilted the scales from seeing the mystery and beauty of love to staring through the dark, hypnotic spell of obsessive sexual drives. Perhaps focusing on pathology distorted his perspective.

Boys and men long to be nurtured. This includes touch. This includes intimacy. This includes feeling fulfilled.

We look to women for this filling. Yet—with respect and appreciation for many wonderful women—no woman can be our total fulfillment! This is a fantasy expectation. A partner can give us wonderful moments. A partner can care for us and give us great fulfillment. But she cannot be our *total* fulfillment.

God is our Supreme Nurturer. Unfortunately, we tend to re-create God in macho images while our passions long for tenderness—the feminine side of God. Perhaps that is what Catholic theology allows by revering the holy Mother Mary. Protestant men have no parallel means to revere the feminine characteristics and nature of the Divine. In our deepest reaches, it is our Creator that we long for. God is our first and ultimate lover.

Jogging late at night I can feel intimate with the Creator. I tell God about my hurts and hopes, my fear and fantasies. On occasion, I have burst into tears while running. God is there. I sense His presence, respond.

Parents were meant to give us hints, glimpses, and tastes of God's nurturing. Committed to a woman, we can experience hints, glimpses, and tastes of God's love. God does not love us invisibly, silently, alone. He calls us to commune with other believers in order to experience aspects of His love. Of course, these relationships do not give us the entire wealth of God's deep love for us—some of this we experience while in communion with God Himself. Yet we can't deny that, through our fellowship with other human beings, God uses the people in our lives to illustrate and to express His love for us.

Sexuality has to do with the whole of our being. It impacts, and is impacted by, the body, mind, emotions, behaviors, styles, attitudes and beliefs. Sexuality includes our expression of feelings and thoughts via words and touch. Sexuality includes commitment to a lover through the intercourse of our bodies and souls. Sexuality teaches us about God.

God is sexual. God created sexuality. The Trinity is more than just "God in three persons": the Father, the Son or Word, and the Spirit or Breath. God is also the interaction of these "persons" of the Godhead. God is expressed in the Scriptures through male, female, and non-sex pronouns and images. In the sense that our sexuality is part of the image of God, we can sense something about the passion and love of God.

Back to *The Sound of Music*. The Captain almost married the Baroness. I, of course, didn't like her. She was too cold, too aloof, too proper. In the end, though, she did the right thing. She intuited the Captain's love for Maria and backed out of their engagement. Thank God!

From my vantage point as a love-struck ten-year-old, marrying the "right" woman for the "right" reasons of social standing seemed like—well, it seemed unbearable to me. Fulfilling external obligations at the expense of internal passion—yuck! In the end, the Captain chose his heart . . . but he certainly cut it close! In the end, he awakened to the stirrings in his soul. He chose Maria. I get teary-eyed during the gazebo scene every time.

At the tender age of ten, my heart ached with love for Maria. For weeks, I thought of nothing else but her. I could barely eat. I could barely play baseball (which was worse than not eating!). No one knew what I was feeling: I was too embarrassed to tell.

The moral lines of our feelings are not always clear. We just know we have these feelings. They hardly wait for our moral judgments to determine if they should appear or not. Still, we are responsible to evaluate the consequences of acting on our feelings. This is our responsibility.

And yet, who can deny that passion and the feelings it provokes are divine gifts? They are good. They are very good. Celebrate passion! Celebrate "wholehearted" sexuality that transcends a single act and impregnates all that we do and are!

OBSESSIVE SEXUALITY

Hiding Our Emotions of Guilt and Shame

The confidence that we possess about our competence and/or attractiveness can be quite fragile, especially during the tumultuous journey from boyhood to manhood. By *competence* I mean our desire to want to do well at "manly" things such as sports, fixing cars or machines, being brave in crises, earning money. By *attractiveness*, I'm referring to our desire to look good to women.

Our masculine confidence is vulnerable to positive—or negative—messages we receive from people we consider significant in our lives. Unfortunately, negative messages are often heard more powerfully. With each positive message, we climb a step. With each negative message, we fall a flight of stairs.

Parents or guardians were the first and primary molders of our pliable self-esteem. If the power of their early messages tilted toward the negative, then we can have deep feelings of guilt or, more painfully, shame.

Guilt and shame are not all bad. Guilt, motivated by our conscience, helps us to follow the laws and rules of society. Stealing ought to make us feel guilty. If we are healthy, guilt will inhibit our thoughts of stealing. Thus we can be responsible citizens and family members. Shame helps us know *how* to be appropriate. We want to be proud of our bodies, for example, but shame reminds us not to flaunt or use our bodies indiscriminately.

One sunny day I was counseling an engaged couple in my office. Suddenly the young groom-to-be hollered, "Wow!" as his eyes stared a hole through the window in my office. He was watching a woman riding a bike down Chapman Avenue in Garden Grove, California, wearing a thong bikini (the wedding still took place, but we spent more than one counseling session on his wandering eyes). Okay, I had to work hard not to stare too, but that's not the point. The point is that the bicyclist ought to have felt ashamed. She lacked class. It was neither the time nor the place. Shame keeps us—well, most of us, anyway—from grandiose ideas about ourselves.

The words *guilt* and *shame* tend to be used interchangeably in our society. When we say "Shame on you!" to a child, we usually mean, "You ought to feel guilty about what you just did." It may seem like a small thing, but whether a child feels guilt, or whether he feels shame, can powerfully impact his social development. This is because—even if our society tends to blur the difference—guilt and shame are not the same thing.

How Do Guilt and Shame Differ?

Guilt is what we feel about what we did.
Shame is what we feel about who we are.
Guilt has to do with our behavior.
Shame has to do with our being.
Guilt is how we learn rules or principles. Usually we learn these from our family, friends, church, or school. For the most part, we are capable of following these standards. When we violate them, we feel guilty. Then we try again to follow the standards.

Shame infiltrates our feelings on what it means to be a man. Somewhere along our paths of life, many of us became convinced that we are less than what a man ought to be. We feel weak, dirty, or less than other men. We feel inferior. Our spirit is wounded. This is shame. Shame can infect a man's whole being so that he loses a sense of his goodness. A degree of hopelessness can set in. Simply trying harder doesn't resolve shame, because shame weaves itself into our very being.

Feeling guilt or shame is psychologically and spiritually innate. They help us to develop the boundaries necessary to live in society. Children need balanced and helpful messages from competent parents or caretakers to help them grow up to be responsible and reasonable.

Yet the world is not a safe place. Most people will accept us, some people will love us genuinely, a few will use us. We soon learn to trust discriminately. Unfortunately, too many corrections, too little affirmation, too much hollering from adults pushes a child into a pit of guilt. And guilt, despite its usefulness when it is experienced in balance, can hurt a child's personality if it is applied too liberally.

Even more devastating is shame. It forms intimate links with our very bodies, hearts, minds, and souls. Shame arises when the core of our being is violated in some manner or another. When a child is sexually violated, she or he feels shame. When a child is beaten, he or she feels ashamed. When a child's competence or attractiveness is assaulted, he or she will feel helplessly ashamed.

Thou Shalt Not Commit Adultery

Ned attended church regularly. He knew the rules. But on a business trip, he drank a bit much and became friendly with a woman in the cocktail lounge of the hotel where he was staying. She looked good. She was kind and friendly.

He had been angry at his wife, Fran, for years. He felt unloved by her. That very morning, in fact, Fran had nagged him about chores undone. Ned felt bitter.

Inhibitions eased by alcohol, it was easy for Ned to slip upstairs with the woman. She left during the night. In the morning, Ned awoke feeling sick. He canceled his morning appointments to deal with his humiliation.

Ned felt guilty. He knew what he did was wrong. He worried about how to handle this. He was scared—would Fran find out? He decided not to tell his wife, and vowed never to do it again! He avoided thinking about God. Uh-oh! Had he committed the unpardonable sin? He didn't think the "unpardonable sin" referred to adultery, but he couldn't remember for sure. Now he felt terrified. Ned tried to block these thoughts from his mind.

Even more than guilty, Ned felt ashamed. He feels helpless with women much of the time. You see, sex troubles Ned. It was a forbidden topic during his upbringing: Dad and Mom simply did not talk about sex which, of course, for Ned only added to the power and mystery of sex and women. Occasionally, Ned feels powerful and has "good sex" with Fran. More often, however, he and Fran avoid sex and avoid talking about it.

Sometimes Ned peeks at porno magazines. He is ashamed about his paradox of powerful and yet "shameful" urges. Yet he carries these conflicting feelings in secret; there is no one he dares talk to about these dark and hidden feelings. He is too ashamed and doubts that any of his friends would understand.

Ned sees no hope in his dilemma. He feels disgusted and excited about his sexuality at the same time. He compartmentalizes his life. When he feels "religious," he feels ashamed about his sexual urges. The shame he feels has become rooted in his person. He knows that sex is supposed to be good—God-given, even. But he doesn't feel that way! His passions feel wrong, bad, and evil.

It's hard for Ned to imagine God approving of sex. Could God really have created such a strange and powerful physical and emotional experience? God and sex? He could not imagine God in this way. And why would God be so malicious as to saddle us with these urges for sex, then allow us to feel so ashamed?

Ned stuffs his sexual feelings, creating even more shame.

Once, as a young boy, Ned was punished when his father caught him, as Ned says, "reading a dirty magazine" behind the barn. "Shame on you! That's trash!" Ned's father screamed at him even as he took a few exhilarating peeks. Ned got whipped immediately. Seeing the pictures had aroused feelings in Ned that made him feel good. Ned was too young and naive to discriminate between his healthy sexual feelings and the way he was learning to satisfy those feelings. His father's punishment taught him to reject good and healthy feelings which are natural!

Ned didn't know it at the time, but his father was fighting his own battle against sexuality! But of course, he couldn't talk with Ned about his feelings. Ned learned by Dad's example—and his punishment—to identify sexual feelings with evil.

What messages about sexuality did you get from your father? And from your mother?

It's not evil to notice a woman's shapely curves. It is, in fact, a God-given awareness. What our eyes, minds and bodies do after we notice, however, is what makes us a mature man, or an adolescent in an adult body!

Fearing Our Feelings: Homophobia

Many men fear their tender emotions because we fear being "effeminate." We particularly fear our tender feelings toward other men.

Yet all men have a feminine side. It's nothing more or less than our normal, human capacity to feel, explore, and express sensitive emotions.

Some men fear touch, feeling especially uncomfortable with tender or soft touching. Some men are terrified to be touched by other men. Yet this is defined by culture, rather than by universal truth: in many places of the world, men touch and kiss naturally.

Some men, as they fear and fight tenderness and touch, confuse vulnerability with homosexuality. Because they are crusading against what they *perceive* as the effeminate within themselves, they become outwardly hostile toward gay men.

Other men discover they are "gay" because, awakened to their need to touch and be touched, they think their need for tenderness with other men must mean they are gay! They, too, might be confused by our narrow social prescription for "acceptable" male emotions. Of course, I am not proposing this as the explanation for homosexuality. Nevertheless, this emotional/sexual confusion is an important dynamic for all men to consider. Feelings of love for another man do not mean sexual expression is right, good, or wise.

It seems to me that our monstrous dilemma has two heads. One head says, "Men should never touch each other!" After all, touch evokes tender feelings and tender feelings make us anxious. Our anxiety overrides our tenderness, and we find ourselves acting aloof to affirm our "male" identity.

The other head tells us that tenderness and touch always have sexual implications. For most men, that translates into the thought that touch has implications relating to the *sexual act*. The confusion between tender, honest touch and sexual desire is a deplorable consequence of this age's hedonistic, user mentality. Ironically, this mentality is perpetuated by both militant libertarian and reactionary fundamentalist extremists, only for different reasons and for conflicting agendas.

In Men at Peace, we huddle at the end of each session. We circle together, putting arms around each others' shoulders or backs. We share final words. They might be words of encouragement for a brother who has shared tender feelings or who faces a struggle ahead. Perhaps it is a prayer. Sometimes we close by saying, "We form this circle because we are a community of men who care about each other, and we touch each other because we do not get touched enough." What a tender, encouraging moment!

Violating Our Feelings: The Use of Pornography

Lost in the national debate about pornography is the tragedy of destroyed lives. Deep, dark wounds are created when we violate our need for tender feelings and sexuality with the harshness of pornography. A legitimate human need for physical expression becomes demeaned when fed poisonous trash.

Pornography is what we read or see to arouse sexual impulses, simply to feed our impulses. It is a destructive cycle. Pornography can be implicit or explicit in its graphic nature or display. Technical debates about explicit or implicit are useless: the effect is the same. Pornography is both a result and a cause of our social perversion. We are all guilty and responsible.

Rampant pornography is the by-product of a society which teaches people to use people and love things. It is the dark side of a hedonistic society. I fear much of American capitalism has degenerated into individualistic hedonism. Hedonism is not freedom! Hedonism is being controlled by pleasure.

Ted Bundy, the serial murderer, warned Americans that pornography helped him to fuel his twisted drives. Unfortunately, it is too simple to say that pornography "caused" his violence. Violence and pornography, however, come from the same roots: wounded self-esteem and profound shame.

We, as a society, have sanctioned certain forms of pornography and even violence in worship of economic gods. Our society preaches to us that it is okay to use and abuse—ourselves and others. Yet we continue to hide our psychic slavery under the umbrella of "free enterprise."

In my view, graphic commercials enticing children to gobble nutrition-free foods are a form of the same societal illness that allows pornography to flourish. It is, in a sense, violence. It violates a child's naivete and innocence. It violates their growing bodies. It relies on the same manipulative techniques that use slinky women to sell cars to men, or implicit sexual messages to sell perfumes to women. The difference is that our children have even fewer defenses than we do; they have a less developed sense of choice. Our children are less responsible and more vulnerable.

As a society, we have embraced manipulation. Too much advertising, for example, taps into our shame and guilt. We are shamed into buying our children the latest toy. Our children feel ashamed when they don't have the very best in athletic shoes. We are shamed into believing our faces are too wrinkly, our bodies are unsightly, our breath stinks, our bodies stink, we stink. We are being used. Is it any wonder that we, in turn, become users of the people around us?

Strictly speaking, pornography obsesses on the act of sex. It elevates erotic love—a legitimate quality of love—to be the most desirable form of love. Yet if a relationship is driven by erotic love alone, it's running on at least three flat tires! Friendship, affection, and charity are among other forms of love necessary to grow a balanced relationship. But perhaps there's the point: pornography scoffs at relationships. Erotic love is worshiped while the person or relationship enabling the erotic expression is devalued.

The destructive heart of pornography lies in its self-absorption and relational destructiveness. It debases our humanity. We become mere animals. We become impulse grabbers. We lose our sense of uniqueness as God's ultimate creatures. Pornography cuts sex from the heart of love and responsible, dignified expression.

Perhaps looking at "dirty pictures" began innocently enough during days of youth. Perhaps it started merely as an adolescent experiment. But what about now? As we mature as individuals and as members of society, we must take responsibility for our choices and actions: we must take responsibility for our passions. The adult person who is addicted to pictures of sexual violence is responsible for his behavior.

So, too, is the minister. He might rail obsessively against "Godless purveyors of pornography," yet if he is too busy to hold his wife tenderly, he, too, has cut away from the sex act the very elements that make it all that God intended. He has joined the pornographer in elevating an act and demeaning a person.

Perhaps we holler most about what we fear in ourselves!

Sex can be used as violence in yet another manner, when it is withheld to manipulate a spouse. It is also violence when a man demands sex constantly, saying, "I can't help it, I have my needs." These are all pornographic uses of sex. Fidelity is betrayed: self-service becomes the primary objective and the real "lover." In contrast, peace requires centering yourself by loving *people* and using *things*. Peace requires swimming against the current stream of our society.

Sexual Gratification: When You Just Can't Wait

Some men are unable, or unwilling, to delay gratification of sexual arousal. The belief is: "If I feel it, I should have it. *Now*."

This may be a problem of impulse control, rooted in a childhood lacking sufficient discipline. By discipline, I mean the parenting limits by which a child learns to delay gratification.

Ken is a thirty-year-old business success story. He is a stockbroker. He drives a Corvette convertible. He enjoys many women friends.

As a child, Kenny was spoiled. He used power plays to get what he wanted from his parents. He screamed, cried, and used every trick in the book to get his way. As a grown man, Ken satisfies his sexual urges whenever he feels like it, in whatever way he feels. He rarely thinks of consequences. And why should he? He has never learned limits.

Unfortunately, "cracking down" on such children is rarely the answer. Becoming harsh or punishing simply doesn't work. Such children usually are duplicating their parents' maturity level, and immature parents "crack down" immaturely. Too often, parents who rant and rave about their children do so because their own impulses are out of control!

The solution for the out-of-control child is not an easy one: his or her parents need to grow up! When that happens, parental discipline will create a context in which the child can actually be helped. If you are the parent of an out-of-control child, get help! Consider therapy—for yourself—or check into some parenting classes.

When Shame Inhibits the Male Identity

Carl, fifteen, was tall, strong, and athletic. At school, he was generally outgoing and poised. His father was around, but emotionally absent. His father taught him bluntly that women are objects to be used. Carl's father used to say about his wife, "I give her what she needs as long as she meets my needs."

Carl and his mother were very close until he was five. Then he rejected her in order to build his identity as a male. This was, after all, what he thought his father wanted. Unfortunately, it created conflicting loyalties within Carl. He loved his mother—but what he seemed to need most of all was to please his father. These conflicting identity needs made him feel crazy! Sometimes when his mother showed him love, he pushed her away even more rigorously. His mother felt rejected.

Sometimes Carl's mother talked to him about her loneliness and need for love. This was entirely inappropriate considering Carl's age and his developing and vulnerable ego. Carl responded by feeling guilty and responsible. He wanted, somehow, to make her feel better. She unintentionally began using him, emotionally, as a surrogate husband. This, of course, complicated Carl's confusion.

On a few occasions, Carl's mother embraced him inappropriately. He felt keenly her need for affection. He felt despair about his desire to make his mother feel better. He felt confused about his sexual boundaries with his mother. These were deeply held secrets that caused him great shame!

Carl became bitter toward his sexual feelings. His solution was to choose to "control" sex by using brute physical strength. He fought tender feelings which he associated with his mother's needs. Such feelings made him anxious. He became "rough" with other male friends to avoid any effeminate signals. Fights further affirmed his fragile masculinity. Carl used sports to vent his frustrations. Carl could not attach himself to any woman—in fact, most women made him feel threatened—and so he continued to see them as objects for sex. He was, in fact, becoming a younger version of his father.

Carl grew to experience all sex as pornography. He used sex to arouse his feelings since, with the exception of sex, he felt pretty numb and dead inside.

Sex and Rage

As a boy, a chronically enraged man received both harmful male-role modeling from his father and inadequate affirmation of his male sexuality from mother. A man or woman (probably a family member) may even have abused him sexually.

In such a man, sex is experienced as power. Power is associated with sexual feelings. This man has little sense of boundaries regarding how to use his body wisely. He does not conceive of sexual experience as part of intimacy in a relationship since using and being used is his life!

He gets power—and dominates or punishes others or himself—through sex. Shame may haunt him at times. If he is psychotic, he might not even feel the shame!

I have heard a man describe how, in the middle of having intercourse with his wife, rage welled up within. He had urges to pummel her with his fists. His feelings had been so attacked, so violated in the past, that any powerful feelings—positive or negative—were experienced as rage. Some men have beaten women during intercourse.

The use of pornography is violence. It certainly is violence toward women who are seen and used as objects. But it is also violence toward men. It violates our sensibilities and tenderness.

Using Others: Incest and Rape

At least one in four women is sexually abused before the age of eighteen. One in ten men is sexually abused before the age of eighteen. Some research suggests even scarier statistics: one in three women, and one in six men. Most of these abuses are perpetrated by men. Most of these men are family members, relatives, or friends.

Each of the following quotes are taken from different, real-life situations. They are answers to questions I've asked during some of my sessions with men:

- *How could you violate your twelve-year-old step-daughter in that way?*
  "Well, you don't know her. She's twelve going on twenty-four. She led me on. She wears revealing clothes. She came to me—I didn't ask for it. She rubbed my shoulders. She smiled at me a lot. She knew what she was doing. It was only after I touched her that she screamed. Now her mother has convinced her that it was totally my fault."

- *Sir, did it occur to you that you were touching your thirteen-year-old daughter inappropriately?*
  "You have a dirty mind, you know that? I wasn't doing anything wrong. She has no mama. She has a lot of pain from her periods. Nobody but I can help her. I try to make her feel better. Besides, who's going to teach her the facts of life anyway? Somebody's got to do it!"

- *Sir, you read my intake form. I am required to inform the authorities when I hear about an incident of child abuse.*
  "What kind of counselor are you? You call yourself a Christian? I came here with good intentions, to tell you I made a mistake. I told you in confidence. I am looking for help. Now you're telling me you'll expose me. My daughter will be just fine unless you ruin and expose our family!"

- *So your daughter had a friend over for the night, and you climbed into your daughter's friend's bed?*
  "Yeah, I couldn't help it. It just sort of happened. I've never done it before and I will never do it again. But you know how it is. She looked so sweet. I tried not to waken my daughter or the girl, but I guess I scared her. I really don't know what came over me. I can't

see that it's a big deal—I mean, there was no sex or anything! I don't think making a big deal out of this will help anybody."

- And this was my response to a "devoutly Christian" man whose wife was dying of cancer, yet he persisted in abusing her sexually and physically: *I will not tell your wife that she must submit to your need for intercourse. She is not able to give that to you now.*
  While his wife sat sobbing hysterically, he said: "You can all go burn! I have needs. She exaggerates—I never hurt her. The Scriptures say she should fill my needs. I am the head of this house."

I supported her desire to move in with her parents so that she could die where she was loved.

Weeks after she died, he made an appointment to see me. I naively hoped he was coming to reconcile, to express peace in honor of, and in respect for, his wife. Instead, he walked into my office and said, "All I have to say is this. You drove my wife away from me. God will deal with you." Then he stormed out, slamming the door.

I walked to my desk and sobbed for minutes. I remember feeling sick to my stomach, and I wondered if I should continue as a therapist. I did.

Only a few men are able to admit, "I violated someone, and I am responsible."

If you have committed rape or incest, you will not be "cured" simply by following the steps in this book. You need special help. Find out who treats men with this problem in your area. Please get help before it is too late for you or your victim.

Using Others: Sexual Harassment

Men play fantasy games in their heads about women; some act out these head games. We fantasize about how they feel toward us. This comes from our insecurity and sometimes the desire to stimulate our bored impulses out of depression. Sometimes, to handle our fear, we try to entice a woman to indicate her interest in us. Her hints of interest might satisfy us enough to leave her alone.

Other men don't know how to back off. They just want sexual conquests. They use women to satisfy selfish needs. Many American men are in denial about this.

Many women who work with men feel incredibly vulnerable. They have already had to overcome discrimination against women to attain their level of success in the business world; now they must fend off sexual advances and harassment. A woman can feel vulnerable to the whims of her bosses. When a man is in a position of authority over a woman, he sometimes feels he has rights with her. Some men have no sense of the limit of power, boundaries of respect and decency, not to mention simple appropriateness. They are users.

Treat *all* persons with dignity and respect. *Always.*

If you are struggling with sexual obsessions or addictions, my heart goes out to you. If you have been sexually traumatized, please seek help. Many men need such help. I have only presented an outline of male sexual dilemmas to help you clarify your issues and pains.

Problems with sexual boundaries are profound because they are shame-based behaviors and attitudes. The perpetrator is a wounded soul.

The antidote to a conscience overburdened with guilt is confession and restitution. Tell God. Tell a confidant. Then try to go back and make things right.

The antidote to shame-based behaviors, however, is conversion and reconstruction. First, you must admit your wrongs. Do what you can to make things right, but do not force reconciliation. Do not force the victim in any way. Second, submit these things to God and submit to reconstruction through competent therapy.

Please remember: You deserve the best possible life. Be responsible with your behavior and feelings! May you find genuine pleasure in a healthy sexual life.

14

Step 7: I Am Responsible for My Passions:
Our Passions for Work

"It has always seemed strange to me," said Doc. "The things we admire in men, kindness and generosity, openness, honesty, understanding and feeling are the concomitants of failure in our system. And those traits we detest, sharpness, greed, acquisitiveness, meanness, egotism and self-interest are the traits of success. And while men admire the quality of the first they love the produce of the second."
—John Steinbeck, *Cannery Row*

Why do men work? Men work because it is in our nature to do so. The book of Genesis portrays work, play, and pleasure as inseparable. Work was part of our created intent. Part of why we live is for work. Yet the misanthropy of our demons splits work from play. Work became toil, sweat, hardship, and left man anxious about his survival and the accumulation of comforts and rewards.

Why do men work? To make money. We have to make enough money to survive, to pay the bills, to put food in our mouths, clothes on our bodies and a roof over our heads. Money first pays the bills. More money buys more comfort.

For many, money represents the value of their work. From there it is a simple step to begin believing that money represents self-value and self-esteem. How much we make begins to impact how we feel about ourselves. Money becomes a measure of success, especially as men compare incomes and benefits, homes, cars, and toys.

Why do men work? Most men hope to do their jobs well. This gives men a sense of emotional satisfaction, a sense of accomplishment, the good feeling of a job well-done. This, too, is a source of self-esteem for men.

Of course, it is possible for personal satisfaction, which leads to self-worth, to come from internal judgments:

- "I did a great job."
- "I handled that well."
- "I am proud of myself."

More often, however, we look for an external source of validation:

- "The boss says I did a great job."
- "They say I have saved the company thousands of dollars."
- "They applauded me for landing the Acme account."

Fortunately or not, our bosses' judgments about our performances determine much about our futures. If bosses were purely objective, these judgments would be fair. But bosses are not wholly objective because they are imperfect humans. The people who judge us have their own needs and motives. This can complicate things!

There are obvious dangers in relying on money and on the judgments of other subjective, imperfect human beings as the very basis for our self-esteem. These are fickle standards by which we measure our worth: our bosses are fickle; economies are fickle. Some men seem to be able to handle the fickleness—they manage to roll with the punches related to their careers. Other men get knocked down or out!

Men have made titles a measure of success in work. If we are successful—which means that we can produce and earn profits for our company—our chances of being promoted improve. At that point, we are given a new job title, greater responsibility, and more stress. We may even be required to devote more time and attention to our jobs.

Another danger in the competitive promotion game is that we can be promoted to a job we know nothing about. Perhaps you have great expertise in a technical field. If you do well enough, you're bound to be promoted to management. This may well be a field you know little about—and perhaps don't even like! Of course, upper management will try to help by sending you to seminars. But your best hope is that you will be assigned to a great secretary or assistant who knows how to run your position and his or hers as well. If you're really lucky, you might discover you actually have a knack for management.

It's quite possible to do well, make money for our companies, earn accolades from our bosses—while selling our personal dignity in the process. We can build our egos on work success while we rip apart the fabric of our moral sanities. Such choices can be terribly complex and subtle.

Harvey's company disposes of toxic wastes through its regular trash pickups because federally required toxic waste dumping would dig into the company profits. Harvey knows his job would be in jeopardy if he objected or blew the whistle. Harvey is in a tough spot.

Rudy knows that his church pads its attendance statistics to show numerical growth. Other churches are impressed. Many of the parishioners are impressed. No one is harmed by the little ruse—technically. Except that Rudy is the pastor—the one who is supposed to be calling society to a moral conscience.

The difficulty of working for others is that we serve their agenda. Any particular religious or moral belief we have might not fit the company agenda. And it's not just beliefs: our personal needs and the needs of our families are also expected to play second fiddle to the good of the company. And so we face a choice: how much of my personal dignity can I sell to satisfy or advantage the company? These can be complex, and even life-changing choices.

Failure and success seem to run in seasons. For most of us, there seems to be a balancing of the two over the years. For others, success breeds more success. For still others, failure seems to fuel more failure. Some seem to succeed despite themselves while, for others, failure seems like their destiny. While success—at least as the corporate world defines it—builds tenuous self-esteem, failure bleeds our self-esteem.

Many men "tolerate" their jobs. They make enough money to be satisfied or comfortable, but they find little personal reward in their work. They experience little creativity or personal enjoyment. The job has become a necessary obligation or a secure habit. Some men survive work to get to their hobbies, friends, or family—those things they truly love.

John Bradshaw says many of us have become "human doings," having lost a sense of our "being." We have lost our sense of creativity, of passions, of bliss, of self-expression, of self-determination. We are just functioning.

HOW WORKAHOLISM BETRAYS US

The great irony is that, in the end, the obsessive drive that propels a man to achieve external rewards rears its ugly head and eats him alive. The goals of fame or fortune become a devouring demon. The monster blackmails us into sacrifices we never imagined. It all begins so innocently, if not nobly. "I wanted us to be happy, to have things," one man said to his wife. The demon hears and responds, "Yes, but to get those 'things' I want your heart! You have come this far. It would be foolish to stop now. The goal is within reach—you can have it all!"

Workaholism cheats us of our souls, while laughing its sinister, snarling laugh. The demon feeds itself on our hearts. Then it turns its back on us, dancing merrily on its way. We are left broken, emotionally spent.

And for what?

Along the trail, imperceptibly at first, our values and ethics, our treatment of others, the sense of wholeness in our lives, begin to slide. Perhaps, looking back, we can't remember being confronted with black-and-white moral or relationship choices. Looking back, perhaps all we can see are the fuzzy choices, the kind that are grey. But the pattern of honoring the demon wears us thin. We become successful people with insignificant lives.

Some men along this path become addicted to their own adrenaline! Adrenaline is the only "drug from within." In other words, it is a drug that our own bodies produce. According to Dr. Archibald Hart, "While 'workaholism' can sometimes mask home problems or basic insecurities, most often it is an addiction to the adrenalin surges brought on by challenge and competition."[1]

Men hooked on adrenaline crave constant, intense activity and often live chaotically. Even their recreation and "rest" may be loaded with drive and competition!

Dr. Redford Williams clarifies which type of person is apt to have harmful adrenaline and stress hormone surges. Previous research, he wrote, suggested that people with Type A behavior—impatient, driven, aggressive—suffered greater risk of heart attack, coronary disease, or other stress-related illness. New studies, however, show that men and women who are hurried and prone to hostility suffer even greater health deterioration.[2]

What are the roots of hostility? Hostility, like aggression, is a learned behavior. Somewhere we learned to mistrust others. Hostile persons react by seeking revenge or by punishing others. Our blood boils when a fellow employee makes even an honest mistake. We curse at anyone cutting us off the road. We fume at an umpire's bad decision. Unfortunately, the mistrusting, hostile person is also a great denier. Like the alcoholic, he is the last person to see his problem, although he is quite adept at seeing everyone else's!

One day, something collapses in our lives. Our child develops behavioral problems. Our physical or mental health takes a nose-dive. We lose the respect of our employees. Or our boss's trust. Perhaps even our wives. The crisis shocks us, and yet it was inevitable. We ignored the symptoms and signs.

We collapse on the shifting, unstable sands of our haughty dreams. Now we stop to assess the price we paid. If we are lucky, someone is still there to love us.

If that is the irony, the paradox is this: *most recent management theory is beginning to disown the old obsessive, workaholic style.* Men who choose genuine love make better employees in the end. They are more stable. They are easier to work with. They are better team players. They make better decisions. They are more comfortable and fun to be with. The obsessive, addictive, volatile types simply wear out!

How are we to assess the fact that the traits that have typically bred "success" in our culture also describe mental illness? Consider these haunting descriptions of borderline and narcissistic personality disorders. Compare these characteristics with personality traits often valued in business and politics:

- *Borderline personality:* Can be highly functional and productive. This person also tends to be able to manipulate others, since he lacks deep and genuine emotion. He attaches to people superficially and mimics behaviors of love. He can fascinate others with impulsive behaviors.
- *Narcissism:* Driven by endless ego needs, he can be insatiably competitive. Needs constant affirmation, since he is quite insecure. World revolves around him and his needs. Can be a great salesperson.

Sheer gall, impudence or luck can make a man rich or famous. However, it takes raw courage, steeled nerves, and an adventurous will to face one's self and to choose peace!

MEN: CONQUERORS AND CREATORS

Men have always been conquerors. This isn't necessarily wrong or evil. This drive, in fact, pushes us to accomplish what otherwise would not happen! It is *how* we conquer and *what* we conquer that gets us into trouble. Conquering need not be hostile or competitive. And we can conquer our own volatile drives.

Many men are driven to succeed to satisfy an insatiable need to win the approval of their fathers. Yet, despite their mighty efforts, it may never happen. Many dads cannot express satisfying approval to their sons. Beneath Dad's crusty exterior, pride may well lurk, but he never learned how to show it openly. Such emotion was too intimate. If you are the son of such a father, it's possible that you gave up trying to force him into awkward expressions of his feelings. Perhaps you've been able to deal with the grief and loss you experienced by never hearing your father's expression of approval and pride in you. It's also possible that, while intellectually you might acknowledge that "Dad will never change," something inside of you remains driven and obsessed. If you can prove that you're good enough, successful enough, rich enough—maybe, just maybe, you'll catch Dad's attention after all.

There are men who are corporate success stories. They are giants in their field. Leaders of America. And yet it matters not. They work to fill the gnawing void where Father's approval was meant to be.

Other men never received Mother's love. Such men have a terrible time with developing empathic feelings toward others. They may also have trouble with intimacy. Their idea of love is based on need, rather than on giving. A man from this kind of background may well want a woman to fulfill his emptiness. He possesses her. He might be addicted to her! His "love" runs wild with fear, possessiveness, and jealousy. The constant insecurity of his self-worth feeds this need endlessly. He is trapped.

Any person wounded from a relationship is bound to approach closeness with caution. But when he does attach, he's like a tic under the skin! He won't leave. Yet despite the apparent closeness, those wounded most deeply build protective barriers to deeper levels of intimacy. The risk of hurt seems too great.

Some men experiencing stress and trouble in their relationships find release by pouring themselves into their work. "At least," they reason, "my job loves me. At least I'm successful here." Work is a great place to hide.

GAINING A HANDLE ON WORK DISSONANCE

Max DePree has written marvelous books on leadership. For many years, Mr. DePree was chairman and CEO of Herman

Miller, Inc., a furniture-making company in the Zeeland, Michigan area. In 1988, *Fortune* Magazine hailed Herman Miller as one of America's "ten most admired companies."[3]

In his book *Leadership Is an Art* Mr. DePree explained that intimacy is a key component in significant leadership. He wrote:

> Intimacy is at the heart of competence. It has to do with understanding, with believing, and with practice. It has to do with the relationship to one's work . . . [and] a key component of intimacy is passion. . . .
>
> We find intimacy [not through a formula but] through a search for comfort with ambiguity. We do not grow by knowing all of the answers, but rather by living with the questions.
>
> Intimacy rises from translating personal and corporate values into daily work practices, from searching for knowledge and wisdom and justice. Above all, intimacy rises from, and gives rise to, strong relationships.[4]

According to Mr. DePree, there are two types of relationships in work situations. The first is "contractual." This covers all the legal and technical obligations and rewards which are established in a job relationship. Yet contractual relationships cannot describe, nor encompass, the freedom of creativity and the power of passion that is essential to enjoyment at work. This is the territory of "covenant" relationships.

> A covenantal relationship rests on shared commitment to ideas, to issues, to values, to goals, and to management processes. Words such as love, warmth, personal chemistry are certainly pertinent. . . . They fill deep needs and they enable work to have meaning and to be fulfilling. . . . They are an expression of the sacred nature of relationships.[5]

I believe that more companies are perking their ears and paying closer attention to the covenantal aspect of employee relations. They are doing this in two ways:

1. "Participatory management" is in vogue, at least in theory. Even large companies like GE are trying to shift from hierarchical to more dialogue-based methods of decision making. Unfortunately, reports are that some older executives and managers are struggling to understand the new processes, have little skill at them, or occasionally seek to sabotage the success of the new participatory methods. Making the shift is not proving easy: it involves, for many, grieving the loss of the old.

The next significant step in participatory organizations will very likely be greater sharing of company profits and losses from the "top" executives to the entry-level employees. Further, some companies are playing a bigger role in contributing back to their communities and to the future well-being of our planet. Ben & Jerry's Ice Cream, silly though they might seem, is a leader in this area. (I have thought of following their lead by painting our church sanctuary white and black to resemble the spots of a cow, and replacing the church chimes with a cowbell and an amplified "moo.")

2. Another way companies are covenanting with their employees is by taking an interest in their personal development and life goals. Rather than firing employees who have areas of relational weakness, for example, some companies are giving employees opportunities for personal growth through seminars, therapy, and/or other training. Some companies have begun day-care centers on premises so that employees can be near their pre-school children. Such companies are to be commended.

RELATIONSHIPS BY CONTRACT

Whether they know it or not, some men and women organize their personal relationships in carefully structured and functional ways. These relationships are more contractual than intimate, more negotiated than felt. Many relationships smack more of business than personal. These "pseudo-intimate" relationships are distinguished by these qualities:

- Prenuptial arrangements, particularly agreements regarding wholly separate finances.
- High expectations of what "I" am going to get out of this relationship. Of course, these expectations are not written in the form of a contract, but they might as well be. When the relationship hits a snag and "contractual" expectations are not met, the result can be low satisfaction and even disillusionment.
- Trust issues that surface regularly. Both partners blame the other for violating trust, documenting such incidents during arguments.
- Communication is usually a two-person monologue instead of a dialogue. The partners simply do not hear each other. Capacity for empathy is low.
- Functional concerns consume much of their time together. Each partner can be dictatorial and demanding.

Contractual relationships are like two people with a cookie jar. They know a lot about cookies—they know what they look like, smell like, feel like—but they never quite dare to eat the cookies. After all, what if they eat the cookies and find they don't like them? True, it's a risk. But it's a risk that genuine love comprehends and relishes without threat. In fact, this risk empowers love.

SOME FINAL THOUGHTS ON MEN, INTIMACY, PASSION, AND POWER

Male and Female Differences

Girls learn to talk early. They talk about feelings. They learn to support each other.

Boys learn to act. They organize plans and structure people into hierarchies of power.

"A boy's conversation revolves around dominance and competitiveness, whereas a girl looks for intimacy and equality," says Aaron T. Beck in *Love Is Never Enough*.[6]

Beck goes on to describe how men and women discuss problems differently. A wife shares a problem, hoping to receive understanding and sympathy. Yet often the husband fails to offer sympathy of any sort. Instead, he thinks about her problem in the same way he tackles any problem at work. He gives practical solutions. He advises her. She feels he doesn't really care. He thinks he has given her a way to "fix" the problem.[7]

Women say, "If we can talk about it, our marriage is working."

Men say, "If we have to keep talking about it, the marriage is failing."

What a contrast!

In his study of male and female differences, psychologist David M. Buss (University of Michigan) says that women complained most that men did not understand their need for intimacy. "Sex has a different meaning for women than for men. Women see sex as following from emotional intimacy, while men see sex itself as a road to intimacy."[8]

Carl Whitaker, the grandfather of experiential system's therapy, comments in *Dancing with the Family*: "Men just have an impossible time with intimacy. [They pursue intimacy through] achievement, acquisition, and possession."[9]

The toys of little boys become, with their manhood, money, sports cars, or companies. "Men dress themselves in accomplishments and successes. Without them, they feel naked and ashamed. [Men] define themselves by what they have, not by who they are."[10]

We wish to have closeness and success. We might gain measures of both, but there is something even better: there is love and significance. We were created by the Creator to be creators ourselves.

Becoming all that we were meant to be includes:

- Reconnecting our hearts to appropriate passions. The demon of lust demands to play its despairing tunes on our despondent spirit. Only you have the power to say No! to the demons and Yes! to responsible, joyful passions.

- Making choices that fill our spirits with significance for God, ourselves and others. We can live again according to the rhythm of God's unique design for us. This is the way of peace and contentment.

I must confess that I am in recovery from an Overly Serious Childhood. I learned to take life far too seriously as a child. Looking back, I wonder if I learned a work ethic based on fear and deprivation through the Dutch conservative communities I was raised in. We talked about joy, but it was a depressingly heavy and humiliating joy. It was the kind of pride and joy one feels for feeling humble. Is it any wonder I was depressed as a kid?

My recovery includes . . .

- Time for imagination—thinking about positive wild ideas and visions.
- Time for humor—laughing about the ironies and paradoxes and just plain absurdities of life.
- Time for joy—seeing and feeling beauty in the seemingly small and the insignificant.
- Time for play—playing catch with my boys, running in the wind, laughing with my friends.
- Time for peace—writing this book and being with my brothers in Men at Peace.

I'll be praying for your recovery, too.

Step 8: I Am Responsible for My Feelings and Thoughts

Men live through their heads. We even "think" our emotions. With an infinite array of emotions available to us, we tend to stick with what we call "facts."

That is not to say, unfortunately, that most men are wise or rational. Rather, we can be quite emotional when we feel rage or depression, two of the few "acceptable" male emotions. Yet our minds tend to rationalize our hurt or fear, rage or depression. We also manage to deny the hurt we do to others by our rage or depression. And we repress a vast world of other emotions that could help us better understand ourselves and other people, and which might clarify our minds and hearts enough to make better choices in life.

Meet Gordon. Gordon says he detests "emotional people." He says this with a great deal of emotion.

Meet Tom. Tom says emotions cloud rational thinking. He is proud of his "great mind" and its ability to find solutions to complex problems even when other minds cannot. Unfortunately, Tom has few friends. He argues regularly with coworkers and acquaintances about issues (often trivial), making sure they are corrected frequently. He is quite emotional underneath his cool exterior in these arguments over what is "right" or which is the correct "fact," alienating many with his insensitivity.

Most of the Men at Peace Steps direct us toward the responsible practice of true emotions. We need to "get out" of our heads in order to feel. As we work through these steps, our first attempts at practicing responsible emotions are likely to be pretty sloppy! Some men might find it hard to believe they even *have* any emotions at all! Be patient. Time and practice pay off. In this chapter, we will explore differences between thoughts and feelings, and we will learn how to make better rational and emotional choices.

*Emotions—which is another word for feelings—*are spontaneous inner responses to things outside of us (another person, place, thing, or event). They can also be responses to things within (an idea or belief). Emotions are felt through our bodies, although men tend to be inhibited in body and emotion.

You have already been working on the emotions of anger and anguish, fear and hurt, grief and joy, and passions. These feelings are expressions of your self as you interact with the world. It is possible to alter our emotional responses through new experiences and beliefs, which we will be examining in greater detail shortly.

Feelings are not right or wrong—they just exist! At the same time, our behaviors in reaction to our feelings have moral and relational consequences, and we are responsible for our behaviors.

It is common for us to have mixed feelings or even contradictory feelings at the same time. This is why learning to recognize our feelings and discriminating them one from another is important. For example, at the very same moment I may feel happy about a new job and scared about how I will perform. We can feel opposites at the same moment—I'm sure you remember this principle from our chapter on joy and grief, for example.

Thoughts, unlike feelings, are judgments, opinions, or ideas about what we experience. Thoughts help us organize our world and our roles in that world. Thoughts allow us to make choices, hopefully based on valid information, on our feelings, and on our subconscious senses or intuition.

Often people confuse thoughts and feelings. Here are three examples of thoughts. Notice that using the word *feel* doesn't magically change the thought into a feeling!

1. I think it is going to rain today.
2. I feel that it is going to rain today.
3. I feel like it is going to rain today.

The thought is the same in all three examples: it is going to rain today! Here, however, are four examples of feelings:

1. I feel wet. (Feeling = wet)
2. I am angry. (Feeling = angry)
3. A cloudy sky makes me sad. (Feeling = sad)
4. I wish it would rain today. (Feeling = wish)

Here are combinations of thoughts and feelings:

1. I hope it rains today so that I don't have to water the lawn.
   (Feeling = hope; thought = don't have to water the lawn)
2. The sky is blue. I like blue skies.
   (Thought = the sky is blue; feeling = like)

Most of our communication combines thoughts and feelings. Some communication theorists suggest most sentences, or at least most ideas, are combinations of thoughts and feelings. We are probably safe in saying that the shorthand for most sentences could be:

I feel _____ (emotion) because _____ (thought).

Remember, most men communicate primarily in thoughts. Our goal in Men at Peace is to communicate clear thoughts *with emotional clarification and expression*. This is important because relationships are built on emotional expression! Learning to express emotions is important for another reason as well: emotions are the stuff that gives our lives breadth and depth, color and vitality.

EXPLORING EMOTIONS AND THOUGHTS

Try this brief exercise to work on exploring thoughts and emotions. As you do, however, keep in mind that thoughts *are not* emotions. Emotions often include words like: happy, sad, angry, hurt, afraid, tired, peace, anxious, lonely, loved, tender, joyful, okay, soft, hard, lazy, and energetic.

Please follow these rules:

1. Explore one sentence at a time. Do not look ahead.
2. Clarify in each sentence what is the thought and what is the emotion.
3. Do not judge or critique what you hear yourself say! The point is to express thought and emotion, not to judge the content of your statement.

Now finish these sentences:

1. At this moment I am feeling _____.
2. When I enter a roomful of people I usually feel _____ _____.
3. I am happiest when _____.
4. The saddest moment of my life was _____.
5. I feel down when _____.
6. I become angry when _____.
7. The emotion I find most difficult to handle is _____.
8. I love _____.
9. What hurts me most is _____.
10. I am afraid of _____.

Once you've finished these questions, you can practice further by doing two things:

1. Write or say your own sentences. Explore your thoughts and emotions further.
2. Listen to other people talk. Figure out what is their thought and what is their emotion.

EMOTION, CONTEXT, AND BODY LANGUAGE

The context of a situation determines much of what is meant. For example, a person might say: "I'll take care of you." Yet this can mean many things depending on context. If it is said by a bank robber drawing a gun on a teller, this is not a good sign. On the other hand, if it is said by a loving wife to her husband, home sick with a cold, then it is a wonderful phrase.

In your mind, give the following sentences different contexts to see how the meaning might differ:

1. I need some space. (Imagine a wife saying these words to a possessive husband. Then imagine a husband asking for room on the kitchen table to do his paperwork.)
2. Let me have it.
3. I know what is best.
4. That's wrong!
5. Let it go.

Body language is one of the ways we determine the context and meaning of what someone is saying to us. Body language is actually said to compose up to ninety percent of our communication! Think about this. Body language can include your voice—how loudly or softly you say something—as well as the tone of your voice. Body language also includes your facial expression—are you laughing or smiling? Angry or mad? Are your muscles tight or loose? And what about the twists and turns of your eyes, mouth, forehead, and cheeks?

For example, think of the simple words *I love you*. Now say these simple words using various voices and tones. Your meaning changes, doesn't it? Your voice reveals the context; it lets us know if you are genuine, sad, angry, or sarcastic. Say the words again, this time with different facial expressions. Again, you can say many different things by merely raising an eyebrow or turning your lips into a frown.

Now think of your whole-body language. You can communicate a lot with your body. Suppose you wanted to communicate the words and message, "I really care what you think, dear!" to your wife. Would you say these words while reading the paper? Of course not! Would you stare at the floor? Would you turn your back to her? Would you cross your legs and arms and look uptight? Yet we make these very mistakes—in big and small ways—often! We don't pay attention to our body language as we communicate. We might *think* we're telling our wives that we care what they think. But we might be saying something altogether different with our bodies.

If you truly want to communicate to your wife that you care about what she thinks, you will want to do the following with your body:

1. Face her squarely. Think of both of you, sitting on either end of a box, your body facing hers directly.
2. Open your posture. No crossed arms or legs. No tenseness in the face. Try talking to yourself in a mirror once. It's scary to watch ourselves and see what kinds of messages we are communicating with tense facial muscles!
3. Sit or stand close together. Body space is very powerful. Sitting or standing close can communicate threat if what you are saying is unwanted or negative; sitting or standing close can communicate intimacy if your message is wanted and positive.

    Imagine trying to teach a seminar entitled "Intimacy and Love" under the following circumstances: your audience of 500 is scattered throughout the 100,000 seat Rose Bowl and you are speaking from the Good Year Blimp as it circles the Rose Bowl with your voice being pumped through a massive public address system. You might be the greatest speaker in the world, and yet the spatial distance would make your content seem absurd. And yet isn't this exactly what we do with our wives? We holler supposedly meaningful things across the room while we're reading the paper! Is it any wonder we aren't taken seriously?
4. Make eye contact. You don't have to stare, but meaningful eye contact is vital.

All of these body signals are very important when you are communicating thoughts—and they are even more critical when you are communicating your feelings or emotions. How have you been communicating with your body? What can you begin to work on?

INTIMACY

Intimacy happens when we learn to communicate what we feel and to appreciate the feelings of others.

Intimacy is built on sharing two kinds of emotions:

1. *Emotions of affection.* Saying "I love you" with words and touch is vital to the development of intimacy! Saying "You know how I feel," or thinking *I shouldn't have to say anything because she should be able to tell from my actions* simply aren't good enough. They may help you avoid expressing your feelings, but they will never build intimacy!

2. *Emotions of vulnerability.* This is what the entire Men at Peace program emphasizes. We need to share our vulnerable emotions, which we categorize broadly as fear and hurt. If we don't learn to express these emotions, our souls starve and our relationships die. Technically, we might stay married, or maintain contact with our best friends, or keep our title of "father." But titles don't mean the relationships are healthy, or even alive. Without shared vulnerability, our relationships simply cannot survive, much less thrive!

TRUTHFUL THOUGHTS

Much of the time, we think we know what is going on around us. We know "the facts." If someone tries to tell us differently—as they often do—we manage to discount them. We think, secretly in our heads or aloud if we are rude, that they are "wrong" at best, and very possibly "stupid."

The truth, however, is that very little in this world cannot be legitimately interpreted in more than one valid manner. Our "facts" are very often just one way of looking at a situation.

Take, for example, the story of a woman running behind a man, who is also running and carrying a black bag. She is screaming, "He has my bag!"

I would assume an innocent woman has had her purse stolen by a male criminal. If I witnessed this scene, I would find myself quickly considering what I should do.

But wait! In such a fast-moving moment, it's possible that I got the facts wrong! What if she is a doctor, racing to the scene of an accident with her assistant, who is carrying her bag of medicines? She yells to those ahead, "He has my bag!" to let them know that the person ahead, who simply happens to be a faster runner, has her supplies. A moment later, they both turn the corner and arrive at the scene of the accident.

A far-fetched story? Perhaps. But catch the point: misperceptions of facts happen often because we judge the "truth" much too quickly and with too little information. Most often, we damage our relationships by judging too much too soon, and listening far too little.

Telling the truth, and thinking honestly, is made possible when we are careful not to misjudge the facts. But telling the truth also demands that we look carefully, not just at the facts, but at our motives.

Think about it. How often do you distort the truth to get your way? To avoid conflict? To be right, even if it costs you peace and happiness? I'm not saying that you consciously and willfully lie—but we all are guilty of distorting the truth, even just a little. We tweak the truth to get what we want, when we want it. And in doing so we lie to ourselves and we damage the trust other people hold in us.

In preparing for honest communication, it's also important to recognize that much of our perception of the facts is skewered by our emotions. For example, I might fear conflict, so I defend myself by believing that I alone have the facts. To think that "I am rational and you are emotional" can quite often be a very emotional judgment!

"I feel that she should not yell at me," is a thought, even though the word *feel* is used. Men often think that they feel just because they use the word *feel* in place of the word *think*. Let's go ahead and clarify the thought, as well as possible feelings attached. What this person is actually saying—and probably feeling—is: "I think she should not yell at me. When she does, I feel aggravated, hurt, or intimidated."

On the other hand, "I think I am sad," is actually a feeling statement, even though the word *think* is used. What this sentence really says is: "As best as I can tell, I feel sad."

Discriminating between thoughts and feelings is important because we can judge our thoughts, but *our feelings deserve to be heard without judgment!* In the same vein, we owe others the right to express their feelings—even if their feelings are about us—without judgment or harmful reactions! We might differ with their thoughts and opinions, and we might be uncomfortable with what they are feeling about us, but we must still take responsibility for how we respond.

Men at Peace has developed a way to handle our side of an argument. This technique has helped countless men. Please read carefully as you think about how you can apply this in your life! For many men, this is a shockingly new idea!

Frequently in Men at Peace, a man will tell us that he can no longer stand his wife yelling at him! Why? "Because it ticks me off!" is a typical first response.

First we explore the circumstances more thoroughly so that he might learn to empathize a bit more with whatever feelings his wife is expressing. We often discover that his wife is home with small children all day long and that she is emotionally and physically exhausted. Or we might discover that his wife is lonely for companionship that he is not providing. Or he may not be listening well to her feelings.

Then we explore the reasons he is so intolerant of conflict or even screaming. Usually we discover that he was wounded previously in his life, frequently in childhood. It's true that his wife is not perfect and has problems too, but he can be stuffed so full of emotions that he can't hear her emotions or those of anyone else.

Finally, we ask a man to try something new. We suggest: "Next time your wife hollers at you, tell her, 'I can see that you're angry with me. Tell me more. I want to hear you.'" Instead of defending himself, his task suddenly becomes to listen carefully *without reacting* like he's used to doing. Stay calm. Listen well.

When she is done, he can say—calmly—"I respect you for telling me what you think and feel even if it hurts. Now I need some time to think about what you are saying. I'll respond _____ " (he names a time).

Keeping his agreement, he returns to the conversation after a Time-Out. The Time-Out helps him make better choices about his response. In fact, it enables him to respond, instead of react. When he returns, he might want to frame his response like this: "I appreciate that you told me how you feel and think. In response, I can do this _____." Or: "I am not ready to do _____, although I *can* do _____." Or even: "Though I appreciate your feelings, I do not agree with your perspective. Most of all, I care about you and how you feel."

Sounds crazy, you say? What is your alternative? I have heard countless men say this new response helped them immensely. And often it has inspired their partners to try the same approach.

CHOOSE YOUR EMOTIONS

Cognitive therapists have taught us how to discriminate between events and our emotional responses to those events. This can be called the A-B-C theory of emotional response:

A = Activating event
B = Beliefs about event
C = Consequent emotion

Activating Event

Events happen to each of us. Some events happen to us without being asked for or provoked by us: we receive a gift, a driver cuts us off on the freeway, someone yells at us. Other events occur because we cause them to happen: we give a gift, we cut someone else off on the freeway, or we yell at someone.

Consequent Emotion

This is what we feel about what happened. We might feel good, bad, happy, sad, hurt, angry, anguished, tired, frustrated, or peaceful.

But here is the key: *Emotions are not evoked directly from events.*
We might *think* our emotions are natural or normal, given the
event. We might even link the two as inseparable in our minds:
"She hollered at me, so of course I got angry!" But the truth is
that we have choices. We choose to get angry. But we could
have also made the choice to be hurt, disappointed, humored,
saddened, or understanding.

Beliefs about the Event

A *Belief* is the powerful middle step between the *Event* and
the *Emotion*. This middle step has become instinctive for most
of us, so we may not recognize it at first. Many of our beliefs
are learned in childhood and are deeply ingrained. These
beliefs, or assumptions—about ourselves, men in general,
women in general, marriage, life, work—can become "laws"
or "truths" through which we filter everything that happens
to us and by us. They are the framework of ideas that cause us
to interpret events as we do. Our beliefs, then, dictate how we
respond emotionally to events.

Example:

Activating event: A driver cuts you off on the freeway.
Belief about event: "Drivers should never cut me off. Such
persons are rude! I have a right to let him know I think he's
rude!"
Consequent emotion: You are angry!

Example of an alternative outcome, based on a different
"middle step":

Activating event: A driver cuts you off on the freeway.
Belief about event: "That driver is crazy. Wow, am I glad I'm
safe!"
Consequent emotion: Fear, then relief!

There are a number of basic beliefs that frequently nudge us into a mode of aggression or depression as our emotional response to events. These beliefs can be categorized as:

- *Universalizing.* We think something or someone is completely good or completely bad, entirely right or entirely wrong. We think in black-and-white, even though the world is mostly gray! Your language can indicate whether or not you are universalizing in your beliefs. Watch for phrases like:

    "She always . . . "
    "She never . . ."
    "I always . . ."
    "I never . . ."

- *Mind reading.* We think we know each other well enough to pinpoint the motives behind something that was said or done. Married couples tend to do this a lot. Language that can indicate you may have fallen into this trap includes these phrases:

    "She did this because . . ."
    "I know *exactly* what she's thinking."

- *Catastrophizing.* We see and believe the absolute worst. We refuse to see the possibilities for change. We blame rather than take responsibility. Language:

    "This is terrible!"
    "This destroys everything!"
    "She can't do anything right!"

- *Shoulds.* These are deeply set internal laws. We learn these as children, sometimes as adults. *Shoulds* block us from seeing other alternatives or points of view. We subject other people—and ourselves as well—to our *shoulds.* Language:

    "People should . . ."
    "She should . . ."
    "He shouldn't . . ."
    "I ought to . . ."

Review in your mind and heart some of your stronger emotional reactions in the past few days. Can you identify some of the beliefs that guided your emotional responses? Continue to think about this in the days ahead. Ask a friend to list what he sees to be your most powerful beliefs. How do these beliefs help you? How do they hurt you? How do they help or hurt others? Monitor your emotional reactions. They point you to your beliefs.

OUR BODIES, OUR MINDS, OUR FEELINGS

We learn very early to disconnect from our bodies when we feel physical or emotional pain: "Big boys don't cry." "Be a man." "You'll just have to tough it out." I remember a high school track coach telling me to "run through the pain." As a result, I further irritated injured disks in the base of my back. My mobility became restricted.

This is not to say that we should always stop when we feel pain. But it means that we can expect to pay a price when we ignore certain signals. Pain tells us that something needs our attention. Sometimes paying attention is enough. Other times pain demands more of a response. Marathon runners, for example, regularly must choose to run with pain. They can make this choice, however, because they pay attention to their pain and know when to run, and when to stop! They run through pain—as long as the pain relates to barriers of performance. They stop, however, if the pain relates to damage of their bodies. Our bodies and emotions are inseparable.

One way to learn what you feel is to get in the habit of listening to your body. Stop your reading for about two minutes. Get into a comfortable sitting position, legs and arms uncrossed. Put the book down after you finish this paragraph and do the following: take five long, deep breaths. Inhale with your nose, exhale with your mouth. Now close your eyes. Do you feel your breathing? Notice how your body breathes in rhythm without your conscious effort. Can you feel your heart in rhythm? What else do you feel? Tension? Where?

Mind and Body Relaxation

Find a comfortable and quiet place. You want to avoid interruptions during this period of relaxation. Make the decision to spend at least ten minutes in this exercise:

Sit comfortably or lie down.

Listen to your body. Where are tension spots? Common places to check are jaws, temples of the forehead, scalp, neck, shoulders, arms, hands, back, buttocks, legs, and feet. Now, mentally go through each of these muscle areas, starting with your feet and moving upward. Tense your muscles in each area, then slowly let the muscles relax.

Now take five long, deep breaths, inhaling through your nose and exhaling through your mouth.

Now imagine you are in a safe and secure place. One of your favorite places. I like to visualize myself near Bear Lake in Rocky Mountain National Park, lying in a nest of clover; or on a deserted beach, lying in sun-warmed sand. What about you? What do *you* feel? Cool breezes? Warm sun? Warm sand? Cool grass? What do you hear? Waves crashing? Birds singing? The wind whistling through the trees? Let your senses take it all in.

If you are carrying a difficult problem with you today, take that problem and set it under a rock. You are free of it for this moment. You can pick it up again when you finish relaxing.

While you are quiet, simply enjoy your feelings. What do you feel? In relaxation, you should experience good feelings like rest (not sleep), safety, calm, peace, comfort.

Relaxing Your Mind

If you have trouble relaxing your mind, first be sure you are truly in a quiet, comfortable place. No interruptions.

Second, realize that learning relaxation takes time. Reconnecting the wires between your emotions and your body takes time. Appreciate what you accomplish each time you try this exercise.

Third, you might try focusing your mind, while you relax, on one of the following:

1. As you visualize being in your favorite place, don't let your mind wander. Instead, focus on a single statement of hope. For example, verbalize aloud, "I am resting . . . I am resting . . . I am resting . . ." Or, "I am safe in God's hands. . . I am safe in God's hands . . ." Or, recite a favorite saying, poem, song, or scripture that makes you feel restful, secure, and peaceful.

2. Focus your mind on a part of your body. For example, in slow-motion, bounce your legs just a bit. Or rhythmically move your arms in a wave motion (this works great in a spa or swimming pool). Or roll your neck slowly.

Another suggestion is for you to listen to a relaxation tape. On occasion, I listen to quiet music. There are also tapes available with sounds of nature, such as waves crashing or rain falling or sounds from a forest. These can be purchased in music stores and some bookstores. Find—and use—whatever helps you!

Using Your Mind to Create Peace

It is common for men to dehumanize a person with their minds and emotions before attacking them verbally or physically. Our minds flatten or belittle someone so that our words—or our fists—can finish the job.

- Think of someone you dislike. Picture him or her as a very large and active person in your mind. What do you see? How does it feel? What does your body feel?
- Now think of someone you like very much. Picture him or her as very close to you. Imagine doing something together that you really enjoy. How does this feel? What does your body feel?
- Now think of someone you have attacked in some way and at some time. Think of him or her in bright, appealing colors, with three dimensions. Picture being together as a positive experience. Picture this person in a positive manner, as a living, caring, sensitive, fragile human being. What are you feeling? Would you want to attack this person now?
- Now imagine a past situation with this person that you did not handle well. Picture, as vividly as you can, how you thought and felt and acted. How does it feel to replay this incident in your mind? Think about how you would have *liked* to have handled the situation. Rerun the tape again, this time picturing yourself thinking, feeling, acting, and reacting the

way you wished you had acted in real life! Replay this new image several times. How does it make you feel?

- Now think of yourself in general. What do you see? Is your mental image in color, or in black and white? Is it flat, or three-dimensional? Is there activity in your picture? Are you happy or sad? Are you feeling chaos or peace? What else do you see? Can you see into your future? If so, what is it like? In your mental image, can you see yourself clearly? Do you "feel" like yourself, or are you having trouble visualizing yourself in your mind?

- Can you imagine yourself as a little boy? Go ahead. Pick an age. What do you see? What is happening? What do you feel? Now imagine someone else walking onto the "scene" in your mind: it is you, as an adult. Can you tell that little boy that you care about him? Can you accept him as he is and understand his pain? Can you see and understand any happiness in his life? Can you hold him? Can you tell that little boy that you love him?

  If your feelings are powerful and cause you pain, be patient. Try this exercise another time and see how close you can get to the child you once were. This might feel painful or frightening; it might feel wonderful and freeing! Tell a trusted friend, or the men in your group, what you are experiencing. If this exercise scares you in any way, wait to do it with a trusted friend or therapist.

- Now think of possible future situations that you want to handle well. Relax yourself. Take deep breaths. Imagine how you want to think, feel, and act. Get away often to practice seeing the "you" you want to become!

Being an observer of yourself in this way can help you begin to see things more objectively. Of course, these images are not meant to provide, verbatim, a script for your future. Don't try to perfectly "play out" your visions. Life cannot be scripted: it is unpredictable and filled with surprises!

Using your mind and imagination, what you *can* do is begin to view others in a new way. Perhaps most importantly, you can begin to see yourself in a new way! Through these exercises, you can begin to dispel some of the old beliefs that, until now, have dictated your emotional response to the events in your life.

Step 9: I Am a Peacemaker

You have reached the point in your progress in which the risk of becoming enraged or depressed should be greatly diminished. If this is true, congratulations! (If not, *don't give up hope*. Indications are that you need rigorous help from a group or therapist to work through your points of hurt and fear. Keep at it, but get the help you need. Patchwork attempts at peace-living do not work. Commit your life to it!)

Regularly refresh your mind and heart with the Steps of Peace. Continue to practice these steps consciously, and before long you will find that you are practicing them intuitively. If you are part of a group, stay with it if at all possible. You will continue to grow as you help yourself and others.

And now we can add a new dimension to our peace-living. Until now, we have focused on our need to live at peace. Yet we have become aware, through hard work, just how hostile and chaotic men's lives can be. Daily, we will continue to be reminded of this fact as we hear other people using abusive language. We will witness people manipulating others through aggression or passivity. We will continue to meet or deal with people in denial or repression of their emotional lives. That hurts!

What can we do? The most basic thing we can do is to maintain our own peace-living. Second, we can become a peacemaker in our world.

What is a peacemaker?

A peacemaker tells others about his progress in peace. He dares to share, with persons who will handle his story respectfully, what his aggressive or passive behaviors used to be, and what he has done to grow into a peaceful person. A peacemaker knows when others need help and encouragement.

A peacemaker is a mentor to men beginning the path of peace. A mentor does not direct the learner's life but, rather, checks in now and then to see how the beginner is doing! He answers questions by giving honest—not heroic—answers. When appropriate, he may even choose to share stories and insights from his own path of progress.

A peacemaker might even begin a Men at Peace group, using the guidelines in Chapter Seventeen. He makes the group a priority in his life, giving it time to grow and develop. He enjoys the rewards of seeing men awaken to this new life. He also bears loss and grief, mourning the men who give the group a brief try but then quit easily, long before they have learned how to live at peace.

Sometimes a peacemaker takes risks. It is a choice we make. Let me share two stories of crazy, spontaneous moments in which I took a risk in order to be a peacemaker.

Several years ago, my wife and I were shopping for groceries in a Lansing, Michigan, supermarket. I went to get a loaf of bread. But as I turned down the bread aisle, I saw two women hitting each other with loaves of bread! One was cursing the other, shouting, "You've had it, lady!" Apparently they had bumped carts. Instinctively—not because I am courageous but because they were hitting each other with bread instead of salamis—I stood between them.

"Cut it out!" I yelled. "Stop it!" I hollered for about a minute until they quit. One woman was crying. The other kept yelling and cursing, flailing her loaf, trying to get a side swipe around me at the other woman. Then she started hollering at me. I asked her to move on or I would call the police. Finally, the store manager came and escorted the hollering woman out of the store. I watched to be sure that she left. I agree, it's hardly the stuff of myths and legends, but I like to think that it was a rescue on some level. In any case, it required a risk, though getting nailed upside the head with a loaf of Webbers may not, to some, constitute much of a risk!

The second story took place on one December Sunday afternoon as my wife and I were driving north on Highway 101, from the South Bay to San Francisco to see *The Nutcracker* at the San Francisco Opera House. Suddenly, ahead in the fast lane, we saw two cars parked precariously at the edge of the lane. Traffic swerved dangerously around them.

Near the cars, two young men were screaming at another man who, with a woman clutching his arm, was waving a knife! The two men yelled and lunged back and forth; the man with the knife took threatening jabs back. The woman on his arm, meanwhile, clung tightly and screamed for help.

I pulled my car to the side of the road, though I doubt the highway patrol would recommend this course of action as a rule! As I got out and approached slowly, the two young men began to back off and move toward their car, still screaming obscenities. I quickly chose a tactic: I began hollering directives as I moved toward the man with the knife. I said loudly, "Be calm. I will help you. Give me the knife," over and over until, a few minutes later, he seemed to calm down. When I was near the man with my right palm extended, he gave me the knife.

The two fellows jumped in their car and sped off. The woman thanked me as I headed back to my car, shaking, with the knife still in hand.

I handed the knife to my wife and drove off, still trembling. A moment later, a car sped by, driven by the man who had wielded the knife. From the passenger window, the woman smiled and waved. I had their knife! I wondered, for a moment, if the driver would stop and try to get it from me, but he drove by and never looked back.

I gave the knife to my dad, who uses it as a fishing knife.

Crazy stories. I would not recommend that we go looking for opportunities to be peace-making heroes. Most often, experts advise us to hand over our cash and avoid raising the ire of hostile or vicious persons. Yet these were two situations in which I chose to try to respond, carefully and alertly. Most of all, they showed me that society is in desperate need of peace!

Some people have been *real* peacemaking heroes. Some have even lost their lives because they did what was right in order to protect others. These are difficult, sometimes spontaneous decisions.

A better long-term plan is to build peace in your community through a Men at Peace group. Do it in honor of those who have sacrificed themselves for peace. Do it for the men you meet who are still in the grasp of the rage/depression/pain that you are learning to conquer. And do it for yourself. Maybe, together, we can even save lives . . . and families. One "man at peace" brings peace to many lives. However you continue your peacemaking, may you be blessed!

CONTINUING CARE FOR YOUR LEGITIMATE NEEDS

The following are legitimate personal and relational needs. Formulate a plan to balance these needs in your life. Choose to work consciously to meet one need at a time. Take one step at a time, meet one need at a time. That's all we ask!

Legitimate Need	Ways to Satisfy This Need
Responsibility	Choose responsibly
	Stop blaming or stuffing
	Tell the truth
Belonging	Approach others first
	Join a men's group
Self-worth	Enjoy learning change
	Read self-esteem material
	Stop negative self-talk
	Try something new without
	putting pressure on yourself
	to succeed

Fun	Play without competing
Freedom	Accept limits Choose and enjoy your choices
Contribute	Say what you think or feel Care for someone else without strings attached
Wisdom	Watch significant movies Read great literature Read self-help books to work on your life Think
Encourage	Affirm others Be kind Smile Trust when possible Love
Exercise	Jog, walk, or ride a bike Swim Do aerobics Take care of your body
Faith	Have intimate times with God Go to church or synagogue Give to others, especially the poor Sing, dance, feel Read faith literature

AFFIRM YOUR POWER AS A PEACEMAKER

All of the Steps you have completed have been character builders. By now you can claim the following new character strengths. You are building a new style of life: a life of peace!

- "I can show my feelings and express my fears and hurts in ways besides anger or anguish."
- "I can change and choose the direction of my changes."
- "I can ask for help when I need it and offer help when I think it is needed."
- "I can ask for what I want, but know that I cannot always have it."
- "I can tell people when I cannot fulfill their expectations of me."
- "I can consider new ways of thinking, acting, and relating to people."
- "I can reject stereotypes of how I am 'supposed' to be."
- "I can express my frustrations, disappointments, and anxieties."
- "I can take responsibility for my actions and not allow other peoples' behavior to push me into choices I don't want to make."
- "I can show my strength by choosing not to battle someone just because that person doesn't meet my expectations."

Pace yourself. Work on past steps and tasks that are still in need of your attention. But most of all, celebrate all that you have learned and changed in your life. Affirm yourself!

God be with you in your life of peace.

Peace!

Men at Peace Groups

HOW MEN AT PEACE BEGAN

In 1984, with Jim Whiting, I started a men's group at a women's center in Loveland, Colorado. Most of our men faced third-degree assault charges: they had been arrested for battering. For these men, joining our group was an alternative to court sentencing. Others heard about us through word-of-mouth and came voluntarily. This was a rather intense therapy group. Some sessions were emotionally and verbally intense.

We found that the connection with the women's center gave us the aura of being a "group for batterers." We found tolerance, but little support for the existence of our group. The board of directors of the center did not have the time, nor the inclination, to understand our purpose. We needed a separate identity with a more positive focus.

The group then moved to my non-profit counseling center at Calvary Church (Christian Reformed) in Loveland. This gave the group a "home" and greater flexibility in how we wanted to be organized and run. For two years, the group averaged seven members. Several men made great progress in learning peaceful behaviors.

Jim and I disbanded the group in August, 1987 because I had accepted a position in Southern California. We spent our last weeks grieving the end of our time together.

In September, I began my new position as a pastor at the Crystal Cathedral in Garden Grove, California. I began a men's group within a few weeks. The group took on the name Men at Peace. We advertise ourselves as offering "Hope for men troubled by anger or depression."

HOW TO BEGIN A MEN AT PEACE GROUP

A Men at Peace group can begin anywhere! Churches, synagogues, and men's organizations are natural "homes." Yet any place where men can meet with some privacy can work.

Men at Peace began with myself and one other man as we met on a chilly Thursday night at my office. Beginnings often appear inauspicious. We decided to meet one night per week. Within a month, we grew to five men. During the past five years, we have averaged twenty-two men per session, and we continue to grow. Our smallest group included three men; our largest was comprised of more than forty men. When a group begins to average ten members, it may be time to start another group! We often split into two or more groups so that intimacy can be maintained.

In the past five years, over 500 men have attended group two or more times. It is an unfortunate fact that about a third of group first-timers don't return. About half of our first-timers attend three or four group sessions; seventeen percent attend six or more sessions.

We advertise each week in the church bulletin. We also submit notices or articles in the "Community News" or "What's Happening" sections of newspapers. Newsletters of men's organizations or even businesses also help spread the word. And of course, word-of-mouth is always effective.

I prefer not to give the exact place of our meetings in our advertisements. I prefer to give a phone number, then briefly interview a man first. I ask what he expects from group. He'll often ask me what we do. A few men just don't fit the group—they might be too timid, hostile, or disturbed. These I refer to a therapist.

Start a group with yourself and at least one other committed person. You may want to work on the *Men at Peace* program for a few weeks yourselves before venturing out as a public group. Personal progress, of course, will build your confidence. On the other hand, closed groups can become repetitive and boring. Advertise as soon as you are ready.

Set a date to begin. Be clear to members and interested persons when and where you will meet. Know what you plan to do. Then show up for six weeks before you decide whether or not your group is taking off.

You need to be bold and enthusiastic! Any hesitation or timidity on your part will turn others off. They are looking for something that works! Be bold! Believe in your group!

MECHANICS OF GROUP GATHERINGS

Time

You can meet anytime: during breakfast, at lunch, after work, in the evening. I prefer evening meetings because evenings tend to be less rushed. Yet it is better to have a group—even during the day when you have less time—than to have no group at all!

Group requires at least an hour. An average amount of time from start to finish is one-and-a-half hours; we go two hours. We meet at seven p.m. and finish at nine p.m.

We meet once each week. Meeting every other week *can* work, but not as well. Men need consistency and regular support.

Place

You can meet anywhere, but privacy adds a good deal of freedom and security. A home is okay if no one traffics through and there is quiet. New members are particularly anxious about privacy; advanced groups tend to feel more open.

Churches and synagogues have lots of rooms. A priest, minister, or rabbi may be able to arrange access, intrigued by your group and grateful that you exist. Business boardrooms can work. Restaurant gatherings can work. Men's organizations have rooms. Club houses at apartments, townhouses, or condominiums can also work. All you really need is comfortable chairs and privacy!

GROUP AMBIANCE

The leader will need to warmly greet each man as he arrives. A handshake and a smile is comforting. Learn first names immediately. Use name tags.

If posters are allowed in your meeting room, display some. Use posters encouraging peace and the expression of emotions, opposing domestic violence, etc. Check a religious bookstore in your neighborhood, or call your local women's center or another men's group for materials.

You may use our name on your literature, or invent your own. If you use Men at Peace, we ask that you follow our format and organization.

Coffee and/or tea—or cold drinks on hot days—relaxes everyone. Respectfully, we don't allow smoking in our groups—too many men use smoking to avoid feelings. Further, smoking offends some men, or triggers allergies.

If you are not meeting in a restaurant, think carefully about snacks. We offer cookies, occasionally. Snacks are okay, but if they are available during group, some men may use them to avoid talking. Other men focus on food if there is too much. They think, "Should I get more to eat?" or "That guy's talking too much—we'll never get to the food!" The messages get sticky. We are there for group, not food.

A bathroom, of course, must be accessible.

GROUP FORMAT

New Members

Warmly welcome each new person. Each first-timer is asked to fill out and sign a Registration Form and to read and sign the Group Rules. Examples of both of these are provided at the end of this chapter. The new member returns the Registration Form to you, but signs and keeps the Group Rules for himself.

Pre-Group Conversation

We support general dialogue before group. Still, we watch for these tendencies:

1. Some men try to "get their stuff out" before group with one or two other men. They may be nervous, impatient, or just prefer to share with one person in particular. Yet if this becomes a habit, they will not learn the value of community, face their fear of the group, and/or learn impulse control! If a brother does not share in group, others become less willing to share also, perhaps resenting the brother who isn't willing to risk. Other men will stay silent in group, then "spew out" their problems or frustrations to whoever will listen *after* group has ended. This has the same effect. Some men need individual therapy as well as group sessions. If you find this happening, chat with the individual in private, being kind but direct about your concerns for him.

2. Men tend to talk about their jobs, women, sports, off-color jokes, their criticisms of others. Any talk before or after group that is disrespectful, negative, competitive, hostile or domineering needs to be confronted. I try to confront the person privately. If several men join in the negative conversation, I speak to the whole group. Such talk demonstrates a lack of integrity in the recovery process, since it works against the entire premise of the Men at Peace group. It also discourages or offends other men. It sets a competitive tone. Men can find that kind of comradery elsewhere.

If I need to confront the group about this, I might say: "Hey guys, our conversation seems to have taken on a negative tone. We're violating the spirit of group. Let's talk about something more positive. How about . . ." This doesn't happen often, but when it does, it must be dealt with.

Obviously, we don't run around checking up on men outside of group time. It is their choice to work the program with integrity—or not to do so. But I want them to respect the program when they are on "group turf." Respect is critical for the group to work.

THE CORE OF GROUP TIME

1. Check-In

We begin promptly. Waiting teaches procrastination. I also want to show respect to the time and schedules of the brothers who attend.

You may begin "Check-in" by going around the circle or by allowing men to speak spontaneously. Often I begin Check-in, but not always. During Check-in, the primary task is for each man to indicate whether or not he would like time that evening to share some of the issues he's dealing with.

The format of Check-in is for each man, in turn, to say:

"My name is _____, and I am responsible for my behavior." He may then say, "I would like some time," or "I do not need any time."

Men are notorious for degrading their needs. Often, during Check-in, we'll hear someone say, "My problems aren't as big as theirs," or "It's not important," or even "I'll take time if there's some time left at the end." Men demean themselves and their problems with these statements. Encourage men to either ask for time, or don't ask for time. Our hope is that they will learn to respect and value their need for time, planning their requests before group begins.

I try to teach men that their choice whether to talk in group about an issue or progress in life is entirely their own. They can't compare their choice to the choices of the other men in group, nor their need to the needs of the other men in group.

Each man is significant. Each man needs to choose to deal with his own life, requesting what he needs for his own recovery.

It is, however, legitimate for a man to say when requesting time during Check-in, "I just need a few minutes." This kind of statement helps the leader of the group plan the evening. Even so, a brother might still insist on adding that he wants to be sensitive to other men whose problems "are bigger than mine." Appreciate his sensitivity, then remind him that it is the group leader's job to balance the time: each man's needs are of equal importance, regardless of the "size" of his problems.

As leader, don't become discouraged: after all these years, I still have trouble convincing men to be straight with their needs during Check-in, so be patient! It might be encouraging to know that in five years of group and more than 250 sessions, I have never had a group meet without someone asking for time. Check-in itself is therapeutic. It teaches men to talk about themselves: they just need to keep working at it!

New members may Check-in last. They are allowed to learn by observation. Their first Check-in statement—"I am _____ and I am responsible for my behavior"—will be awkward, but that is okay. You might want to explain Check-in briefly if a new person seems particularly nervous.

Men need rituals and good habits. Check-in gives the group consistency and direction.

If a brother regularly does not ask for time, I might ask him, "I was wondering how _____ is going in your life? Would you be willing to talk about it later?" Usually he will say yes.

Often new members, during Check-in, are asked: "What brings you here tonight?" We allow a few minutes during Check-in to hear his answer. Or, if he has a lot to say, we ask him to fill us in on the rest of his story later in the evening.

Newcomers who say "I just want to watch" are allowed that privilege for one week. At the end of his first group session, I often will ask: "Is there anything you'd like to say about tonight?" This is a non-threatening question that will often help him break the ice in addressing the group for the first time. If he returns the next week, we encourage him to share a bit more about his life.

As the group "ages," you may choose to have men identify, in their Check-in statement, the program step they are currently working on. For example, someone might say, "Hi, my name is Bob and I am learning to articulate my feelings." This helps men see progress in each other and motivates them to progress within themselves.

2. Talk Time/Teaching

Once Check-in is completed, I recount the names of the men who asked for time. This reminds everyone to use his time wisely. Then we begin talk, or "sharing" time.

When a man asks for time, he is asking:

1. To *inform* the group about what is happening—problems or progress—in his life. Progress deserves affirmation and encouragement!

2. For *feedback* on a situation, issue or problem. When we give feedback, *we do not advise.* Advice is "fixing" or "caretaking." We do not tell a brother what to do, or what is right (unless he violates rules). We do not tell brothers how to get jobs. I have had men ask for money. We do not say, "What you ought to do is . . ." or "What I would do is . . ."

Feedback permits us to:

1. *Mirror what we hear.* We ask questions to understand or to help the brother think through his situation. We are not detectives or analysts. During feedback, the kinds of statements and questions that are appropriate include: "What I hear you saying is _____. Is that accurate?" Or "What happened when _____? How did you handle that?"

2. *Ask about feelings.* Men often talk facts. "What did you feel then?" or "What do you feel now?" are important questions during feedback. Even when asked directly for their feelings, men tend to talk thoughts. During feedback, don't be afraid to push for feelings. When a man does talk about feelings, understand and empathize with his spoken feeling. Do not try to "fix" or disagree with feelings, except to help a man find his feelings behind his anger or anguish.

3. *Make tentative suggestions.* This is as close as we get to advice. We might say, "What if . . ." or "It seems to me that . . ." The key word here is *tentative.* We respect each man's responsibility to make his own choices, whether they are right or wrong in our views.

4. *Support and celebrate.* "Terrific!" "Great job!" are affirmations that mean a lot. We support big steps and small ones too! Even approximations of peaceful living are supported. We are not perfectionists. We covet opportunities to tell each other, "You are making progress!"

5. *Confront.* This is the toughest part of group, especially for the leader. Most confrontation is tender, such as: "Bill, I wonder if you are . . ." Occasionally confrontation is tough. When you see a bother in heavy denial, there comes a time to challenge him. Examples include:

- "Bill, I care about you *and* [don't use the word *but*] I think you are hurting yourself."
- "If that happened to me, I would be afraid."
- "You *look* angry even if you don't *feel* angry!"
- "What are you fearing?"

Most confrontation needs to be finished with affirmation:

- "You have a lot going for you. You can make it!"
- Or simply: "I care about you."

A few brothers talk with tons of details. Their stories get confusing or chaotic, which also may indicate their style of life and/or their inability to develop friendships. This also tends to indicate passivity or feelings of victimization.

Occasionally, I become directive: "What do you want from group with regard to this?" Or, "To focus in, what is critical to you about what happened?" Or, "What did [or do] you feel about that?"

On rare occasions, a man tries to dominate group time with his insights. I try to be patient, but will stop him by saying, "Thank you—now others need time." If he does this chronically, first I will ask him privately, outside of group time, to allow others to have more time. If he persists, I will confront him during group: "George, I'm wondering if you see that you are dominating the group." If this is not effective, I will ask him to leave the group. Often other men in the group will confront him long before I need to do so; a group that confronts in this way is a healthy group!

Men at Peace groups focus on the path of peace. This includes practicing communication and peace skills. We cannot do everything for each person. We focus on active listening, understanding, empathizing, exploring and articulating feelings, giving tentative suggestions, celebrating, and confronting. We do not "fix" people's lives.

The best skill we can learn in this program is Time-Outs. Remind brothers to practice and use their Time-Outs. When a brother is "slipping," it usually means he's not using this and other basic skills. Ask brothers to share stories about their Time-Outs to encourage others and keep each man alert to using this skill.

Teaching

About once a month, we follow Check-in with a teaching/learning time. When a group is relatively new, teaching establishes the direction and work of the group. New members need to learn the basic skills. We go over Time-Out guidelines in group or after group with new men. Even old-timers benefit from the review.

The topics in this book were gathered from the topics I have addressed during teaching times. There is enough material here to last for years. You can also find great books and magazine articles in bookstores and libraries.

We do not have speakers come to group. Our primary purpose is to articulate feelings in the context of a caring community of men. We try to avoid the quest for a "guru," which would defeat the purpose of group interaction. The group can, however, sponsor a special public event featuring a speaker—perhaps even someone from the group—to be held at a different time than regular group meetings.

I prefer that men do not spontaneously share articles or books without getting approval from the leader first. Occasionally a man will try to dominate group with insights or details about other methods or programs of recovery.

Sometimes the material presented is extremist, or promotes a single view or form of therapy. To say "This has helped me" is good group dynamics—to say "This will work for you" is not.

I affirm men when they gain personal insight. Their attitude and enthusiasm at such times is more valuable to the group than the particular content they found helpful. Affirm how they did it for themselves.

Some of your men may be in Alcoholics Anonymous or other groups. Of course, if he is a recovering alcohol or chemical abuser, that is necessary. I support any outside program or experience which genuinely helps a man. Yet it is not helpful for men to push other programs or experiences in our group. That takes the focus off our purpose and dilutes what we are there to do. In extreme cases, a man may need to choose which group suits his present needs best.

Time-Keeping

Someone, usually the leader, is the chief time keeper. It can be a tough job, but it's critical. Without coming across as a score keeper, you must keep group moving with fairness. Without being too obvious, you must watch the clock to balance each man's time. Gauge in your mind at the beginning during Check-in who needs time, who needs less time, and who needs priority because he has been shorted in the past.

The time keeper must be bold and tough without being a bully. Often I'll say, "Thank you for sharing openly. Now we need to move on to give others time." It's typical to have, in the same session, two or three men share for twenty to thirty minutes, and several men share for five to ten minutes each.

Beginning groups need the leader to be more open with his own "stuff." Be bold in showing men—through personal example—how to share their issues, how to make progress, and how to give feedback.

When our group began, I gave 75 percent of the feedback. Then I started to ask others what they thought or felt about someone's story or issues. This helped stimulate dialogue. When I knew I would have to miss group for a week or two, I asked the two most mature brothers to lead in my absence. Their boldness grew immensely through the experience! Now

I am able to sit quietly and marvel at the wisdom and love of other men as they interact with each other. It's just plain wonderful to watch!

When a brother is working on Step Six or beyond, he might be ready to begin leading group. Encourage men to become mentors for the newest members. Some brothers may be ready and willing to start their own groups.

Having a co-leader relieves you of stress during group times. It also gives you time to think and observe while the group remains in progress. Outside group, a co-leader supports you, and vice versa. Talk about your own personal issues with your co-leader. Think together about the path your group is taking.

I occasionally take time for myself in group. The benefit to briefly sharing one of my own concerns, issues, or progresses is that this keeps me "alive" to myself. Still, I only share deeply in group if I think my stuff helps the brothers see how to deal with their own issues and joys. I shared my grief when I lost a friend. I shared loneliness. I have talked about the wonder of the birth of our sons.

This means I depend more on co-leaders, outside group time, for support and confrontation in my life. Sometimes men who are advanced in the program benefit from an advanced group. They can lead or co-lead the regular groups, yet meet together at other times for support from other leaders and co-leaders like themselves.

3. Closing Group

If group talk stops, we stop. Usually, however, time runs out and I have to stop the group since we try to end right at closing. Only once or twice in five years have I closed group early because the men ran out of things to say!

Usually someone will say, "Why don't we go longer!" Yet experience has taught me that this doesn't work. Why? Men eager to continue are often newcomers bursting with enthusiasm and caught up in the newness of "sharing their hearts." However, if they share too much, too eagerly, and too soon they may feel embarrassed. Some will not return to that group, feeling vulnerable and "out of control." Remember:

what feels good to a man can also cause him anxiety and fear in private.

Also, one and a half hours is a long attention span—people tire. Some men have things to do after group. If the group ends at different times each week, the men feel uncertain about what to expect. Help the group know what to expect: don't burn them out or make them feel insecure. Consistency and honesty pay off. That is one of the premises of peace. Some of the men may choose to go out for coffee after group—that's great!

If your group needs more time, consider adding half an hour. But two hours should be the maximum.

To close group time, form a circle. We put our arms around each other's shoulders, forming a huddle.

In the huddle we say only positive things. We encourage a brother who is struggling. We pray for a brother or the group as a whole. We might say the Lord's Prayer or the Serenity Prayer—"God, grant me the serenity to accept the things I cannot change, courage to change the things I can, and wisdom to know the difference."

Often we say together, "We form this circle because we are a community of men, and we touch each other because we don't get touched enough. Have a good week!"

Usually, I say the last prayer or words.

OTHER CONCERNS

Confidentiality

It is absolutely necessary for brothers to maintain confidentiality outside the group. That means we don't use people's names outside of group, even to our spouses. We don't talk about others' issues to anyone, *including group members*, outside group. If we have issues with a brother, we bring them up in group. We can tell our spouses what we are learning through group about ourselves, and we can share the skills we are working on.

The only exceptions are:

- If a man feels too embarrassed or afraid to share an issue with the group, but needs to talk, I will listen to him and help him decide if and when to share his issue with the group.
- The co-leaders may share thoughts about the progress of a particular brother in the group. This is not a license to hyper-analyze anyone, but rather an opportunity to share thoughts or insights that might help the leadership as they direct and encourage that member in his progress. The group must understand, and be told ahead of time, that this is within the bounds of confidentiality.

From time to time, group members need to be reminded of the importance of confidentiality.

Hand-Outs

The "Time-Out Steps" may be photocopied without obtaining permission, and given to members of a Men at Peace group. Please acknowledge the book as your source. The other materials in this book are best used in context, so they may not be copied.

Brothers with Special Needs

We would like to think that our group is good for all men, but this just isn't true. Men who have chronic patterns of violence or depression need specialized help. They can use some of this material, but they may need further help. Some men are too troubled for group and need therapy. You must protect your group. If a man is domineering or his life is too chaotic, he can sap the enthusiasm or time of the group. I try to work with him. If problems persist, I direct him to seek other help, guiding him to such help if possible.

Topics Acceptable in Group

Group is a time to talk about *you*. We do not talk about our wives or partners, except as they relate to our stories and feelings. Never do we accept that a man's problem is caused by someone else. He is in the group to change himself. I know that many wives have trouble believing this. They ask their husbands, "So what did you say about me in group tonight?"

Yet we do not give men information on how to change their spouses. We do not spend group time talking about our partners or "their problems." What is discussed about others is incidental to working on our *own* issues.

We also don't allow men to expound on what "all women" are like. Stereotypes are simply not helpful. A man may need to accept his partner's personality and behaviors. He may even face difficult choices about how to work out his relationship with her. But we do not support simplistic generalizations as a way to blame someone else for our problems.

Despite all this, some men are bound and determined to blame. We confront blame immediately. This pattern will not allow him to progress until he faces his own choices and his fears and hurts.

Given these guidelines, men may talk in group about most any topic in their lives. The kinds and numbers of topics are endless! For this reason, every week group is a totally new experience.

Preparing Members for Changes at Home

If a brother seems driven to talk about stresses in his relationship with his partner, it might be a good time to acknowledge that as men change, their partners can get angry. This happens for two reasons:

- When a man begins to get well, the relationship begins to change. The partner, who may have gotten used to being a victim, has lost her source of chaos. This can actually hurt her and make her angry as she loses "the problem out there" and is forced to face her own problems. I must tell you that some of my feminist friends vehemently oppose this explanation!
- A more frequent occurrence is that some partners have repressed their hurt and anger so deeply and for so long, that as their husbands begin to get well,

pent-up feelings become released. These partners have been wounded deeply, and deserve time to deal with their own hurts and fears, which are suddenly surfacing and being experienced as anger. This, of course, puts the tenderly-recovering man in a real test of his new-found skills of peace.

We teach men not to accept violence toward themselves, and to stay non-violent toward others.

Friendships Outside the Group

Some men in group become friends outside group. We encourage this as long as group confidentiality is not compromised.

I tend not to form friendships with brothers in group, other than my co-leaders. Realistically, I can't be friends with every man. More importantly, during the week I need a little emotional space from the intensity of group.

Activities Other Than Regular Group Discussion

Sometimes we have group picnics or go to baseball games together. We do this only occasionally, and we do this simply to have fun together. Men are not particularly good at simple, clean fun, so the practice can be helpful!

Jim Whiting had a group which went on Outward Bound wilderness weekends together. They had good experiences learning to trust each other.

Our group, one summer, spent the evening at a California Angel's baseball game. The next week at group, however, one of the brothers was angry. He had chosen not to join us for the game, and reported: "While you guys were all out having fun, what if someone new had shown up for group and wanted to kill himself? Don't you guys care?"

On the surface, this sounded like a caring, concerned attitude—but I noticed that this brother hadn't volunteered to show up for any theoretical, suicidal newcomer—he was simply blaming everyone else. I might have supported his concern if he were actually suggesting a solution, rather than blaming. He preferred, however, to be angry with us, rather than choosing to be responsible with his concern. Later, he admitted that he was jealous that we were out having fun together. Of course, he knew several weeks in advance that we were going to the game and had chosen not to come: he didn't like baseball.

The group is not God. We have limits. We help as we are able, keeping ourselves healthy first.

Being the Group Leader

The success of the group, particularly in its early stages, depends on the leader. The group will tend to take on the leader's personality, attitudes, and agendas. This may seem a little scary, but look at it another way: the group will grow as far as you do! And watching others grow is tremendously rewarding.

Beginning groups need bold leadership. Don't be afraid to lead. Believe in yourself and your progress in peace. We want to influence men with the power of peace. They need someone to imitate.

To enjoy leadership even more, look for a co-leader. If you don't have a friend to help you lead, look for a co-leader to emerge from the group. Give him time to grow, but when you think someone is ready, give him the honor of being your co-leader. Make clear what you expect from him in his new capacity. Begin giving him simple steps and tasks. For example, he might begin by leading Check-in. Then he might serve as the time keeper. Then he might teach a topic. Finally, he might take on a greater role during feedback.

When you take a week off, it's an opportunity for him to try his new skills leading the group solo. Later that week, meet with him to review what happened. I believe a good leader is someone who makes himself unnecessary! Teach others to do your job as well or even better than you do! You will benefit, your co-leader(s) will benefit, and the group as a whole will be stronger too.

The beauty of having a co-leader is that you can do more as a leader. The advantages are:

- With your co-leader keeping time, you have more time to think and adjust your feedback during a group session.
- You use less emotional energy during group.
- Your co-leader will see things you don't see regarding various brothers. He will balance your perspective. He will support or confront in ways that did not occur to you.
- With a co-leader you can model good communication. You can even have modest differences during group and talk them out in front of the other men. Do it in a respectful manner and reach a compromise or conclusion. Some men have never heard another man reach a graceful compromise, such as: "I think you're right. I change my mind. Let's have our teaching time at the end of group tonight."
- With a co-leader you can role play. Example: you play the role of a group member and have your co-leader play the role of the member's wife. Let the brother observe, through your demonstration, how he handles situations now, and perhaps how the situation could be handled differently, with better communication skills.
- Your co-leader can be a friend and confidant. You can share concerns about another brother or the group as a whole. You can share triumphs and disappointments. You can brainstorm together. You can make plans.

Above all, your power and success as a group leader come from:

- *Enjoying the men in your group.* Your attitude is important to the success of the group. You can have great structure and technique, but if you don't care for the people in your group, your success will be limited. Men long to be liked and to be with people who like them, so it is critical that you like the brothers.

In addition, have fun with your group! Fun is powerful. See the humor in situations even as you cry with a brother. This creates an environment for change.

- *Modeling peace.* We model peace through honesty. We tell the truth. We genuinely practice truth in our lives at home and work.

We model peace through working on good communication skills. We do what we teach, we say what we mean, and we speak assertively but kindly.

We model peace by sharing our hurts and fears. We express our anger or anguish calmly, objectively. Men are not used to this—they think anger is supposed to be volatile, not calm. But we stay calm.

We model peace through our openness and vulnerability. We do not get defensive. A good leader accepts criticism. A liked leader often gets teased by the group. Accept their barbs. Be a fool for fun. Tell your foibles without humiliation.

We model peace through non-violent attitudes and behaviors.

- *Working hard.* It is tough to lead. It takes courage to confront. It takes work to keep the clock for the group. The leader must organize: the buying of coffee, setting up the room, copying handouts . . . The little things mean a lot.

Group leadership is much like parenting. The rewards are not always visible immediately. But your love for these brothers and your joy in their progress makes the effort well worth it. And as a bonus, you will grow and have fun in the process. There's simply nothing like it!

MEN AT PEACE GROUP RULES

1. Abuse of alcohol or drugs at any time are grounds for expulsion from group. Alcoholics and other addicted persons must be recovering and in treatment. Any use of alcohol or nonprescription drugs on the day of group is prohibited. Chemicals alter our moods, feelings, and inhibitions, making our group work ineffective.
2. No smoking during group time.
3. Group meetings are wholly confidential. Outside group time, you may only talk about what *you* are learning in group. Never discuss others' names or details of their lives outside group.
4. We do not tell other group members how to live their lives. We do not give advice. We support each other and make tentative suggestions to others when appropriate. We do not ask for money or do business during group time.
5. Threats made to harm yourself or others may be reported to the appropriate officials. Child abuse must be reported to child protection agencies. Crimes committed and revealed may be reported to civil authorities.
6. Abusive language, swearing, or cursing is prohibited.
7. Acts of violence committed while being a member of group may be grounds for expulsion from the group. You must be committed to following our basic tool: Time-Outs.
8. By attending this Men at Peace group, I am making a commitment to peace in my life. I will ask the group for feedback to help me progress in peace. I will remember to be a representative of peace outside the group.
9. I will abide by these rules.

_____   _____
Name   Date

MEN AT PEACE REGISTRATION

Name: _____

Street Address: _____

City: _____ Zip: _____

Phone: (Home) _____ (Work)_____

I have read and am responsible for the Group Rules.

Signed: _____ Date: _____

Endnotes

Chapter Two: Power and Passion: Cravings that Clash

1. "Careers Start Giving In To Family Needs," by Cathy Trost and Carol Hymowitz, *The Wall Street Journal*, June 18, 1990, "Marketplace."
2. Karen Tumulty, "The Dead-End Kids," *Los Angeles Times Magazine*, 28 October 1990.
3. David Gelman with Carolyn Friday, "Overstressed by Success," *Newsweek*, 3 June 1991, 56.

Chapter Three: Walking Toward the Pain

1. "Lee Atwater's Last Campaign," by Lee Atwater with Todd Brewster, *Life*, February, 1991, 67.
2. George Tomas Kurian, *The New Book of World Rankings* (New York: Facts on File, Inc., 1984), 384-385.
3. Quoted in "Why Won't Crime Stop," by James Fyfe, *The Washington Post*, March 17, 1991, "Outlook."
4. *Uniform Crime Reports for the United States*, 1989, Department of Justice, Federal Bureau of Investigation.
5. This estimate, made in 1988, comes from the National Coalition Against Domestic Violence and has been consistently confirmed by other sources.
6. "Helping Husbands Who Batter," *Social Casework: The Journal of Contemporary Social Work*, (Vol. 65, No. 6) June, 1984, 348.
7. Ibid.
8. Sandra Blakeslee, "Anger and Cynicism Can Kill You, Doctor Finds," *The Orange County Register*, 16 January 1989.

9. Robert Bly, interviewed by Bill Moyers for "A Gathering of Men," PBS Broadcast, January 1990.
10. Ibid.

Chapter Six: Step 2: I Am Responsible for My Anger

1. Carl Cannon, "Decades of Research Renew Debate on TV Violence," *Orange County Register*, 30 May 1989.
2. Ibid.
3. Doris J. Rawot, "Men's Roles in Child Care," *Family Therapy News*, November/December 1984.
4. Samuel Osherson, *Finding Our Fathers: How a Man's Life Is Shaped by His Relationship with His Father* (New York: Fawcett Columbine, 1986), 6.
5. Ibid.
6. Ibid., 8.
7. Ibid., 10.
8. Jack Balswick, *The Inexpressive Male* (Lexington, Mass./Toronto: Lexington Books, 1988), 99.
9. Ibid., 111.

Chapter Seven: Step 3: I Am Responsible for My Anguish

1. Paul Ciotti, "How Fathers Figure," *L.A. Times Magazine*, 18 June 1989.
2. Leo Tolstoy, *Resurrection* (New York: The New American Library, 1961), 102-104.

Chapter Nine: Step 4: I Am Responsible For My Fear

1. Joseph Campbell with Bill Moyers, *The Power of Myth* (New York: Doubleday, 1988), 51.
2. Judith Wallerstein interviewed by David Van Biema in "Learning to Live with a Past That Failed," *People Magazine*, 29 May 1989, 87.
3. Lillian B. Rubin, *Intimate Strangers: Men and Women Together* (New York: Harper and Row, Inc., 1983), 57.

Chapter Ten: Step 5: I Am Responsible For My Hurt

1. Van Biema, "Learning to Live with a Past That Failed," 87.
2. Craig W. Ellison, "Loneliness: A Social Developmental Analysis," *Journal of Psychology and Theology* 4 (1978), 8.
3. Ibid.
4. Henry Nouwen, *The Wounded Healer* (Garden City, New York: Image Books, a Division of Doubleday and Company, Inc., 1972), 83.
5. Ibid., 84-85.
6. Quoted in Robert N. Bellah et al., *Habits of the Heart: Individualism and Commitment in American Society* (Berkeley: University of California Press, 1985), 158.
7. Ibid.
8. Campbell, *The Power of Myth*, 8-9.
9. Quoted in Robert Coles, *Harvard Diary* (New York: The Crossroad Publishing Company, 1988), 14.

Chapter Eleven: The Antidote to Fear and Hurt: Forgiving Yourself; Reconciling with Others

1. Lewis Smedes, *How Can It Be All Right When Everything Is All Wrong* (New York: Harper and Row, Inc., 1982), 51.
2. Lewis Smedes, *Forgive and Forget: Healing the Hurts You Don't Deserve* (New York: Harper and Row, Inc., 1984).

Chapter Fourteen: Step 7: I Am Responsible for My Passions: *Our Passions for Work*

1. Quoted in "Addicted to Adrenalin," *Focus on the Family Magazine*, April 1986, 4. His book is entitled *Adrenalin and Stress* (Irving, Texas: Word Books, 1986).
2. Dr. Redford Williams, "Your Anger Can Kill You," *Reader's Digest*, August 1989, 183-188
3. Max Depree, *Leadership Is an Art* (New York: Doubleday, 1989), xvii.
4. Ibid., 45-49.
5. Ibid., 50-51.

6. Dr. Aaron R. Beck, *Love Is Never Enough* (New York: Harper and Row, 1988), 83.

7. Ibid., 84.

8. Daniel Goleman, "Conflicts Between Sexes Linked to Subtle Contrasts," *The Orange County Register*, 13 June 1989.

9. Dr. Carl A. Whitaker and Dr. William M. Bumberry, *Dancing with the Family* (New York: Brunner/Mazel, Inc., 1988), 125.

10. Ibid.